CONSUMER PROTECTION LAW

IN A NUTSHELL

Third Edition

By

GENE A. MARSH
Professor of Law
The University of Alabama
School of Law

WEST
GROUP

ST. PAUL, MINN.
1999

Nutshell Series, In a Nutshell, the Nutshell Logo and the West Group symbol are registered trademarks used herein under license.

COPYRIGHT © 1976, 1981 WEST PUBLISHING CO.
COPYRIGHT © 1999 By WEST GROUP
       610 Opperman Drive
       P.O. Box 64526
       St. Paul, MN 55164–0526
       1–800–328–9352
All rights reserved
Printed in the United States of America

ISBN 0–314–23168–4

 TEXT IS PRINTED ON 10% POST CONSUMER RECYCLED PAPER

2nd Reprint — 2006

TO MY WIFE, JENELLE, AND
MY SONS, NATHAN AND ELLIOTT

Gene A. Marsh

*

PREFACE

Consumer protection laws today reflect fundamental changes in the way individuals obtain credit,
pay their bills and make purchases. In the past,
consumers purchased most goods and services
through local merchants in face-to-face transactions,
and borrowed money in established relationships
with local depositary institutions. People were more
conservative in their use of credit and lenders often
required significant down payments, strong credit
records and an established history of employment.
Consumers paid in cash, occasionally wrote checks,
and dealt in a paper world of bank notes and credit
sales contracts.

Much has changed. Consumers continue to trade
with local merchants, but they also make purchases
from telemarketers, catalog sellers and companies
marketing their products over the internet. Many
cars are leased and some appliances are rented. The
"paper world" in consumer credit and payment systems is still with us, but individuals now pay some
of their bills electronically. They use credit cards,
debit cards, stored-value cards and they access cash
through an ATM rather than a teller.

Credit is now available to consumers who have
shaky credit records, although the price of the credit
may be high. Usury laws no longer exist in some

places. And although depositary institutions such as banks, credit unions and a variety of mortgage lenders remain dominant, there are many nondepositary subprime lenders serving individuals who have a history of slow payments and default. The supply of credit to the subprime market has been bolstered through the bundling and securitization of subprime loans, attracting investors in search of higher returns.

Consumers pay more bills electronically, but they also receive payments by means other than the transfer of paper. The federal government is sending Social Security and other federal benefit checks electronically, and a growing number of people have their payroll checks deposited directly in their checking accounts. However, the storage and transfer of information electronically raises concerns about unauthorized access to consumer accounts, credit reports and other personal information.

This Nutshell treats the traditional areas in consumer protection, but also introduces new state and federal laws that reflect the changes noted above. Although there was little activity from Congress in the 1980's in enacting new consumer protection laws, there was a resurgence of activity in the 1990's. The new laws reflect a change in the political climate and the need to provide some procedural protections and additional disclosures, as prices were deregulated in a number of markets. This Nutshell explores the development of the subprime credit market, dealer-arranged financing and the explosion in the use of open-end credit by consumers. The "fringe banks," such as pawnshops, payday lenders and rent-to-own operations are also discussed. Arbitration and class actions in consumer disputes are also discussed, although more complete coverage of these subjects must be found elsewhere.

The author acknowledges the excellent research assistance provided by law students Beth Bosquet, Gregg Curry and Hope Stewart. Typing and technical help were provided by Wanda Elliott. The author also appreciates the research support provided by The University of Alabama Law School Foundation and the George M. and Mary C. Akers Fund. Finally, the author acknowledges the excellent work of Professor David Epstein and Professor Steve Nickles, whose 1981 second edition of this Nutshell stood the test of time and was appreciated by many law students and professors who explored this area of the law.

PROFESSOR GENE A. MARSH
THE UNIVERSITY OF ALABAMA

*

OUTLINE

Page

PREFACE --- V
TABLE OF CASES --- XXI

Chapter One. Introduction to Consumer Transaction Law

Section

A. What Is a Consumer Transaction?------------ 1
B. Common Law Remedies: Limitations and Problems of Proof------------------------------ 3
C. Modern Consumer Protection Statutes: An Overview----------------------------------- 6

Chapter Two. Public and Private Actions to Regulate Consumer Markets

A. Overview-- 12
B. State Agency Enforcement --------------------- 12
C. The Federal Trade Commission: A Brief History --- 15
D. Private Actions Using State Law ------------ 21
 1. General--- 21
 2. Who May Sue? ----------------------------------- 23
 3. Who Can Be Sued?------------------------------- 24
 4. Procedural Obstacles to Suit ------------------ 25
 5. Remedies--- 25

Page

Section

D. Private Actions Using State Law—Continued

  6. Attorney's Fees Under State Statutes 26

E. RICO as a Civil Suit Option for Consumers -- 27
F. Class Actions--------------------------------- 29
  1. Overview ----------------------------------- 29
  2. Basic Requirements for Certification 30
  3. Potential for Abuse in Class Actions 33

G. Arbitration ----------------------------------- 35

Chapter Three.   Methods of Inducing Consumer Transaction

A. Advertising --------------------------------- 40
  1. Common Law Actions ---------------------- 40
  2. Federal Trade Commission's Regulation of Advertising ----------------------------------- 42
  3. Bait and Switch Advertising------------------ 45
  4. Applying States Statutes to Advertising 48
  5. The Truth in Lending Act's Advertising Provisions ----------------------------------- 50
  6. Racketeer Influenced and Corrupt Organization Act Advertising Provisions 51
  7. Class Actions Based on Deceptive Advertising ----------------------------------- 52

B. Other Sales Practices ---------------------- 53
  1. Door-to-door Sales ---------------------- 53
  2. Telephone Sales ---------------------------- 54
  3. Mail and Telephone Order Sales ------------- 57
  4. Unsolicited Goods------------------------- 58

Page

Section

B. Other Sales Practices—Continued
 5. Referral Sales 58
 6. Pyramid Sales 59
 7. Auto Sales 59
   a. Repair Regulations 59
   b. Sale of Used Cars 60
 8. Auto Leases 61

Chapter Four. The Consumer Credit Market

A. The Growth of Consumer Installment
     Debt 63
B. The Consumer Lending Industry 65
 1. Overview 65
 2. Payday Loans 67
 3. Pawnshops 67
 4. Rent-to-Own 68

C. The Subprime Credit Market 72
 1. Overview 72
 2. Abusive Lending Practices in the Sub-
     prime Market 74

D. Dealer-Arranged Financing 75
 1. Overview 75
 2. Lender Liability Theories Involving Deal-
     er Paper 76
 3. Problems With Dealers in Home Improve-
     ment 79
 4. Financing Dealer Contracts 83
 5. Unfair Lending Practices in Dealer Fi-
     nancing 86

Section   **Page**

D. Dealer-Arranged Financing—Continued
6. A Benchmark Case in Dealer Financing   90

**Chapter Five.   Credit Reports, Identity
Theft, Credit Repair, and Equal Access to
Credit**

A. Credit Reports-------------------------------   98
1. Use---   98
2. Common Law Protection ----------------------   100
3. State Laws----------------------------------   102
4. Fair Credit Reporting Act -------------------   102
    a. Scope -----------------------------------   102
    b. Requirements for Furnishers of Infor-
        mation-----------------------------------   105
    c. Requirements for Consumer Credit Re-
        porting Agencies ------------------------   107
    d. Requirements for Users of Consumer
        Reports----------------------------------   110
    e. Rights of Consumers ----------------------   114
    f. Administrative Remedies ------------------   118
    g. Criminal Remedies-----------------------   119
    h. Civil Liability ----------------------------   120

B. Identity Theft Act---------------------------   122
C. Credit Repair Organizations Act ------------   124
D. Discrimination in Access to Credit ----------   127
1. Scope of Equal Credit Opportunity Act -----   127
2. Discrimination in Obtaining Information
    in Credit Applications -----------------------   128
3. Discrimination in Evaluating Credit Appli-
    cations -------------------------------------   129

Page

Section

D. Discrimination in Access to Credit—Continued

4. Notification --- 131
5. Effect of Equal Credit Opportunity Act on
   State Law --- 132
6. Remedies --- 133

Chapter Six. Disclosure of Terms in Consumer Credit Transactions

A. Need for Disclosure Legislation -------------- 135
B. Federal Truth in Lending Act ----------------- 137
 1. Introduction ----------------------------------- 137
 2. Regulation Z and the Official Staff Commentary --- 137
 3. Scope of Application of Truth in Lending -- 138
    a. Amount of Credit --------------------------- 139
    b. Purpose of Credit --------------------------- 139
    c. Status of Debtor --------------------------- 140
    d. Business of Creditor ------------------------ 140
    e. Imposition of Finance Charge ------------ 143
 4. Organization of Truth in Lending Act and
    Regulation Z ----------------------------------- 143
 5. General Disclosure Requirements ----------- 145
 6. Closed-end Credit Disclosures ----------------- 147
    a. Time for Disclosure ------------------------- 147
    b. Disclosure of the Finance Charge ------- 149
 7. Credit Insurance ----------------------------------- 153
 8. Burying Finance Charges in the Cash
    Price --- 155
 9. Annual Percentage Rate ----------------------- 162
10. Other Disclosure Requirements -------------- 165

Section

B. Federal Truth in Lending Act—Continued

11. Additional Disclosures in Certain Residential Mortgage Transactions 168

12. Additional Disclosure Problems 171
   a. Location of Disclosures 171
   b. Security Interests............................ 172

13. Open-End Credit 174
   a. Disclosures in Applications and Solicitations................................... 174
   b. Initial Statement 175

14. Periodic Statements 177

15. Recent Problems in Open–End Credit and Marketing of Consumer Goods 180
   a. Overview of the Litigation................. 180
   b. Marketing Flaws............................ 181
   c. "Spurious" Open–End Credit 186

16. Real Estate Transactions and TILA........... 187

17. Federal Enforcement of TILA.................. 191
   a. Administrative Enforcement.............. 191
   b. Criminal Actions........................... 193

18. Consumer Remedies.............................. 194
   a. Introduction................................ 194
   b. Standing to Bring Claims for Damages 195
   c. Measure and Purpose of Damages 196
   d. Multiple Tila Statutory Damages......... 198
     (1) Multiple Violations Generally........ 198
     (2) Refinancings........................... 198
     (3) Multiple Obligors 199
     (4) Multiple Creditors: Assignee Liability 200
   e. Violations Giving Rise to Statutory Damages................................... 201

OUTLINE

Page

Section

B. Federal Truth in Lending Act—Continued
  (1) Generally 201
  (2) Specific "Disclosure" Violations: What Is a Penalty Violation And What Is Not 202
  f. Recovering Both Tila Damages and State Law Damages 204
  g. Recoupment and Set-off 206
  h. Statutory Damages and Recission 206
  i. Rescission Generally 207
  j. Actual Damages 208
    (1) Background 208
    (2) Standards For Proving Tila Actual Damages 208
    (3) Practical Approaches to Obtaining Actual Damages 212
      (a) Generally 212
      (b) Restitutionary damages 213
      (c) Damages for consumer's missed opportunity 214
      (d) Consequential damages: emotional distress 215
19. Defenses 216
  a. Statute of Limitations 216
  b. Bona Fide Error 217
  c. Correction of Error 217

C. Truth in Savings Act 218
D. The Consumer Leasing Act 220
  1. Introduction 220
  2. Required Lease Disclosures 221
  3. Remedies for Cla Disclosures 223

XV

OUTLINE

Page

Section

E. The Interstate Land Sales Full Disclosure
Act 224
F. Real Estate Settlements Procedure Act 226
G. The Home Ownership and Equity Protection Act of 1994 229
  1. Introduction 229
  2. The Apr Trigger 231
  3. Point and Fees Trigger 231
  4. Disclosure Requirements 232
  5. Additional Substantive Protections and
  Penalties 233

**Chapter Seven. Regulating the Cost of
Credit**

A. History of Rate Regulation 235
B. Should There Be Rate Ceilings? 239
C. Problems in Proving Usury 242
  1. Intent 243
  2. Should Loans and Credit Sales Receive
  Different Treatment? 244
  3. Has the Maximum Legal Rate Been Exceeded? 247

D. Types of Lenders and Credit 248
E. Federal Preemption 249
F. Computing the Maximum Amount That
Can Be Charged 251
G. Other Computation Problems 255
H. What Charges Are Considered Interest? ... 263
  1. Loan Origination and Closing Expenses 264

Page

Section

H. What Charges Are Considered Interest?—
    Continued
   2. Commitment Fees ------------------------------ 264
   3. Charges Payable by the Debtor on Default 265
   4. Prepayment Penalties -------------------------- 266
   5. Is It Really a Credit Transaction? ----------- 267
   6. Which State Rate Law Applies? -------------- 268

I. Remedies--- 271

Chapter Eight. Regulation of Other Terms in Consumer Transactions

A. FTC Credit Practice Rule---------------------- 273
   1. Introduction ----------------------------------- 273
   2. Remedies for Violations of the FTC Rule--- 274
   3. Prohibited Practices Under the FTC Rule   275

B. Flipping -- 280
   1. The Increase of Loan Renewals -------------- 281
   2. Employee Incentives and Marketing Strat-
       egies in Loan Renewals ---------------------- 284
   3. Add-on Interest and the Rule of 78THS ---- 287
   4. Observations on Flipping----------------------- 289

C. Credit Insurance--------------------------------- 294
   1. Introduction ----------------------------------- 294
   2. Regulation of Credit Insurance -------------- 295
   3. Credit Life Insurance ------------------------- 298
   4. Credit Disability Insurance (Accident &
       Health) --- 301
   5. Involuntary Unemployment Insurance ----- 302
   6. Credit Property Insurance -------------------- 303
       a. Overview ----------------------------------- 303

Page

Section

C. Credit Insurance—Continued
    b. Excess Property Insurance Coverage.... 305
  7. Non-filing Insurance 308
  8. Force-Placed Insurance 312
  9. Voluntariness 313

D. UCC Limitations on Interests in After–Acquired Consumer Goods 322
E. Yield Spread Premium Financing Arrangements 324
F. Additional Complaints Regarding "Upcharges" and Itemization of the Amount Financed 330
G. Unconsionability 333

Chapter Nine. Post-Transaction Problems

A. The Holder in Due Course Doctrine 337
  1. Introduction 337
  2. The Loss of Holder in Due Course Status in Certain Consumer Lending 343
  3. Should the Ftc Rule Limit Affirmative Recovery? 350

B. Defenses in Credit Card Transactions 360
  1. Defenses Arising From the Underlying Transaction 360
  2. Unauthorized Use 364

C. Electronic Fund Transfer Act 368
D. Billing Problems 381
  1. Fair Credit Billing Act 381

OUTLINE

Page

Section

D. Billing Problems—Continued
    a. Billing Errors 382
    b. Billing Period 387
  2. Billing Systems 389

E. Default 393
  1. Common Law Limitation on Collection Efforts 394
  2. The Fair Debt Collection 398
    a. Introduction 399
    b. Persons and Transactions Covered 399
    c. Validation of Debts 401
    d. Prohibitions Against False or Misleading Information 402
    e. Harassment or Abuse 404
    f. Additional Restrictions on Communications With the Debtor 405
    g. Civil Liability and Bona Fide Error Defense 405
  3. Other Statutes 406
  4. Judicial Collection Efforts 406
  5. Exempt Property 408
    a. State Law 408
    b. Title III of the Consumer Credit Protection Act 411
  6. Obtaining Judgments 414
  7. Special Rights of Lien Creditors 416
    a. Repossession in General 416
    b. Actions Under Article 9 417
      (1) "Breach of the Peace" Under Section 9–503 417

OUTLINE

Section   **Page**

E.   Default --- 393
        (2) Retention or Resale Under Article
              9 --- 418
        c.   Limitations on Deficiency Judgment ---- 420

F.   Warranties --- 424
  1. Uniform Commercial Code ------------------- 424
  2. The Magnuson–Moss Warranty Act --------- 430

INDEX --- 437

TABLE OF CASES

References are to Pages

Abele v. Mid–Penn Consumer Discount, *199*

Adiel v. Chase Federal Sav. and Loan Ass'n, *211*

Allied–Bruce Terminix Companies, Inc. v. Dobson, *36, 37*

Amoco Oil Co. v. Ashcraft, *335*

April v. Union Mortg. Co., Inc., *160*

Armstrong v. Edelson, *357*

Arneill Ranch v. Petit, *258, 259, 260*

Arnold v. United Lending Companies Corp., *38*

Aztec Properties, Inc. v. Union Planters Nat. Bank of Memphis, *262*

Badie v. Bank of America, *37*

Balderos v. Mercury Finance Co., *161*

Barash v. Gale Emp. Credit Union, *195*

Barrett v. Stamford Motors, Inc., *197*

Bartholomew v. Northampton Nat. Bank, *216*

Bell v. Loosier of Albany, Inc., *266*

Benion v. Bank One, Dayton, N.A., *187*

Bigelow v. RKO Radio Pictures, *210*

Blaisdell Lumber Co., Inc. v. Horton, *366*

Bristol–Myers Co. v. F.T.C., *44*

Brooks v. Home Cable Concepts of Tennessee, Inc., *180*

Brookshire v. Longhorn Chevrolet Co., *266*

Brown v. Austin Area Teachers Federal Credit Union, *249*

Brown v. Investors Mortg. Co., *251*

Brummer, In re, *258*

Campbell–Salva v. Direct Cable of Mobile/Pensacola, Inc., *180*

Cantrell v. First Nat. Bank of Euless, *204*

Castano v. American Tobacco Co., *33*

Chancellor v. Gateway Lincoln–Mercury, Inc., *160*

Clark Leasing Corp. v. White Sands Forest Products, Inc., *421, 422*

Cochran v. American Sav. and Loan Ass'n of Houston, *244*

Colgate–Palmolive Co. v. F. T. C., *44*

Commercial Credit Corp. v. Chasteen, *266*

Commonwealth ex rel. v. _____ (see opposing party and relator)

Cook v. Frazier, *269*

Cosby v. Southeastern Cable Systems, *181*

Cripe v. Leiter, *24*

DeBlase, In re, *266*

Deer Creek Const. Co., Inc. v. Peterson, *26*

de Jesus v. Banco Popular de Puerto Rico, *27*

Dennis v. Handley, *198*

Dominguez, In re, *260*

Draiman v. American Exp. Travel Related Services Co., *367*

Dryden v. Lou Budke's Arrow Finance Co., *194, 205*

Duty v. General Finance Co., *394*

Eachen v. Scott Housing Systems, Inc., *356*

Elder–Beerman v. Nagucki, *365*

Emery v. American General Finance, Inc., *293*

Evans, In re, 120 B.R. 817, p. *196*

Evans, In re, 114 B.R. 434, p. *196*

Ex parte (see name of party)

Fairley v. Turan–Foley Imports, Inc., *194*

Fifth Third Bank/Visa v. Gilbert, *366*

First American Bank & Trust v. Windjammer Time Sharing Resort, Inc., *265*

First Trust Nat. Ass'n v. Daruka, *195*

Florida Bar v. Went For It, Inc., *49*

Ford Motor Credit Co. v. Milhollin, *146, 212*

Ford Motor Credit Co. v. Morgan, *350*

Ford Motor Credit Co., Ex parte, *327*

Foreign Commerce v. Tonn, *243*

Foremost Ins. Co. v. Parham, *5*

TABLE OF CASES

F.T.C. v. Bunte Bros., Inc., *15, 16*
F.T.C. v. Pantron I Corp., *46*

Gallegos v. Stokes, *140*
Gennuso v. Commercial Bank & Trust Co., *173*
Gibson v. Bob Watson Chevrolet–GEO, Inc., *332*
Goldman v. First Nat. Bank of Chicago, *217*
Gray v. American Exp. Co., *382*
Green v. Continental Rentals, *71*
Greenlee v. Steering Wheel, Inc., *200*
Gresham v. Termplan, Inc., West End, *173*
Groseclose v. Rum, *258*

Hanley, In re, *70*
Heintz v. Jenkins, *400*
Hemauer v. ITT Financial Services, *198, 204*
Henley, In re, *264*
Henningsen v. Bloomfield Motors, Inc., *426*
Henslee v. Madison Guar. Sav. and Loan Ass'n, *265*
Hogg v. Ruffner, *245*
Home Sav. Ass'n v. Guerra, *350, 358*
Hyland v. First USA Bank, *362*

In re (see name of party)
Iuteri v. Branhaven Motors, Inc., *211, 215, 216*
Izraelewitz v. Manufacturers Hanover Trust Co., *362, 364*

James v. Home Const. Co. of Mobile, Inc., *196*
Jensen v. Ray Kim Ford, Inc., *194*
Jeter v. Credit Bureau, Inc., *210*
Johnson v. Mercury Finance Company of Alabama, *158*
Johnson v. Rutherford Hospital, *196*
Jones v. Approved Bancredit Corp., *340*
Jones v. Federated Financial Reserve Corp., *102, 113*
Joyce v. Cloverbrook Homes, Inc., *173*

Kenderdine, In re, *173*

Ladick v. Van Gemert, *400*

Lawrence v. Credithrift of America, Inc., *194, 205*

Lewis Refrigeration Co. v. Sawyer Fruit, Vegetable and Cold Storage Co., *429*

Maddox v. St. Joe Papermakers Federal Credit Union, *195*

Marquette Nat. Bank of Minneapolis v. First of Omaha Service Corp., *270*

Marshall, In re, *197*

Mastrobuono v. Shearson Lehman Hutton, Inc., *36*

McAnally v. Ideal Federal Credit Union, *249*

McCoy v. Salem Mortg. Co., *211, 212*

McCullar v. Universal Underwriters Life Ins. Co., *299*

McCullough v. Bank of Stamford, Inc., *195*

Meierhenry, State ex rel. v. Spiegel, Inc., *269*

Melvin, In re, *147*

Minskoff v. American Exp. Travel Related Services Co., Inc., *367*

Mitchell v. Industrial Credit Corp., *311*

Mourning v. Family Publications Service, Inc., *197*

Murphy v. Household Finance Corp., *197*

Najarro v. SASI Intern., Ltd., *244*

National Petroleum Refiners Ass'n v. F. T. C., *17*

Nevels v. Harris, *257*

Nickel, Commonwealth ex rel. Zimmerman v., *205*

Palace Industries, Inc. v. Craig, *266*

Patrick v. Union State Bank, *122*

Pentico v. Mad–Wayler, Inc., *258*

Perez v. Briercroft Service Corp., *81*

Perino v. Mercury Finance Co. of Illinois, *160*

Preston v. First Bank of Marietta, *211*

Public Finance Corp. v. Riddle, *204*

Ransom v. S & S Food Center, Inc., *211*

Rathbun v. W. T. Grant Co., *246*

Richardson v. Citibank, *271*

Riley v. Ford Motor Co., *429*

Rodash v. AIB Mortg. Co., *197*

Rodgers v. Rainier Nat. Bank, *267*

Roper v. Consurve, Inc., *250*
Russell, In re, *209, 210, 211, 214*
Rust v. Quality Car Corral, Inc., *216*

Sampson v. Mercury Finance Co., *160*
Semar v. Platte Valley Federal Sav. & Loan Ass'n, *140*
Simpson v. Termplan Inc. of Georgia, *199*
Singer v. Chase Manhattan Bank, *362*
Smiley v. Citibank (South Dakota), N.A., *271*
Smith v. Cotton Bros. Baking Co., Inc., *414*
Snow v. Jesse L. Riddle, P.C., *400*
Spears v. Colonial Bank of Alabama, *294*
Spiegel, Inc. v. F.T.C., *415*
Spiegel, Inc., State ex rel. Meierhenry v., *269*
Sprouse, In re, *266*
State ex rel. v. _____ (see opposing party and relator)
Steinbrecher, In re, *206*
Stewart v. Travelers Corp., *414*
Stewart, In re, *209*
Stieger v. Chevy Chase Sav. Bank, F.S.B., *365*
Story Parchment Co. v. Paterson Parchment Paper Co., *210*
Sutliff v. County Sav. and Loan Co., *211*

Tanner Development Co. v. Ferguson, *258*
Tashof v. F. T. C., *46*
Taylor v. Quality Hyundai, Inc., *201*
Tinker v. DeMaria Porsche Audi, Inc., *357*
Towers World Airways Inc. v. PHH Aviation Systems Inc., *366*
Transamerica Ins. Co. v. Standard Oil Co. (Indiana), *366*

Unico v. Owen, *340*
Union Mortg. Co., Inc. v. Barlow, *90, 93, 94, 95, 96*
United States Finance Co. v. Jones, *82, 342*
Universal Bank v. McCafferty, *366*

Vickers v. Home Federal Sav. and Loan Ass'n of East Rochester,
211, 212

Walker v. Wallace Auto Sales, Inc., 155 F.3d 927, p. *161*

Walker v. Wallace Auto Sales, Inc., 1997 WL 598149, p. *161*

Walsh v. Ford Motor Co., *33*

Warehouse Home Furnishings v. Whitson, *310, 311*

Warner–Lambert Co. v. F. T. C., *45*

Weinberger v. Great Northern Nekoosa Corp., *33*

Wetherby v. Retail Credit Co., *101*

Whitaker v. Spiegel Inc., *245*

Williams v. Public Finance Corp., *194, 205*

Williams v. Walker–Thomas Furniture Co., *324, 334*

Zachary v. R. H. Macy & Co., Inc., *390*

Zapatha v. Dairy Mart, Inc., *334*

Zenith Radio Corp. v. Hazeltine Research, Inc., *210*

Zimmerman, Commonwealth ex rel. v. Nickel, *205*

CONSUMER PROTECTION LAW

IN A NUTSHELL

Third Edition

*

CHAPTER ONE

INTRODUCTION TO CONSUMER TRANSACTION LAW

A. WHAT IS A CONSUMER TRANSACTION?

A consumer transaction occurs when a person obtains goods, real property, credit, or services for personal, family, or household purposes. Examples include:

(1) John and Beth Simpson see a television commercial for home improvement work, with easy financing available. After they call a telephone number posted in the ad, a salesperson calls on them at home and makes a contract for siding and roofing. The work performed by the company is defective, but the finance company holding the installment sales contract insists on being paid, even though the roof leaks and the siding is falling off the house.

(2) Nathan buys an old, used cadillac from Dale's Used Auto for $2,750. He finances the deal at the car lot. The credit manager tells Nathan that in order for the credit to be approved, the deal must include an extended service

contract on the car and credit life insurance on Nathan's life.

(3) Steve Berry needs $200 cash, but has no relationship with a bank or traditional lender. In order to raise the money he goes to a pawn shop and pawns his automobile title. Steve continues to drive the car, but the pawn shop holds the car title. Although the state usury law sets the maximum permissible rates on $200 consumer loans at 20 percent, the title pawn dealer charges Steve 300 percent interest on the transaction. The state pawnshop law permits the 300 percent interest rate.

In each circumstance, the ordinary rules of contract law apply. However, since each is also a "consumer transaction," special consumer protection statutes and rules may be in play as well. Since consumer transaction law is primarily statutory law, this nutshell will focus on consumer transaction statutes. In addition, tort theories such as fraud, defamation and conversion will also be discussed.

This Nutshell does not examine consumer transactions and consumer protection policies outside of the United States, but there is a growing consensus of international opinion on what good consumer laws and practices should be. In 1985 the United Nations adopted *The United Nations Guidelines for Consumer Protection*. The UN Guidelines have had a significant influence on consumer policy actions undertaken by governments and consumer groups, across many cultures. There is a growing body of literature on consumer law and consumer protection activities across the globe. An international focus on consumer law has become more relevant as free markets develop throughout the world and transactions move more easily across international boundaries, due to electronic funds transfer and the growing use of the internet to place orders for goods and services.[1]

B. COMMON LAW REMEDIES: LIMITATIONS AND PROB-LEMS OF PROOF

In the 1960's and 1970's many consumer protection statutes were enacted at the state and federal level. Prior to that time most consumer transactions were governed by the ancient rule of caveat emptor or "let the buyer beware". Some protection was available for consumers where false information was used to market a product. For instance, a deceived buyer could bring an action for fraud against a manufacturer who falsely advertised a product. Although the technical elements required to establish fraud vary, most of the states require that the buyer establish at least the following elements:

(1) A false representation of a material fact;

1. For a thorough treatment of consumer protection in transnational and emerging markets, *see Consumer Law In The Global Economy: National and International Dimensions* (Ian Ramsay, ed. 1997).

(2) Knowledge or belief by the seller that the advertisement is false or knowledge that he or she lacks sufficient information to make such a claim in an advertisement;

(3) An intention by the seller to cause the buyer/plaintiff to act in reliance on the advertisement;

(4) Justifiable or reasonable reliance by the plaintiff; and

(5) Damages caused by the plaintiff's reliance.

The first requirement is troublesome for some plaintiffs because the misrepresentation must be one of "fact" rather than "opinion." An opinion has been described as, "[a] statement ... which either indicates some doubt as to the speaker's belief in the existence of a state of facts ... or merely expresses his judgment connected with the facts, such as quality, value, authenticity and the like.... " W. Page Keeton, et al., *Prosser and Keeton on the Law of Torts* § 109, at 755 (5th ed. 1984). So, a fraud action cannot lie against a car dealership which advertises a car as "the best one on the market."

This so-called "puffing" exception has obvious effects on the informational value of advertising. An advertiser may escape fraud liability by avoiding specific, factual information while opting for broader quality claims.

The reliance requirement may also prove difficult to establish in a fraud claim. The "justifiable reliance" standard allows for consideration of the individual characteristics of the borrower, giving consideration to such matters as the buyer's mental capacity, educational background, relative sophistication and the bargaining power of the parties. Under the justifiable reliance standard, consumers are given more leeway in the analysis of whether their reliance was reasonable, even though hindsight may show they could have been more careful or made a further inquiry before deciding to buy a product or service. Some courts have moved from "justifiable reliance" to "reasonable reliance," where a more objective standard is used to measure whether reliance on the part of the buyer was reasonable. *Foremost Ins. Co. v. Parham*, 693 So.2d 409 (Ala.1997). The reasonable reliance standard is not as forgiving for consumers and is generally favored by defendants who sell consumer goods or make consumer loans.

Another limitation on common law protection against false advertising is the cost of litigation. Even where a consumer could make a legitimate case, litigation costs could often outweigh the potential damages, except for big-ticket items. Given this fact, finding an attorney to bring the case could prove quite difficult. Additional problems encountered by plaintiffs attempting to use a fraud theory in false advertising cases will be discussed more thoroughly in Chapter 3.

C. MODERN CONSUMER PRO-TECTION STATUTES: AN OVERVIEW

The surge in consumer protection legislation, particularly in the late 1960's and 1970's was in part a response to the problems encountered under tort theories, but also a function of the politics of the time, when "too much government" was a rallying cry for business. Although there was very little new legislation in the 1980's, most of the statutes remain with us today and are frequently amended to address issues raised by consumer groups, regulators and those in industry.

The workhorse of modern consumer protection law is The Consumer Credit Protection Act of 1968 (CCPA). Title I of the Act has as its short title, The Truth in Lending Act (TILA). The Act requires creditors who extend consumer credit to disclose essential credit terms, especially the costs of obtaining the credit, before the credit is extended. Furthermore, Truth in Lending regulates the terms of credit advertising and provides a framework for sale of products related to the credit transaction, such as credit insurance, as well as, person-to-person transactions. The Act is considered *infra* at pages 135-179, and The Truth in Lending Simplification and Reform Act of 1980 is considered *infra* at page 136.

Title II of the Consumer Credit Protection Act (labeled "Extortionate Credit Transactions") was aimed at curtailing income gained by organized crime from extortionate credit transactions. "Loan sharks", who extend credit at usurious interest rates and then use force to collect due amounts, are the primary targets of Title II. Title III ("Restrictions on Garnishment") limits the amount of a person's earnings subject to creditor garnishment and prohibits an employer from terminating an employee because of one garnishment.

Credit card provisions were added to the Consumer Credit Protection Act in 1970 and 1974. The 1970 act prohibited distribution of unauthorized cards and established a fifty dollar limit on cardholder liability for unauthorized use of his or her credit card. The 1974 amendments make credit card issuers subject to defenses arising out of the transaction between a merchant and a cardholder. Additional provisions have been added to regulate payment systems other than credit cards.

The Fair Credit Reporting Act, added in 1970, regulates both the content and confidentiality of the credit reports of "consumer reporting agencies", and provides for consumer access to the reports. If a consumer's denial of credit, insurance, or work is based, in whole or in part, on consumer report information, the user of the report must inform the consumer of this fact and provide the consumer with the name and address of the agency that furnished the report. The consumer may then request a copy of his credit report from the reporting agency. If the consumer challenges the accuracy of the information, the agency must investigate and make any necessary changes. See *infra* at pages 102-122.

The Equal Credit Opportunity Act and the Fair Credit Billing Act were added in 1974. The former prohibits creditors from discriminating on the basis of sex or marital status. *See infra* at pages 127-134. The latter dictates that creditors maintain procedures whereby consumers can make complaints about billing errors. Once a complaint is lodged, the creditor must explain the bill or correct it. *See infra* at pages 376-388.

Congress added the Fair Debt Collection Practices Act in 1974. The Fair Debt Collection Practices Act governs the conduct of certain debt collectors who are engaged in the business of regularly collecting debts owed to another party. *See infra* at pages 399-406. In recent years the Fair Debt Collection Practices Act has been expanded to cover areas outside the ordinary consumer credit contract, such as an attempt to collect a condominium association fee.

Although there was little activity from Congress in the 1980's in enacting new consumer protection laws, there has been a resurgence of activity in the 1990's. This can be explained by a change in the political climate, as well as filling the need to provide some procedural protections and additional disclosures, as prices were deregulated in a number of markets.

In 1994 Congress passed the Home Ownership and Equity Protection Act (HOEPA), which was designed to protect vulnerable consumers from predatory home equity loans, made by sub-prime lenders. HOEPA does not establish interest rate ceilings, but requires certain disclosures and prohibits certain predatory practices that had become a problem in home mortgage loans involving the high rates and excessive fees that are common in subprime lending. HOEPA will be discussed *infra* at pages 229-234.

In 1991 Congress enacted the Truth in Savings Act (TISA), which is intended to allow consumers to make informed decisions about deposit accounts at depositary institutions. The required disclosures are designed to make consumers more aware of rates on the savings side, just as Truth in Lending was enacted to allow consumers to better understand the costs of consumer credit when they get consumer loans, buy goods on closed-end credit, or use a credit card. The Truth in Savings Act will be discussed at pages 218-220.

In 1998, Congress enacted the Identity Theft Protection Act. This law provides for the imposition of fines and imprisonment for individuals found guilty of stealing an individual's personal information with the intent to commit an unlawful act. This new law will be discussed at pages 122-124.

Other federal statutes also affect consumer transactions. Section 5 of the Federal Trade Commission Act (FTC Act) regulates "deceptive" or "unfair" trade practices. Title II of the Magnuson–Moss Warranty–Federal Trade Commission Improvement Act expanded the FTC's jurisdiction and enforcement power. The role of the FTC is considered more fully *infra* at pages 42-48.

Title I of Magnuson–Moss provides minimum disclosure standards for written product warranties. If a seller issues a written warranty, it must comply with these standards and any supplemental rules established by the FTC.[2] Written warranties for consumer goods costing more than $10 must be designated either "limited" or "full". The meaning of these terms and other Magnuson–Moss requirements are discussed *infra* at pages 430-436.

Another important federal statute is the Real Estate Settlements Procedure Act. *See infra* at pages 226-228. This act protects buyers and sellers of residential real estate from unreasonably high settlement costs by requiring advance disclosure and outlawing certain "kickbacks".

Beginning in the 1960's, most states passed consumer statutes, *e.g.*, rate regulation measures and consumer credit disclosure laws. The states also passed UDAP ("unfair or deceptive acts and practices") statutes designed to parallel and supplement the FTC Act. The FTC and Commissioners on Uniform State Laws recommended that the states enact these UDAP statutes out of a belief that effective regulation of unfair and deceptive acts could not

---

2. Magnuson–Moss confirmed the FTC's power to issue regulations and detailed the procedures the FTC must observe in establishing such rules. For an in-depth consideration of these procedures, *see* Kinter & Smith, *The Emergence of the Federal Trade Commission as a Formidable Consumer Protection Agency*, 26 Mercer L.Rev. 651, 670–675 (1975).

occur without state aid and private lawsuits. The types of statutes and the particulars of the statutes vary considerably from state to state, and an extensive body of case law has emerged to interpret the reach of the various statutes. These statutes will be discussed more thoroughly in Chapter 2.

The Uniform Commercial Code (UCC), with a few exceptions (*c.f.*, §§ 9–505 and 9–507), does not treat consumer transactions differently from commercial transactions. The UCC sections that have most affected consumer transactions, § 2–302 Unconscionability and the warranty provisions of §§ 2–312 through 2–317, are not limited to consumer transactions. These sections are discussed *infra* at pages 424-430.

In response to abusive marketing practices involving the use of the telephone, in 1994 Congress passed the Federal Telephone Consumer Protection Act (FTCPA) which regulates the hours during which telemarketing calls can be made. And the Telemarketing and Consumer Fraud and Abuse Prevention Act (TCFAPA) of 1994 was enacted to provide some substantive protections, addressing deceptive telemarketing for the sale of goods and services, as well as contests and prizes. And the Telephone Disclosure and Dispute Resolution Act of 1992 (TDDRA) regulates abuses that were common in the use of 900 numbers.

CHAPTER TWO

PUBLIC AND PRIVATE ACTIONS TO REGULATE CONSUMER MARKETS

A. OVERVIEW

The emergence of public agencies as the enforcement arm in the consumer transaction arena was, in part, due to problems with private enforcement of consumer protection at common law. Now in the area of consumer transactions, various state and federal agencies have a wide array of responsibilities. Part B of this chapter will provide a brief overview of state agency enforcement, but most of this chapter focuses on the Federal Trade Commission. State statutes which allow for private actions based on unfair and deceptive acts and practices encountered by consumers will also be discussed, while Chapter 3 will provide a more detailed analysis of the application of these statutes to deceptive advertising.

B. STATE AGENCY ENFORCEMENT

There are a number of state agencies which regulate consumer transactions. Within any state, the attorney general and agencies such as the state

banking department and state insurance department may be charged with the responsibility to
license and regulate businesses within their respective industries.

As is true at the federal level, some state legislatures enact laws, but grant the authority to the
appropriate state agency to promulgate regulations,
license the businesses and hire examiners to conduct audits and investigate consumer complaints.
Across the country, state regulation is often uneven,
based on legislative authority, budgetary constraints and the politics of the state.

In some states, the attorney general takes on a
high profile in consumer regulation, and is expected
to serve as a guardian for the public. In other
states, the office of the attorney general plays almost no part in consumer protection. This difference in the profile of state attorneys general was
recently demonstrated in the litigation against tobacco companies, where some AG's aggressively
pursued actions, while others sided with the industry and in some cases took political contributions
from tobacco interests. Also, some states present
very low regulatory hurdles due to the nature of the
state laws and agency inactivity, which make them
havens for businesses engaging in sharp practices.

Often, state regulatory agencies are hindered by
budgets which do not allow for effective enforcement. Some states fund the agencies through licensing and examination fees. Others impose taxes on
such items as the insurance premiums collected by

the insurance companies or assessments against businesses that are licensed under state law.

The state office of the attorney general and departments that regulate industries such as consumer credit or insurance may have the authority to issue injunctions or cease and desist orders against unlawful business practices. In some cases, consumer hotlines are established to help mediate positive outcomes for consumers who have a complaint with a business. In other states, agencies refer cases to private attorneys in a collaborative effort to represent the interests of consumers.

In states where effective and aggressive state regulatory enforcement is generally rare, the void is often filled by federal agencies such as the Federal Trade Commission. However, real teeth in enforcement and consumer protection is usually found in private litigation, where plaintiffs use state and federal laws, as well as class actions to seek redress for fraudulent practices and statutory violations found in the marketplace. Indeed, many state and federal laws empower consumers to act as a "private attorney general" in the policing of markets and enforcement of consumer protection laws. This is particularly true where the statutes provide for attorneys fees and costs, in addition to damages for the harm caused by the illegal business practice.

C. THE FEDERAL TRADE COMMISSION: A BRIEF HISTORY

The Federal Trade Commission Act of 1914 led to the formation of the FTC in 1915. Five Commissioners are appointed by the President to sit for a term of seven years. Under the Act, no more than three Commissioners may be members of the same political party.

Aside from its other myriad enforcement responsibilities, section 5 of the FTC Act grants consumer protection responsibilities to the FTC. As originally passed, section 5 prohibited unfair methods of competition in commerce. Section 5 was amended in 1938 to cover "unfair or deceptive acts or practices in commerce." Soon thereafter, in *FTC v. Bunte Bros., Inc.*, 312 U.S. 349 (1941), the Supreme Court held that the phrase "in commerce" conferred less than the Constitutionally permissible jurisdiction which Congress has over interstate commerce. The FTC charged Bunte, an Illinois manufacturer, with violating section 5 by selling "break and take" packages in Illinois. The amount the purchasers received from these packages were based on chance. In holding that the FTC lacked jurisdiction, the Court reasoned that:

"The 'commerce' in which these methods are barred is interstate commerce. Neither ordinary English speech nor the considered language of legislation would aptly describe the sales by

Bunte Brothers of its 'break and take' assortment in Illinois as 'using unfair methods of competition in [interstate] commerce.' When in order to protect interstate commerce Congress has regulated activities which in isolation are merely local, it has normally conveyed its purpose explicitly.... This case presents the narrow question of what Congress did, not what it could do. And we merely hold that to read 'unfair methods of competition in [interstate] commerce' as though it meant 'unfair methods in any way affecting interstate commerce,' requires in clear view of all the relevant considerations, much clearer manifestations of intention than Congress has furnished."

Taking its cue from the Court's language in *Bunte Bros.*, Congress has since furnished a much clearer indication of its intention. The Magnuson–Moss Warranty–FTC Improvement Act (Magnuson–Moss) amended section 5 to read: "unfair methods of competition in or affecting commerce, and unfair or deceptive acts or practices in or affecting commerce, are declared unlawful." The Senate Commerce Committee Report noted that this expansion of jurisdiction is intended to permit more effective policing of the market place by bringing within reach practices which are unfair or deceptive and which, while local in character, nevertheless have an adverse effect upon interstate commerce.

But, what is an "unfair or deceptive act or practice"? The FTC has long issued interpretive "industry guides" to describe acts or practices in a particular industry which the FTC considers a violation of a section 5 prohibition. However, these industry guides do not have the force and effect of law.

Thus, in 1962, the FTC enacted "trade regulation rules" to specify practices which the commission deemed to violate the Act. These rules are delineated in Title 16, Subchapter D. Unlike the industry guides, which are merely interpretive, violations of the trade regulation rules are violations of the statute from which the regulation is derived.

The difference between industry guides and trade regulations is demonstrated in the following example. Assume that the FTC issues a trade regulation which requires all aspirin advertisements to state that "ALL ASPIRIN IS ALIKE." If the FTC then decided to prosecute a rule violation against an aspirin manufacturer, the complaint would merely need to allege a failure to include the required statement—thus lessening the FTC's burden of proof. In other words, the FTC would not have to prove that the omission constituted a deceptive act. However, if the FTC only issues an industry guide, any action by the FTC would have to show that such violation is a deceptive act. Alleging a violation of the industry guide would simply not be sufficient.

The FTC's power to issue trade regulation rules was challenged but upheld in *National Petroleum Refiners Ass'n v. FTC*, 482 F.2d 672 (D.C.Cir.1973). In that case, the regulation declared that failure to post octane ratings on gasoline pumps would be a "deceptive practice" violation. The court held that FTC substantive rule-making power was consistent with the plain language of the FTC Act and was a reasonable means of accomplishing the Act's purposes.

In the 1970's Congress significantly increased the remedies available to the FTC. Before 1973, the only enforcement option under section 5(a) of the FTC Act was the cease and desist order. Under this procedure, if the FTC believes that a person is violating section 5(a) and if the FTC determines that action would serve the public interest, then it can give the party involved an opportunity to either "consent" to a formal cease and desist order or to agree informally to discontinue the prohibited practice. "Consent," in this context, refers only to future practices and does not imply an admission of past violations. If a case is not settled by a "consent" order or an informal agreement, the FTC can then issue a complaint and notice of a hearing. After the complaint is filed, a public hearing is held before an administrative law judge of the FTC. This trial type hearing has all the safeguards provided for in the administrative procedure provisions of 5 U.S.C. §§ 556–557.

After hearing testimony, the administrative law judge drafts an initial decision for the FTC. If the FTC then determines the act violates section 5(a) it can issue a cease and desist order to the charged party. The order then becomes final on the 60th day after its issuance unless the charged party files a petition for review with the appropriate U.S. Court of Appeals. If review is sought and granted, the FTC order only becomes final after the order is affirmed by the Court of Appeals or by the Supreme Court, if taken to that court for review. A case may therefore take years from the filing of the original complaint before the cease and desist order becomes final.

Before Magnuson–Moss was signed into law in 1975, only a violation of a cease and desist order could be punished. There was no penalty available for the first violation which gave rise to the cease and desist order. Furthermore, a second violation (that is, a violation of the order itself) received only a $5,000 civil penalty.

Then, in 1969, Ralph Nader's "Raiders" published a report criticizing the FTC's consumer protection efforts. Soon thereafter, a special American Bar Association Commission studied the FTC and rendered a report which generally supported the Nader findings. Both reports urged additional statutory authority to allow the FTC broader consumer protection powers. They specifically recommended that the FTC be given the power to obtain preliminary injunctions against unfair or deceptive acts or practices against consumers.

In response to these recommendations, Congress expanded the FTC's power in section 408 of the Alaska Pipeline Act. This Act empowered the FTC to obtain restraining orders and preliminary injunctions against violators or those who threatened to violate *any provision* administered by the Commission. Section 408 also increased the penalty for violations of cease and desist orders and gave the

FTC the right to bring a civil action through its own attorneys if, after notifying the Attorney General and giving him or her ten days to take the action proposed by the FTC, the Attorney General failed to proceed.

Congress further strengthened the FTC's authority in the consumer protection field with the passage of Magnuson–Moss. As already noted, the Act confirms the FTC's power to issue trade regulation rules. In addition, section 5(m)(1) of the FTC Act, *as amended* by Magnuson–Moss, imposes civil penalties for a first violation if (1) it is a *knowing* violation of a trade regulation rule or (2) if it is a *knowing* violation of a cease and desist order issued against another person. In other words, assume the FTC issues a cease and desist order to General Motors which prohibits the advertisement of mileage tests performed by professional drivers without disclosing that the drivers were professionals. The FTC could then seek civil penalties against Ford if they showed that Ford, with knowledge of the cease and desist order against GM, advertised mileage test results without disclosing that the tests were conducted using professional drivers.

Section 19 of the amended FTC Act also authorizes the FTC to seek *damages* for persons injured by unfair or deceptive acts or practices in two situations:

  (1) for violations of existing trade regulation rules defining unfair or deceptive acts or practices; or

(2) for violations of the FTC Act where the violation led to a cease and desist order *and* where a reasonable person would have known under the circumstances that the act or practice was *dishonest* or *fraudulent*.

The Act does not define what types of practices are considered "dishonest or fraudulent". Presumably, it is a stricter standard than "unfair or deceptive" since Congress would not otherwise have added the new test.

A section 19 action for redress does not preclude the FTC from also bringing a section 5(m) civil penalty action; nor does a 5(m) claim affect the Commission's power to seek redress under section 19. Thus, the FTC can, without resorting to a cease and desist order proceeding, file an action for civil penalties and for redress of injuries resulting from the same rule violation.

D.   PRIVATE ACTIONS USING STATE LAW

1.   GENERAL

Every state now has at least one statute aimed at protecting consumers against unscrupulous or misleading trade practices. However, these statutes vary widely in the types of relief they offer to injured consumers. Because these laws regulate a whole array of "unfair or deceptive acts and practices," they are commonly called "UDAP statutes."[1]

1. For a thorough background on the history, scope and remedies available under UDAP statutes, including a state-by-

A large majority of the states have statutes which expressly allow consumers to sue those engaged in prohibited practices for damages or to obtain other relief. These statutes frequently allow rescission of proscribed transactions, and most allow the prevailing consumer an award of attorney's fees. The attorney's fees provision encourages enforcement of the statute by helping consumers attract competent counsel and encouraging them to protect their rights. Attorney's fees are discussed more fully in section 6, *infra* at page 26. All the state statutes which allow a private cause of action allow recovery of actual damages. While some statutes allow only recovery of actual damages, others allow recovery of multiple damages. Remedies are discussed in section 5, *infra* at page 25.

One difficulty posed by consumer claims under UDAP statutes is that the statutory claim often overlaps with traditional areas of tort, contract, and property law. For instance, since many of the statutes allow recovery of multiple damages and attorney's fees to the successful plaintiff, the incentive is great to bring suit alleging a statutory violation even when the injury is of a kind traditionally remedied in tort or contract. Courts have reached varying conclusions and formulated differing standards when wrestling with this problem.[2] Still, since

state analysis of the law, *see* Unfair and Deceptive Acts and Practices, National Consumer Law Center (4th ed. 1997).

2. For an excellent review of the case law in this area, *see* Dunbar, *Consumer Protection: The Practical Effectiveness of State Deceptive Trade Practices Legislation*, 59 Tul.L.Rev. 427, 449–455 (1984).

state deceptive practice statutes grant a private right of action for most goods bought and sold, it is inevitable that they are used as a remedy for private wrongs even when a remedy is available elsewhere in the law.

2.   WHO MAY SUE?

Not all purchasers of goods may sue under state UDAP statutes. For instance, some states allow retailers or "business buyers" a private remedy as "consumers." Others exclude business plaintiffs from the statutory coverage. Some states allow only "natural persons" to sue, thereby excluding corporations and associations.

A further limitation on who can sue for a deceptive marketing practice may emerge when courts consider an advertisement's tendency to deceive. The question may hinge on whether the court adopts a test which looks to the most sophisticated buyer or the least sophisticated buyer. When faced with deceptive advertisement claims, state courts have typically followed the FTC's original "least sophisticated reader" standard, thereby creating a broad right of action for injured consumers. Then, during the anti-regulatory 1980's, the FTC narrowed the definition of deceptive advertising to require proof that a "reasonable consumer" had suffered injury before a suit against the advertiser could lie. This, of course, reinstated one of the difficult elements of fraud into the deceptive advertising equation: reasonable reliance.

3. WHO CAN BE SUED?

Nearly all UDAP statutes exclude from their coverage some class of defendants. Almost all exempt mass media advertisers who merely publish claims made by others. Several states specifically exclude categories of service providers, particularly professionals such as architects, accountants, attorneys, clergy, doctors, banks and insurance companies. Some only exclude one or two professions, while others speak of professional service providers in general in their exemption clause.

The applicability of a UDAP statute to lawyers may be limited by a statutory exemption. Where there is no express exemption, some courts have been reluctant to apply UDAP statutes to legal practice because to do so would, in the minds of some, diminish the professional status of the practice of law if legal services are viewed merely as one more element of "trade or commerce." Representative of such a view is the opinion of the Illinois Supreme Court in *Cripe v. Leiter*, 703 N.E.2d 100 (Ill.1998), where the court held that an attorney's alleged overbilling is not actionable under the consumer fraud act. The court noted that the billing of a client is not simply a business aspect of the practice of law, but it is linked to the attorney's fiduciary obligation to the client. The fiduciary nature of the attorney-client relationship is different than the typical merchant-consumer relationship, which UDAP statutes were designed to regulate.

4. PROCEDURAL OBSTACLES TO SUIT

A few states require the complaining consumer to give notice of the complaint or to give the defendant a demand letter before actually filing the complaint with the court. The defendant is then allowed a certain number of days to make a settlement offer. Should the consumer nevertheless elect to go to court, multiple damages and attorney's fees may be denied if the consumer is not awarded damages *substantially in excess of the settlement offer*. The apparent purpose of such a procedural requirement is to further judicial efficiency by denying large damage awards to plaintiffs who make no attempt to settle.

5. REMEDIES

The state UDAP statutes are divided into four basic categories when it comes to available remedies. From the point of view of the consumer-plaintiff, the best statute requires an award of treble damages to a successful plaintiff without requiring proof that the violation was knowing or willful. Such liberal relief is available in only two states by statute (although the Texas Supreme Court has interpreted its statute to allow such relief as well). Next best, are statutes dictating the recovery of multiple or punitive damages if the plaintiff proves the defendant willfully engaged in an unfair act or practice. A less attractive statute to the consumer, adopted in several states, leaves the award of multiple damages to the court's discretion. The least desirable statute provides only for recovery of actual damages or some statutory minimum. Seven states have taken this approach.

6. ATTORNEY'S FEES UNDER STATE STATUTES

The consumer who wishes to bring suit under a state UDAP statute will, as a practical matter, usually do so only if the statute provides for recovery of attorney's fees. Once again, each state's statute varies significantly. In twenty-five states, a prevailing plaintiff will always receive attorney's fees. In nine states, the successful plaintiff may need to show that the defendant willfully violated the statute before attorney's fees will be awarded. Fifteen states allow a prevailing *defendant* to receive attorney's fees if he or she shows that the lawsuit was frivolous. Four states simply allow recovery of attorney's fees to the *prevailing party*, whether plaintiff or defendant. And, in two of these states, such recovery is left to the discretion of the court, while in the other two, recovery is automatic.

Clearly, the statutes which allow recovery of attorney's fees only to successful plaintiffs are the most attractive to would-be consumer litigants. Conversely, statutes allowing attorney's fees to prevailing defendants are much more likely to chill consumer utilization of the statutory cause of action. For instance, in *Deer Creek Construction Co. v. Peterson*, 412 So.2d 1169 (Miss.1982), a home buyer sued a builder, asserting both a breach of contract and false advertising under the UDAP statute. While she prevailed on the contract claim, receiving a $3450 damages award, she lost the consumer claim. As a result, she had to pay the defendant's attorney's fees for that part of the suit, for a net loss to her of $484. Obviously, whether a statute allows for attorney's fee recovery (and *which party* the statute allows to recover) will often determine whether the consumer will bring a UDAP claim.

The importance of the availability of attorneys fees has also been recognized under federal law, where consumers are empowered to act as "private attorneys general" in bringing cases. In addition, provision for attorneys fees is particularly important in class actions where the amount of damages at stake in an individual case would be too small to support the lawsuit if the consumer had to absorb the cost of the attorney's fee. *See, e.g., de Jesus v. Banco Popular de Puerto Rico*, 918 F.2d 232 (1st Cir.1990) (construing the Truth in Lending Act).

E. RICO AS A CIVIL SUIT OPTION FOR CONSUMERS

In 1970, Congress enacted the Racketeer Influenced and Corrupt Organizations Act (RICO). The purpose of the Act was "to seek the eradication of organized crime in the United States by strengthening the legal tools in the evidence-gathering process, by establishing new penal prohibitions, and by providing enhanced sanctions and new remedies to deal with the unlawful activities of those engaged in organized crime." Pub.L.No. 91–452, 84 Stat. 922, 923 (Congressional Statement of Findings and Purpose).

Among the means used to prosecute RICO violations, the Act opened the door to the use of state and federal fraud statutes to pursue violators. Furthermore, the law allowed private litigants to recover treble damages, costs and attorney's fees if they established that the form of fraud amounted to "a pattern of racketeering activity." Increasingly, RICO remedies have been sought in cases where no direct link to "organized crime" (at least in the classic "Mafia" sense) is proven. Thus, the potential use of the statute in more conventional commercial litigation is vast and offers a defrauded consumer a remedy far more attractive than that traditionally provided for in tort or contract law. For instance, if a plaintiff shows a pattern of statutory fraud violations by a defendant (e.g., repeated fraudulent claims made in a national sales campaign), he or she may choose to bring a claim under RICO. In addition, by bringing a RICO claim, a plaintiff, who lives in a state with a UDAP statute which awards attorney's fees to the "prevailing party", avoids the risk of paying such fees while retaining a cause of action.

The increased use of RICO by civil plaintiffs who allege violation of fraud statutes to meet the statutory "predicate acts" requirement has generated criticism. The critics claim, among other things, that (1) RICO was intended to be used to prevent the infiltration of legitimate business by organized crime, not ordinary commercial fraud and (2) that the threat of treble damages forces many defendants to settle questionable or unmeritorious claims out of court. Proponents of the widespread use of RICO counter by arguing that (1) Congress intended the use of the statute against any criminal "enterprise", not merely organized crime and (2) that out of court settlements are evidence of RICO's merit in filling gaps left in statutory and common law remedies against fraud.

So far, efforts to neutralize or remove RICO's fraud provisions have been unsuccessful. While they remain, RICO's popularity with civil plaintiffs will almost certainly grow. In the 1990's, RICO claims have been particularly common in consumer credit cases, including disputes involving credit insurance products, loan brokers, mortgage escrow accounts, loan flipping (frequent loan renewals), documentation fees and charges to consumers who pay off loan balances before the loan matures. The application of RICO to false advertising claims will be discussed in Chapter 3.

F. CLASS ACTIONS

1. OVERVIEW

Class actions play an important part in the enforcement of consumer protection laws. In cases where individual consumer claims would produce a small award of damages, a class-based effort may provide the appropriate incentives to bring the action. Attorney's fees may also be available and may be substantially higher in a class action than in an individual case or in individual joined actions, due to economies of scale.

Class actions may also be more effective than individual claims in forcing defendants to modify their behavior. A company may be willing to risk continuing a predatory business practice if the odds are that only infrequent individual claims will be filed. However, the filing of a statewide or national class generally raises both the stakes and the publicity surrounding the business practice. Class actions make it possible for individual consumers, who would otherwise be out-resourced in individual claims to join together and take on economically powerful interests.[3] However, pursuing a class action can be both time consuming and expensive, and will require an analysis of the merits of the case, the costs and the scope of the case (nationwide or statewide class) before proceeding.

2. BASIC REQUIREMENTS FOR CERTIFICATION

Rule 23 of the Federal Rules of Civil Procedure provides the prerequisites for certification of class actions in federal court. Most state laws are identical to the federal rule governing class certification. Rule 23 provides:

(a) **Prerequisite to a Class Action.** One or more members of a class may sue or be sued as

3. For a comprehensive treatment of class actions for consumer claims, *see Consumer Class Actions*, National Consumer Law Center (3rd ed. 1995).

representative parties on behalf of all only if (1) the class is so numerous that joinder of all members is impracticable, (2) there are questions of law or fact common to the class, (3) the claims or defenses of the representative parties are typical of the claims or defenses of the class, and (4) the representative parties will fairly and adequately protect the interests of the class.

(b) **Class Actions Maintainable.** An action may be maintained as a class action if the prerequisites of subdivision (a) are satisfied, and in addition:

(1) the prosecution of separate actions by or against individual members of the class would create risk of

(A) inconsistent or varying adjudications with respect to individual members of the class which would establish incompatible standards of conduct for the party opposing the class, or

(B) adjudications with respect to individual members of the class which would as a practical matter be dispositive of the interests of the other members not parties to the adjudications or substantially impair or impede their ability to protect their interests; or

(2) the party opposing the class has acted or refused to act on grounds generally applicable to the class, thereby making appropriate final injunctive relief or corresponding declaratory relief with respect to the class as a whole; or

(3) the court finds that the questions of law or fact common to the members of the class predominate over any questions affecting only individual members, and that a class action is superior to other available methods for the fair and efficient adjudication of the controversy. The matters pertinent to the findings include:

(A) the interest of members of the class in individually controlling the prosecution or defense of separate actions;

(B) the extent and nature of any litigation concerning the controversy already commenced by or against members of the class;

(C) the desirability or undesirability of concentrating the litigation of the claims in the particular forum;

(D) the difficulties likely to be encountered in the management of a class action.

An in-depth analysis of the procedural hurdles to class certification will not be undertaken here.[4] However, note that the Rule 23(a) prerequisites of numerosity, commonality, typicality and adequacy must be met, as well as at least one of the requirements under Rule 23(b).

Variations in state law often present a difficult hurdle for plaintiffs whose claims may be based on a claim such as fraudulent misrepresentations or fraudulent suppression. In determining whether

4. For a detailed treatment of procedural issues in consumer and other class actions, *see* 1 *Newberg on Class Actions* (3rd. ed. 1992).

class treatment is appropriate, courts "must consider how variations in state law affect predominance and superiority." *Castano v. American Tobacco Co.*, 84 F.3d 734, 741 (5th Cir.1996). Defendants may be able to defeat class certification by showing that state law variations present "insuperable obstacles" to a purported nationwide class. *Walsh v. Ford Motor Co.*, 807 F.2d 1000 (D.C.Cir.1986).

3. POTENTIAL FOR ABUSE IN CLASS ACTIONS

Although class actions provide a powerful tool for consumers, there has been growing criticism of class actions where attorneys come away with multi-million dollar fees, while consumers are left with nothing or little as a class member. One court stated the problem precisely, noting that "the [class] lawyers might urge a class settlement at a low figure or on a less-than-optimal basis in exchange for red-carpet treatment for fees." *Weinberger v. Great Northern Nekoosa Corp.*, 925 F.2d 518, 524 (1st Cir.1991).

Some judges have refused to approve settlements where the defendant offers the class little, while offering the class counsel a large amount in fees. This is particularly true in cases where a proposal was made that class members should receive coupon settlements, while class attorneys would receive millions of dollars in fees. Often the coupon could only be used at the very establishment that was cited as having injured the consumer, and in some cases the terms for use of the coupon made redemption unlikely. Thus, the consumer became victimized by both the business and the attorney's, both in the initial consumer transaction and in the "friendly" settlement.

In response to several abusive class action settlements, in 1997 the National Association of Consumer Advocates (NACA) developed and published a set of guidelines to protect consumers. *The National Association of Consumer Advocates' Standards and Guidelines for Litigating and Settling Class Actions*, published at 176 Federal Rules Decisions, addresses ten topics in class action practice, including coupon settlements, attorneys fees and the legitimacy of "settlement classes." NACA is an organization of more than 350 individuals who represent plaintiffs in individual litigation and class actions. The NACA guidelines should provide good guidance to courts and counsel in considering class outcomes that will be fair to consumers who have been harmed by illegal business practices.

It is important to note that most class actions provide an appropriate remedy to consumers, while fairly compensating the lawyers, who often took a terrific risk in bringing the case. However, there have been some collusive and abusive settlements, harming both the consumers involved and bringing considerable public scorn of the lawyers who gave the clients a coupon, while negotiating a sweetheart deal for fees. The 1997 NACA guidelines are one of the most important developments in consumer law, and can provide both lawyers and judges a benchmark for working through the very difficult fairness issues that can occur in class actions.

G. ARBITRATION

Retailers, lenders and assignees of installment sales contracts increasingly are requiring consumers to sign arbitration agreements at the time of contracting. In some cases, businesses attempt to add arbitration provisions to the contract through "bill stuffer" provisions included in a monthly statement, where the original contract lacks an arbitration provision.

In its purest form, arbitration is a procedure employed by parties who choose to have a dispute determined by an arbitrator of their own selection. Each party presents evidence to the arbitrator in writing or through witnesses. Arbitration proceedings are generally more informal than court proceedings and adherence to the rules of evidence is usually not required. The arbitrators award may or may not be binding on the parties, depending on the terms of the arbitration agreement.

The concept of arbitration is ancient and is mentioned in writings dating back to ancient Greece. Arbitration has been used in the United States since the 18th century and has received considerable attention in consumer settings since the mid–1990's, when the United States Supreme Court issued several important decisions supportive of arbitration.

In *Allied-Bruce Terminix Companies v. Dodson*, 115 S.Ct. 834 (1995), the Court held that the Federal Arbitration Act applies to state courts to enforce an arbitration provision if the contract involves or affects interstate commerce. The test for "affects interstate commerce" is as broad as it is in cases of constitutional law and federal jurisdiction. In *Mastrobuono v. Shearson Lehman Hutton, Inc.*, 115 S.Ct. 1212 (1995), the Supreme Court upheld an arbitrator's award of punitive damages, even though the state law permitted only courts, not arbitrators, to award punitive damages. Since these U.S. Supreme Court cases, the use of arbitration provisions has grown, but the survivability of arbitration agreements in consumer contracts has varied once they are tested in the courts. Some jurisdictions have embraced the concept, while others have expressed serious concerns for the welfare of consumers in the implementation of mandatory arbitration.

Arbitration is often confused with mediation. In mediation, the mediator does not make a decision. The mediator works with both parties and their representatives in the attempt to reach a voluntary agreement. The essence of successful mediation is compromise. On the other hand, in arbitration, the arbitrator reaches a decision that is usually binding.

Consumer advocates have become increasingly critical of mandatory arbitration provisions incorporated in consumer contracts, where the businesses will not deal with the consumer unless the arbitration provision is included in the agreement.[1] Consumers have no real choice in those situations, particularly where the arbitration provision has swept the industry through the work of a trade association, such as a state automobile dealer association. In some cases, the automobile dealer representatives fail to describe the concept of arbitration and present as a "take-it-or-leave-us" choice. This is at odds with the notion that arbitration is a process chosen by the parties to resolve their disputes. The lack of consumer choice in many consumer settings is magnified when a consumer is required to waive access to a jury trial.

Although the U.S. Supreme Court hastened the appearance of arbitration provisions in consumer contracts through cases such as *Terminix*, state law will continue to play an important part in determining the survivability of provisions requiring consumers to waive the right to a jury trial. For example, in *Badie v. Bank of America*, 79 Cal.Rptr.2d 273 (Ct.App.1998), the California Court of Appeals ruled that a credit card issuer cannot impose binding arbitration on its cardholders through a "bill stuffer" notice in a monthly statement, even though the original contract included a statement that "all terms are subject to change." The court found that a change requiring consumers to resort to binding arbitration was different than changes to terms such as the interest rate, late charges and other

1. See Mark E. Budnitz, *Arbitration of Disputes Between Consumers and Financial Institutions: A Serious Threat to Consumer Protection*, 10 OHIO ST. J. ON DISP. RESOL 267 (1995).

open-end credit terms. An after-the-fact limitation
on judicial remedies represents such a fundamental
change that questions are raised regarding the
bank's good faith and fair dealing, and raise a
question whether the contract is so one-sided as to
be illusory. A bill stuffer hardly represents a meaningful "agreement" on arbitration and does not
produce knowing consent.

In another case favorable to consumers, the West
Virginia Supreme Court, in *Arnold v. United Lending Companies Corp.*, Clearinghouse No. 52119 (W.
Va. Dec. 14, 1998), held that a clause is unenforceable where it requires that the borrower's claims be
presented to binding arbitration, but allows the
lender to pursue a court action or foreclosure without first going to arbitration. The Court held that a
provision makes the agreement unconscionable and,
therefore, void and unenforceable as a matter of
law.

In May of 1998 the American Arbitration Association published the *Consumer Due Process Protocol
for Mediation and Arbitration of Consumer Disputes.*

Principle 11 of the *Protocol* provides:

Consumers should be given:

(a) clear and adequate notice of the arbitration
provision and its consequences, including a statement of its mandatory or optional character;

(b) reasonable access to information regarding
the arbitration process, including basic distinc-

tions between arbitration and court proceedings, related costs, and advice as to where they may obtain more complete information regarding arbitration procedures and arbitrator rosters;

(c) notice of the option to make use of applicable small claims court procedures as an alternative to binding arbitration in appropriate cases; and,

(d) a clear statement of the means by which the Consumer may exercise the option (if any) to submit disputes to arbitration or to court process.

There are fifteen principles in the *Protocol* that draw attention to the concerns of consumers in the arbitration process. The principles were developed to establish clear benchmarks for conflict resolution processes involving consumers.

CHAPTER THREE

METHODS OF INDUCING CONSUMER TRANSACTION

A. ADVERTISING

1. COMMON LAW ACTIONS

An action for fraud is one common law cause of action that provides a remedy for the injured consumer. The first and most common fraud claims are tort-based claims for deceit or false and misleading advertising. A buyer may bring an action on deceit against a seller for falsely advertising a product if he can prove all of the following elements: (1) that the seller made a false representation of a material fact; (2) that the seller had knowledge or belief that the representation was not based on known information or that seller had a reckless disregard for known facts; (3) that the seller intended for the buyer to rely on the representation made; (4) that the buyer reasonably relied on the representation and (5) that the buyer suffered damages because of the reliance.

The most difficult element to prove in a fraud action is proving that a representation is one of fact, and not one of opinion. This is because advertisements usually consist of exaggerated claims used to boost the sale of a product. Therefore, a common and often successful, defense asserted by sellers is the "puffing" exception defense. The "puffing" defense exempts a harmless exaggeration of opinion which is not intended to deceive the consumer from being considered as a fraudulent misrepresentation. Courts generally look to several factors to determine whether a representation can be considered as "puffing," including: (1) how specific the representation is; (2) whether the advertisement describes virtues about the product that do not exist; (3) whether it is common practice in the industry to make such assertions and (4) how knowledgeable the buyer is about the product. Generally, a representation made with very specific details regarding the product will be considered as a representation of fact rather than opinion.

A cause of action under false advertising may also be asserted as a breach of warranty claim. A seller has made an express warranty if he makes "[a]ny affirmation of fact or promise ... to the buyer which relates to the goods and becomes part of the basis of the bargain ... UCC § 2–313(1)(a)." If the goods do not conform to the affirmation or promise, then the buyer may have a claim for breach of warranty. Since a breach of warranty action requires the plaintiff to show that the defendant made an affirmation of fact or promise, like an action on deceit, the "puffing" exception is available as a defense. Unlike an action on deceit, however, the buyer does not have to prove that the seller intended to deceive him. What is required is proof that the seller's representation was part of the basis of the bargain.

Although common law actions may be difficult to prove because of the strict element requirements, common law actions have several advantages for the consumer. First, most fraud actions allow the consumer to seek punitive damages which may be unavailable under other statutory remedies. Secondly, the common law element requirements are less strict in those states which have liberalized and broadened the scope of the intent and factual requirements of statutory causes of action.

2.   FEDERAL TRADE COMMISSION'S REGULATION OF ADVERTISING

Section 12 of the FTC Act expressly prohibits false advertising. Section 12 makes unlawful the dissemination of false advertising by mail or other means that directly or indirectly induce consumers to purchase food, drugs, services or cosmetics. 15 U.S.C. § 52 (1994). This provision expressly brings false advertising under the provisions of section 5, so that a false advertisement is automatically considered as an unfair or deceptive practice. Section 15 defines the term "false advertisement" as an advertisement that is materially misleading. Although the term "misleading" is not defined, section 15 provides that:

"in determine whether any advertisement is misleading there shall be taken into account (among other things) not only representations made or suggested by statement, word, design, device or sound is misleading, but also the extent to which the advertisement fails to reveal facts material in the light of such representations or material with respect to the consequences which may result from the use of the commodity to which the advertisement relates under the conditions prescribed in the advertisement; or under such conditions as are customary or usual."

15 U.S.C. § 55 (1994).

The FTC provides three primary sources for interpreting the FTC statutory sections: (1) the FTC rules and regulations; (2) the FTC Guides and (3) case law. Paramount to the exercise of the FTC's authority in regulating advertising is the duty to protect the public and to act in the public's best interest. In light of this duty, the courts have developed standards to determine whether an advertisement is false or deceptive within the meaning of sections 5 and 12 of the FTC Act. The present standard used by the FTC is set out in a three-pronged test. A false or deceptive advertisement is one which contains a material fact or omission that is false or misleading to a consumer and upon which a consumer relied. The determination is based on the consumer's overall impression of the advertisement. Therefore, an advertisement which does not contain false information may still mislead a reasonable consumer.

The FTC Act also gives the FTC authority to seek specific remedies against violators. Since private

action is not available under the Act, the FTC has
the discretion to choose the remedy which will best
protect the public's interest. One possible remedy is
injunctive relief which is granted to the FTC by
section 15 of the Act and is usually obtained
through cease and desist orders. Also, the FTC may
temporarily enjoin any deceptive act with a temporary restraining order. The temporary restraining
order will be effective until the cease and desist
order becomes final, a complaint is dismissed or the
temporary restraining order is set aside. Additionally, under section 19, the FTC may commence a civil
action against any individual, corporation or partnership engaged in unfair or deceptive practices. A
court, under subsection (b) of section 19, has the
authority to grant such relief as is reasonably necessary to redress the injury to consumers. Section 19
also provides a nonexclusive list of possible remedies, including the following: (1) recession or refor-
mation of contracts; (2) refunding of money or
return of property; (3) payment of damages and (4)
public notification of the unfair or deceptive act or
rule violation. However, punitive or treble damages
are not among the available remedies.

The scope of the orders issued by a court or the
Commission must be limited. For example, in *Bris-
tol-Myers v. FTC*, 738 F.2d 554 (2d Cir.1984), the
Second Circuit held that a cease and desist order
must be reasonably related to the alleged
violation. In contrast, however, in *Colgate-Palmo-
live Co. v. FTC*, 310 F.2d 89 (1st Cir.1962), the First
Circuit held that the FTC may frame a remedy in

such a way as to extend beyond the specific illegal conduct.

Although not expressly listed under section 19, corrective advertising is an important implied remedy for false or deceptive advertising. This implied remedy was recognized in *Warner-Lambert Co. v. FTC*, 562 F.2d 749 (D.C.Cir.1977). In that case, the court held that the FTC has the authority to require a violator to affirmatively disclose in future advertisements unfavorable facts regarding the product to remedy the lingering deceptive effects of previous misleading advertisements and to prevent future deception.

3. BAIT AND SWITCH ADVERTISING

The FTC exercises its regulatory powers over deceptive advertisements in many areas. One major source of regulation concerns bait-and-switch sales. The FTC's "Guides against Bait Advertising" sets out the scope and definitions of bait-and-switch advertising. *See* 16 C.F.R. § 238. Bait advertising is defined as:

"an alluring but insincere offer to sell a product or service which the advertiser in truth does not intend or want to sell. Its purpose is to switch consumers from buying the advertised merchandise, in order to sell something else, usually at a high price or on a bases more advantageous to the advertiser. The primary aim of a bait advertisement is to obtain leads as to persons interested in buying merchandise of the type so advertised."

16 C.F.R. § 238.0.

In essence, the "bait" is a bogus offer to sell a product. Whether an advertisement is for a bogus offer or for a bona fide offer depends on certain factors such as: (1) the disparagement of the advertised product; (2) the showing of a defective or an unusable product; (3) an insufficient supply of the advertised product, compared to anticipated demand or (4) the method of compensation or penalty given to salespersons as an incentive or disincentive to sell the higher priced product versus the advertised product. 16 C.F.R. § 238.3. For example, in *Tashof v. FTC*, 437 F.2d 707 (D.C.Cir.1970), the FTC found that a seller had engaged in deceptive practices when it was shown that out of fourteen hundred total pairs of eyeglasses sold, less than ten pairs were sold at the advertised price.

Another growing area of regulation addresses the lengthy product commercials commonly known as "infomercials." Infomercials are usually five to thirty minute television commercials that are designed to appear like reporting programs or talk shows. The deception caused by the infomercials occurs when consumers rely on the information presented in the program as factual. This deception is possible because the commercial is portrayed in a form that appears to be an objective description of the advertised product. Uninformed consumers are unaware that the representations made in the commercials are really biased, persuasive and promotional, rather than factual. For example, in *FTC v. Pantron I Corp.*, 33 F.3d 1088 (9th Cir.1994), the court found that a seller had engaged in deceptive practices by representing in its infomercials that scientific studies supported the corporation's claim that the product's formula promoted new hair growth in balding persons.

A third major category of advertising controversy, and one with which every person has had some exposure, is celebrity endorsement. After all, advertisers know that fame sells products. The product's credibility is boosted by being associated with and directly linked to the reputation of a favorite celebrity. These celebrity endorsements are not exempt from liability. A misleading endorsement is a deceptive act or false advertisement if an endorser makes a false or misleading representation in the advertisement, whether knowingly or unknowingly. The danger of a misleading endorsement is that potentially large numbers of consumers will be induced to buy the advertised product by relying on a celebrity's representations as factual merely because of the celebrity's famed status. In response to the large market of celebrity endorsements and the potentially widespread injuries resulting from fraudulent advertisements, the FTC issued "Endorsement Guides" to prevent the use of misleading endorsements in advertisements. *See* 16 C.F.R. § 255. The Guides require that (1) the advertisement reflect the present opinion of the endorser; (2) the endorser be a bona fide user of the product at the time of the advertisement and (3) required disclosures be given to consumers if the celebrity has a direct financial interest in the sale of the product beyond the reasonable expectations of the consumer. If an endorsement is found to be fraudulent, the advertiser, advertising agency and the endorser may all be liable under the FTC Act if each had control and knowledge of the misleading representation. An injured consumer may also pursue a private action against any of those parties under state UDAP laws or under common law fraud.

4. APPLYING STATES STATUTES TO ADVERTISING

Many states have adopted legislation to regulate deceptive or misleading advertising under state UDAP statutes, as discussed in Chapter 2 of this nutshell. In discussing the application of advertising regulation, it is important to keep in mind the three major variations of UDAP statutes adopted among the states: (1) states that model the FTC Act and broadly prohibit unfair or deceptive acts; (2) states that provide a per se laundry list of prohibited conduct that may or may not include a catchall provision and (3) states that provide for private actions under the UDAP statute offering various types of damages. Among those states that have adopted a per se variation, many expressly include misleading advertising within the laundry list of prohibited acts.

Most UDAP statutes expressly exclude from liability parties that are responsible for distributing advertising materials within a particular media from liability. For example, printers, publishers, magazines, newspapers and television stations are generally held not liable for deceptive advertising contained within a printed or televised advertisement. This protection, however, is very limited. Specifically, the parties must act in good faith to be exempt from liability. If the parties are shown to have actual or constructive knowledge that the distributed advertisement is deceptive, the party may be found liable.

A common defense under both UDAP statutes and the FTC Act is the right to freedom of speech under the First Amendment. The Supreme Court has spoken on this issue in detail and has held that commercial speech is afforded only some protection under the Constitution. The protection, however, is limited and is less than that afforded to noncommercial speech. In *Florida Bar v. Went For It, Inc.*, 515 U.S. 618 (1995), the Court held that the FTC may freely regulate commercial speech that is misleading. Therefore, false and misleading advertisements are not protected by the First Amendment. The Court held that such regulations, however, must be narrowly tailored to meet the following three-pronged test: (1) the government must have a substantial interest in the regulation; (2) the limitations on the commercial speech must materially advance that interest and (3) the regulation must be narrowly drawn.

5.   THE TRUTH IN LENDING ACT'S ADVERTISING PROVISIONS

Sections 141–147 of chapter 3 of the Truth in Lending Act ("TILA") sets forth provisions for advertisements of credit plans. 15 U.S.C. § 1661–67c. The FTC has the authority to enforce the provisions under that chapter, but no right for private action is granted. Additionally, sections 226.16 and 226.24 of Regulation Z of the TILA sets out the required disclosures in credit plan advertising. 12 C.F.R. § 226.16 and § 226.24.

Chapter 3 of the TILA divides the requirements for credit plan advertisements into two main categories: open-ended credit plans and credit ads other than open-ended plans. The requirements are organized according to the disclosures required once the section is triggered. For example, if an advertisement of a credit plan includes specific terms of the credit plan, then the advertisement must include only those terms that are being offered or will be arranged. 12 C.F.R. 226.16(a). Also, if an advertisement for a credit plan discusses a finance charge or periodic rate, then the rate must be disclosed as an annual percentage rate. Additionally, advertisements for consumer leases must disclose any fees, charges or terms of the lease, if the ad mentions any of those terms. 15 U.S.C. § 1667c. Disclosure requirements under TILA will be more thoroughly treated *infra*, at pages 145–152.

6. RACKETEER INFLUENCED AND CORRUPT ORGANIZATION ACT ADVERTISING PROVISIONS

A fifth source of remedy for consumers injured by false advertising is the Racketeer Influenced and Corrupt Organization Act ("RICO") found in 18 U.S.C. §§ 1961–68 (1994). RICO makes it unlawful to receive any income from a person or entity engaged in racketeering activity. *Id.* § 1962(a). To maintain a cause of action under RICO, the consumer must prove the following elements: (1) that the defendant has received money from a pattern of racketeering within the past ten years, including mail or wire fraud; (2) that the defendant invested that money in an enterprise; (3) that the consumer suffered injury as a result of such activity and (4) that the acting entity affected interstate commerce. *Id.* False advertisement actions under RICO are commonly based on mass mailings or telemarketing fraud that form a "pattern of racketeering." *Id.* The consumer has certain advantages for asserting a RICO claim such as the possibility of recovering of attorneys' fees and treble damages. In addition, since RICO is a federal statute, jurisdiction is granted to federal courts which may be better able to provide an unbiased forum for the plaintiff. However, it is often very difficult for the consumer to prove the existence of a pattern of racketeering. Also, like all false advertising claims, the "puffing" exception is available as a defense.

7. CLASS ACTIONS BASED ON DECEPTIVE ADVERTISING

A class action is a very useful tool for consumers in pursuing a false or misleading advertising claim. Class actions were discussed in more detail at pages 29-35. Since most states provide for private action under UDAP statutes, an individual consumer may take advantage of punitive and treble damages. However, a few states, such as Alabama, do not allow consumers to use class actions where their claim is based on the UDAP statute. Individual consumers, however, are sometimes reluctant to file a claim for false advertising because the injuries are usually small but the cost of litigation is high. Therefore, class actions are ideal for individual consumers because they allow consumers to economize the high costs of litigation by spreading those costs throughout the class. Furthermore, an individual may join in a class action suit even if the individual's injury is de minimis.

A class may be certified under UDAP actions, especially when the advertisement is distributed through the mass media. When advertisements are distributed via the mass media, the advertisement is distributed simultaneously to listening, reading and viewing consumers. Therefore, a common deceptive practice can be shown for each member of the class who received the advertisement. The uniformly deceptive message of an advertisement may assist a plaintiff attempting to meet the standards for class certification. Consumers may file a class action if (1) it is impracticable for the class to be joined individually because of the large number of consumers; (2) the same questions of law and fact are common to all of the class members; (3) the claims or defenses of the representative class members are typical of the class as a whole and (4) the representative members will protect the class's interests adequately and fairly.

B.   OTHER SALES PRACTICES

1.   DOOR-TO-DOOR SALES

Most people are familiar with the traditional method of door-to-door sales. From vacuums to insurance, a variety of products are promoted through door-to-door sales. The risk of deception in door-to-door sales is great because of the nature of the sale itself. First, the salesperson typically approaches a consumer at his home, a place where he is vulnerable and cannot easily leave. Secondly, the salesperson generally uses high pressure tactics to induce the consumer to purchase the goods or a service. Third, the consumer will feel compelled to buy into the gimmick and purchase the good just to end the encounter. Therefore, because of the history of door-to-door sales and the abundant opportunities to deceive consumers, the FTC issued the Cooling–Off Period Rule under 16 C.F.R. § 429.

The Cooling–Off Period gives the consumer the right to cancel any sale resulting from a home solicitation within three days after the sale. In addition, the seller must provide the buyer with a written copy of the sales contract and attach to the contract two copies of a notice of the buyer's right to cancel. The Rule requires that the contract include the same terms as used to make the sale. An oral disclosure of the right to cancel must also be given. A consumer cannot waive this right to cancel and the seller must not misrepresent this right. A home solicitation includes any personal contact from a sales representative at a person's home or other locations outside the home such as a motel room, but excludes a place of business.

2. TELEPHONE SALES

The promotion or sale of a product by telephone is a primary source of fraud. There are two major categories of telephone fraud: 900 numbers and telemarketing. On-line scams are closely related to telephone fraud and are frequently regulated under telephone advertising provisions. Telemarketing is a booming industry which is also a haven for scams. Typically, telephone scams take the form of (1) a phoney business investment opportunity that promises unrealistic returns in exchange for high risk or false ventures; (2) prizes or awards promised in return for a fee or (3) "recovery room" scams that target victims of scams and promises to recover the lost prize or investment in return for a fee. Victims usually possess some vulnerable characteristic, such as, the poor or elderly, and calls are usually made during odd hours of the day. This lucrative industry is, however, confined by strict federal and state regulations.

First, the Federal Telephone Consumer Protection Act ("FTCPA"), 47 U.S.C. § 227 (1994) authorizes the Federal Communications Commission ("FCC") to regulate telemarketing corporations. The Act requires that phone calls be made only between 8 a.m. and 9 p.m. local time of the person called. No calls can be made to emergency or health facilities, cell phones or digital pagers. Additionally, the Act allows consumers to bring private actions in state courts for violations and makes available treble damages for willful conduct or injunctions for losses greater than $500.

A second source of regulation is the Telemarketing and Consumer Fraud and Abuse Prevention Act ("TCFAPA"), 15 U. S.C. § 6101 (1994), which places specific limitations on the time, place and manner of telemarketing calls. The TCFAPA authorizes the FTC to regulate the telemarketing industry and specifically prohibits deceptive and abusive telemarketing acts or practices. Telemarketing is defined within the statute as any plan, program or campaign designed to induce the purchase of a product or service advertised. Mandatory disclosures are also required, including the identification of the seller and purpose of the call. The FTC issued a rule that requires that an offer of goods or services be accompanied by a description of their nature. If a prize is offered, then the seller must inform the consumer that it is not necessary to purchase the good or service to enter the contest and qualify to win a prize. Additionally, all costs, fees, restrictions, limitations, conditions or refund limitations must be disclosed. Coercive means used to induce participation, threats, intimidation and harassment by repeated calls are expressly prohibited.

The TCFAPA grants authority to state agencies and attorney generals to sue parties in federal courts for violations and to seek injunctive relief. Additionally, telemarketing fraud is well within the actions available under state UDAP statutes as a deceptive practice. In fact, many UDAP statutes include telemarketing fraud as a per se category of deception. States also have regulations for telemarketing under expansions of their door-to-door statutes. Finally, a common law action for fraud is always available for any type of fraud.

The use of 900 numbers creates another widespread problem. These 900 numbers lure customers with an endless array of gimmicks. For example, a 900 number might promise to give a consumer an opportunity to receive large discounts, when it is actually providing the consumer with long-winded useless advice at a charge to the consumer of so much money per minute for the call. Therefore, substantial regulation of 900 numbers is in place to prevent and prosecute such fraud. The Telephone Disclosure and Dispute Resolution Act ("TDDRA"), 47 U.S.C. § 228 (1992), authorizes the FCC and FTC to enforce the provisions of the Act. The Act prohibits phone companies and long distance carriers from disconnecting a customer's service because of unpaid 900 number charges. Phone companies are also required to itemize 900 number charges and to provide customers with an option of blocking 900 number access from their phones.

Since enforcement of the Act's provisions are solely within the authority of the FCC and FTC, no right to a private action is available under the Act. However, 900 number fraud is actionable under state UDAP statutes and, of course, common law fraud. Many states also have included the use of 900 numbers as a per se category of deception and have imposed criminal liabilities for such fraud.

3.   MAIL AND TELEPHONE ORDER SALES

The FTC also regulates the sale of products by mail or telephone order under the Mail or Telephone Order Merchandise Rule, 16 C.F.R. § 435. This Rule protects consumers' expectations regarding the time and delivery of goods and services ordered by mail or telephone. The Rule requires that the delivery of the ordered merchandise be made within thirty days from the date that the order was placed. This time period is only a default period. The seller may be bound to comply with a shorter time period if the seller so specifies or promises. The time limit may also be extended beyond the thirty days if the consumer expressly consents to an extension. If the seller cannot meet the thirty-day rule, then the consumer must be contacted, at which time, the consumer may either consent to an extension or cancel the order and demand a refund. State UDAP statutes also regulate mail and telephone sales with similar time restrictions and required disclosures.

4.   UNSOLICITED GOODS

Another category related to mail order sales is the sale of unsolicited goods. Unsolicited goods are those goods which are mailed to the consumer without any prior telephone or written contact by the consumer. Often the consumer mistakes these goods as free gifts when the consumer receives the goods by mail. The delivery of the goods, however, is actually an offer to sale the goods to the consumer. The seller bets on the probability that the consumer will fail to return the goods because such failure acts as an acceptance and binds the consumer to a financial obligation to pay for the goods. It is very likely that the consumer will not return the goods, considering the expense and inconvenience associated with having to return the goods. Fortunately for consumers, federal law prohibits the delivery of unsolicited goods by mail and considers such deliveries as a per se violation of the FTC Act. Therefore, the consumer may, in fact, treat any unsolicited goods as a free gift.

5.   REFERRAL SALES

Referral sales may also be a per se violation of UDAP regulations or the FTC Act as a deceptive practice. A referral sales plan is a scheme whereby the seller offers large, often impossible and insincere discounts to consumers on products contingent on some future event. That future event typically requires the consumer to provide the seller with a referral list of other consumers who must also purchase the product for the first consumer to get the discount promised. The problem is, however, that often even if the consumer satisfies the contingency, he does not receive the promised discount.

6. PYRAMID SALES

Pyramid sales are schemes whereby the seller seems to be offering to sell a product at a discounted price when he is actually selling rights to sell new memberships to obtain the discount. The sales scheme is named for its "pyramid" effect. The earliest "investors" are the real beneficiaries of the plan because they are the few who reap the largest percentage of profits as more memberships are sold by the members beneath them. The layers of membership increases as each top layer creates new generations of members beneath them. Because profits are distributed from the top down, however, the members at the lower levels may never recoup their original investment.

7. AUTO SALES

a. Repair Regulations

UDAP statutes typically require automobile repair shops to provide the customer with a written estimate of the costs and repairs of the job. If any work to be done on a car goes beyond the estimate given to the consumer, the shop must get the consent of the consumer before proceeding with the extra work. Some state statutes also give the consumer a right to refuse to pay for repairs agreed upon orally. Therefore, the shop owner's only remedy to collect for the work completed is under a quantum merit theory. This creates an incentive for shop owners to comply with the regulations.

b.   Sale of Used Cars

The most common abuse in the used car industry is the sale of a used car as a new car. The FTC issued the Used Car Rule, 16 C.F.R. § 455, to regulate such abuses in the used car industry. The Rule requires that every used car for sale include a "Buyer's Guide." The "Buyer's Guide" is a packet of information which must disclose the following information:

1.   Warning: spoken promises should be in writing b/c of difficulty in enforcement.

2.   Meaning of "as is."

3.   Box checked for no warranty or "as is," if applicable.

4.   Box checked for warranties.

5.   Clear and conspicuous disclosure of the terms and conditions of any warranty.

6.   Information concerning the scope of any available service contracts.

A common problem which arises in the used car industry is "lemon laundering." Lemon laundering is the resale of used cars that have low mileages, but that have been returned to the manufactures because of some defect. The dealerships will repair the defects and sell the car without any disclosures. By not disclosing the fact that the car had been repaired for defects, the seller engages in fraud.

8. AUTO LEASES

In the late 1980's, only about one in ten new vehicles rolling off dealer's lots were leased. A decade later, one-third of new cars obtained by consumers were under lease programs. Lease programs allow a consumer to drive away a car with little money down and a monthly payment that may be lower than the same deal made with an outright purchase.

However, auto leasing has not been without controversy, and particularly relating to the advertising of lease deals. Some dealers have been accused of making false or misleading claims about the obligations incurred in a lease, as well as engaging in bait-and-switch advertising for lease programs.

In 1976 Congress amended the Truth in Lending Act to require disclosures in connection with consumer leases. Although the consumer leasing provisions are a part of TILA, most people refer to those provisions as the "Consumer Leasing Act." Although the Consumer Leasing Act (CLA) applies to leases of consumer goods such as furniture and appliances, the most important application of the CLA is to automobile leases. The CLA is discussed more thoroughly in Chapter 6, at pages 220-223.

CHAPTER FOUR

THE CONSUMER CREDIT MARKET

A. THE GROWTH OF CONSUMER INSTALLMENT DEBT

On September 18, 1958, the Bank of America "dropped" 60,000 credit cards on the city of Fresno, California.[1] Although "the Fresno drop" did not end until more than 2 million cards were placed in circulation over 13 months, this first mass mailing of credit cards resulted in a disaster for the bank. Fifteen months after that September day in 1958, the Bank of America had officially lost $8.8 million on the new credit card program, with the real figure estimated by some to be as high as $20 million, in 1960 dollars.

Bank of America and its competitors learned from the mistakes that were made in this first mass mailing of credit cards. Before the practice of mass mailings of cards was outlawed, banks would blanket the country with roughly 100 million new cards. Many people point to "the Fresno drop" as the first crack in the Depression mentality, that even as late

1. For a history of the birth of the credit card, *see* Joseph Nocera, *The Day the Credit Card Was Born*, The Wash. Post Magazine, December 4, 1994, at 7.

as the 1950's caused consumers to be wary of taking on personal debt.

Consumer installment debt (auto loans, personal loans, closed-end home equity loans, home improvement loans and credit card balances) increased from $106 billion in 1971, to $333 billion in 1981, and to $729 billion in 1991. Peter J. Letsou, *The Political Economy of Consumer Credit Regulation*, 44 Emory L.J. 587 (1995). As of 1990, the average consumer had 9.1 credit cards with a total combined unpaid balance of $2,042. Economists report that by 1997, the average household had over $4,000 in credit card debt. Also, a relatively new feature in the consumer credit market is credit card debt secured by a second mortgage on the home through a home equity line. Although many economists and business people point to the growth of consumer credit as a critical element in building the economy and furthering the sale of automobiles, appliances and other basic consumer goods, others warn that there is too much emphasis on consumption, rather than savings and investment among American households. *See, e.g.,* Dale Ellis, *Introduction to the Symposium: Why Consumer Bankruptcies Will Continue Like a Plague–Structural Forces that Institutionalize Bankruptcy as a Way of Life in America*, 47 Consumer Fin.L.Q.Rep. 391 (1993).

B. THE CONSUMER LENDING INDUSTRY

1. OVERVIEW

Although most of us view a loan as a different animal than a typical sale of goods or services, a loan or the credit element of an installment sales transaction is really nothing more than the sale of money for a price.[2] The price of a loan is the interest rate that the loan carries, along with the other associated charges that may or may not be disclosed as a "finance charge" under various state and federal laws.

It is a fact of life that in the purchase of goods and services, the expectations we hold regarding the quality of the goods and total benefit we expect to receive increase as we pay a higher price. Quality consumer goods may carry an exquisitely high price, while inexpensive goods may be a "watch" or a "stereo" in name only. Goods are for sale along a range of prices and merchants cater to buyers at all levels, generally based on the buyer's preferences and ability to pay.

The consumer lending industry, where the commodity is money, is not unlike the market for the sale of goods in that the price tag on a loan varies widely. Money is for sale at very low rates to credit-

2. For a more thorough analysis of the marketing of consumer credit, *see* Gene A. Marsh, *The Hard Sell in Consumer Credit: How the Folks in Marketing Can Put You in Court*, 52 Consumer Fin.L.Q.Rep. 295 (1998).

worthy customers, while high risk borrowers face very high rates in what is today a largely unregulated market, at least with respect to the interest rates that may be charged. Simple usury cases are not common in modern times because interest rates are not regulated in many areas of lending. To the extent that there are any lids in place, they are found in state consumer credit laws that apply to small loans. However, if a usury violation is found and the actions of the creditor are viewed as intentional, disastrous consequences may follow. Usury laws are more thoroughly discussed in Chapter Seven.

The financial institutions servicing the consumer credit industry range from large banks, credit unions, mortgage companies and other depositary institutions, to small community banking institutions and, increasingly, so-called fringe banking services, such as pawnshops, check-cashing services, and payday loan shops.[3]

Standing between the banks and fringe-banks are an array of consumer finance companies. Many consumer finance companies are subsidiaries of banks or bank holding companies, insurance companies, automobile manufacturers, consumer retailers and other industrial corporations. Finance companies generally make loans at rates that are higher than those available at commercial banks, but not anywhere near the rates of pawnshop loans, where

3. For an excellent treatment of the various entities that operate as fringe banks, *see* John P. Caskey, Fringe Banking (1994). *See also*, Michael Hudson, Merchants of Misery (1996).

the interest charge may approach or even exceed 100 percent per year.

2. PAYDAY LOANS

The recent growth of payday loans (also called post-dated check loans, deferred presentment loans or cash advances) is typical of the short-term, installment credit variations that have appeared in the consumer credit market, largely due to the elimination of interest rate caps and a general trend toward deregulation. Typically, a customer comes to a check casher who has advertised "payday loans" or "payday advances." The customer may need to obtain $100 cash, so he or she writes a check in the amount of the cash needed plus the fee charged by the check casher, which may be $15 to $25, or higher. Both parties agree to defer negotiating the check for 14 days or until the customer's next payday. Implicit in this agreement is the understanding that the customer's check is "worthless" until then. The check may or may not be postdated. On or near the due date, the check casher negotiates the customer's check, or the customer may come back to redeem the check or to renew the transaction for an additional fee. These check cashers are often not licensed under small loan acts or otherwise regulated for this activity.

3. PAWNSHOPS

A relatively new concept in pawnshops is the automobile title pawn, where the consumer continues to drive the car but pawns the car title. Permissible interest rates on auto title pawns around the country range from small loan act rates, up to 300 percent per year. Many automobile title pawnshops charge the maximum rate and although they advertise that the first month is free, borrowers who return to the pawnshop to repay the debt at the end of the first month are often encouraged to keep the credit outstanding, thus triggering the high rate.

4.   RENT-TO-OWN

Another arrangement which approximates a credit transaction, but usually escapes scrutiny under usury statutes is a rent-to-own (RTO) contract. The rent-to-own industry is another example of a subprime market, where most of the consumers who enter into these contracts are unable to purchase the item through a typical credit arrangement and installment sales contract. An individual who does business with a rent-to-own company often also uses the services of a pawnshop, check cashing outlet and other "fringe bank" entities.

In a typical rent-to-own arrangement, the consumer is able to rent an item such as a couch, microwave or refrigerator, for $10 to $15 dollars a week, and often with little or no money down. Typically, a "no credit check" pitch is made in advertisements and no adverse entry is made in a credit report if an individual returns the item after using it for weeks or months. The usual RTO transaction includes a purchase feature which allows the consumer to own the item outright after making the weekly rent payment for a year or more. When you match the stream of payments under a typical RTO arrangement against the payments one would make to own the item outright under a typical credit transaction, the effective annual percentage rate on the transaction is 200 percent or more.

This industry has managed to flourish and escape scrutiny under most attacks based on usury because it did a preemptive strike in many states and lobbied for legislation to validate a RTO transaction as a stand-alone concept, and avoid scrutiny as a small loan, a secured transaction (Article 9 of the Uniform Commercial Code), or be tested under other consumer protection statutes. There are 43 states which "validate" RTO transactions and typically only require disclosure of the total of payments, whether the goods are new or used, and who has the "risk of loss" during the term of the RTO transaction.[4] Some states do require disclosure of the cash price or fair market value of the item.

Due to the state legislation which attempts to validate RTO transactions and immunize them from scrutiny under consumer protection statutes, consumer advocates have had a difficult time invalidating RTO arrangements. The most common theories in RTO litigation are based on the idea that a typical RTO deal is really credit transaction, raising

4. For a comprehensive discussion of RTO transactions, *see* Consumer Credit Law Manual, National Consumer Law Center, Chapter 7 (1998).

issues of protection under Article 9 of the UCC, the Bankruptcy Code and usury. Where a lessee agrees to pay a sum equal to or exceeding the value of the goods, under which there is an option to purchase for nominal consideration, the transaction may be viewed as a credit sale, in certain cases, requiring Truth in Lending disclosures. 15 U.S.C. § 1602(g).

The industry counters that the state law validates the arrangement as a stand-alone concept and that the typical RTO arrangement is not a true "credit transaction" because the consumer is always free to return the item and walk away, with no further obligation. That is, a true RTO arrangement is "binding" only week-to-week and creates no absolute legal obligation for a stream of payments. In that way, a RTO deal is unlike a consumer note or installment sales contract which creates a legal obligation to repay the sum of weekly or monthly payments.

It is the ability of the consumer to terminate the typical RTO deal, in most cases without further obligation or penalty, that insulates most of these transactions from scrutiny under Truth in Lending or the Consumer Leasing Act, discussed in Chapter 6. The Consumer Leasing Act applies only to leases greater than four months in duration. Most RTO agreements are not covered under the Consumer Leasing Act because the arrangement is terminable without penalty before four months. *In re Hanley*, 111 B.R. 709 (Bankr.C.D.Ill.1990).

Whether TILA applies directly to a RTO contract will depend on the specific facts of the arrangement. TILA Reg. Z § 226.2(a)(16) states that a covered credit sale includes certain leases unless they are terminable without penalty to the consumer. One creative argument is that if a consumer pays on a RTO deal for a long period of time, but then terminates the arrangement, the forfeiture of the consumer's "equity" constitutes a penalty, within the meaning of Regulation Z. *Green v. Continental Rentals*, 678 A.2d 759 (1994). Another angle in the attempt to apply TILA coverage is to argue that the RTO transaction is really just like an installment sales contract, resulting in ownership, rather than a mere lease of the product. If TILA does apply, then the disclosures and remedies discussed in Chapter Six would apply.

This picture of consumer lending is not meant to suggest that there are bright lines that can be found in analyzing the practices of lenders along the lending chain. For example, some banks and other depositary institutions provide services to low income borrowers, while some very wealthy people have been known to get a quick loan at pawnshops. However, economists, lenders and regulators generally accept the model of the consumer finance industry that is described above, with consumer finance companies falling somewhere in the middle of the market.

C. THE SUBPRIME CREDIT MARKET

1. OVERVIEW

While the term "fringe banks" generally refers to businesses such as pawnshops and payday loan shops that charge very high rates for their services, probably the fastest growing subset among the more traditional lenders are those that operate in what is usually called the "subprime" market.[5] Although there is no universally accepted industry standard for credit grades, most lenders use categories such as "A," "A-," "B," "C," "D" and "F." Consumers with "A" ratings generally have no late mortgage payments and no credit card payments over 30 days delinquent in the last year. At the other end, consumers with "F" ratings are currently in bankruptcy or foreclosure. Although the term "subprime" lending means different things to different people, most lenders use the term when referring to "B," "C" and "D" credit. Consumers with "D" credit ratings are generally described as experiencing problems that are severe. The use of information to develop credit ratings and credit reports is more thoroughly discussed in Chapter Five, at pages 129–131.

In recent years there has been a considerable boom in subprime lending activity involving automobiles, home mortgages and even credit cards. In

5. This overview of the subprime credit market is taken from the testimony of Professor Gene A. Marsh, before the United States Senate Special Committee on Aging, March 16, 1998, Senator Charles Grassley, Chair.

the auto industry there were approximately 25 subprime lenders in 1991. In 1998 there were more than 150. Mortgage lenders are also vying to make loans to people with shaky credit and subprime mortgage loans are being bundled and securitized. According to one industry publication, the securitization of subprime mortgages increased by 50% from 1996 to 1997.

Even in the sale of consumer products such as satellite television reception equipment, private label credit card issuers have established separate programs to identify and market credit cards to customers who were previously turned down. In some cases the credit card issuers created the programs in response to dealer complaints that too many customers were refused credit in an initial application. As one would expect, the risks inherent in subprime lending are reflected in higher interest rates. Subprime borrowers are described in industry material as borrowers who often do not shop around or haggle over terms. Subprime borrowers may be relegated to finding credit *at any price*.

Lending to subprime borrowers was once considered the province of small loan companies, finance companies and "fringe banks." However, the subprime market is now also served by large mortgage companies, national banks and credit subsidiaries of automobile manufacturers. Several of the largest national banks provide financing for auto purchasers with impaired credit records, buying used-car loans at a discount from face value. Purchasing the contracts at a discount is also a common practice in subprime mortgage lending and even in the acquisition of credit card paper. In some recent cases, lawyers for consumers have challenged this deep discount financing and have alleged that retailers have hidden finance charges in the sales price of automobiles and other consumer goods, in anticipation of selling the consumer paper at a discount. These cases on hidden finance charges and discounts will be discussed in Chapter Six, *infra* at 155-162.

The very high returns initially experienced in the subprime market drew many entrants and investors, but this was followed by an industry shake-out which led to some business bankruptcies and shareholder lawsuits. In some cases, the aggressive accounting strategies used by subprime lenders created a house of cards which collapsed when new entrants caused margins to shrink and borrowers with spotty credit histories (typical subprime borrowers) started experiencing trouble in repayment of the loans. Both the Securities Exchange Commission and the FDIC have warned accounting firms and financial institutions that they must do a more thorough job in how they book profits from loans that are repackaged and how they reflect the risks posed by subprime loans.

2. ABUSIVE LENDING PRACTICES IN THE SUBPRIME MARKET

Some of the lending practices in the subprime market have been the subject of considerable criticism by regulatory agencies and consumer groups.[6] Among the most harmful practices is "equity-stripping." This occurs when a loan is made based on the equity in the house, rather than on the borrower's ability to pay. Consumer advocates claim that the loan is designed to fail and will result in foreclosures, with the lenders acquiring the borrower's home equity.

Another problem in the subprime market is packing, where credit insurance and other extras are added to the loan. Lenders and dealers often retain a large part of the premiums charged for credit insurance products. The problem of packing of credit insurance products will be more fully discussed in Chapter Eight, pages 294-322.

And in many cases, loans are frequently renewed and restarted, in a practice that is known as "flipping." In many cases, the lender triggers a loan renewal and restarts the loan, causing the debtor to make little progress against the loan amount. The impact on the consumer of flipping will also be discussed in Chapter Eight, at pages 280-293.

D. DEALER-ARRANGED FINANCING

1. OVERVIEW

As consumers became more comfortable with carrying larger debt levels and using nontraditional

6. Home equity lending abuses in the subprime mortgage industry were featured in a Prepared Statement of the Federal Trade Commission, in testimony before the Senate Special Committee on Aging, March 16, 1998, Senator Charles Grassley, Chair.

sources for credit, they often turned to the dealers of consumer goods, such as the sellers of cars, jewelry, furniture and appliances, to either sell the goods on credit in a buy-here pay-here arrangement, or to arrange financing from a third party, such as a finance company. Credit sales made in this way can be beneficial for consumers, who find it convenient to shop for goods and credit at one location. However, where a dealer engages in a fraudulent sales practice or misrepresents the terms of the credit, the assignees of the installment sales contracts who provided the credit are often pulled into the litigation. This is particularly true in situations where the dealer is itinerant and is not a deep pocket for recovery. The finance company or other creditor that provided the credit to make the transaction go may face liability under one of the many "lender liability" theories that started to appear in the 1980's.[7]

2.   LENDER LIABILITY THEORIES INVOLVING DEALER PAPER

The term "lender liability" is not a distinct theory but an aggregate of traditional theories applied to the debtor-creditor relationship.   Judgments against lenders have been obtained using a range of theories based on common law and statutory provi-

7. This material on dealer-arranged financing is generally drawn from a law review article written by Gene A. Marsh, *Lender Liability for Consumer Fraud Practices of Retail Dealers and Home Improvement Contractors*, 45 Ala.L.Rev. 1 (1993).

sions. Common law claims include negligence, fraud, conversion, breach of contract, breach of fiduciary duty, alter ego liability, duress, and interference torts. The most common statutory claims are those under the Racketeer Influenced and Corrupt Organizations Act (RICO), state and federal securities laws, environmental laws, and the Bankruptcy Code. Several large judgments obtained against lenders in the mid–1980's, combined with the economic downturn and a more aggressive litigation environment caused borrowers to attempt to pass their losses from failed transactions back to financial institutions. In the 1980s, juries regularly returned multimillion-dollar verdicts against financial institutions. Due to these experiences, the term lender liability became a phrase much on the mind of every loan officer during this period.

The climate for lenders in the early 1990s improved due to a recovering economy and because many of the early lender liability judgments were reversed on appeal, particularly where the cases were brought on contract-related claims. However, claims against lenders predicated upon tort theories and other common law claims remain a serious threat.

One prominent area of lender liability is described as "control liability."[8] Although there are several theories under which control liability may

8. *See* J. Dennis Hynes, *Lender Liability: The Dilemma of the Controlling Creditor*, 58 Tenn.L.Rev. 635 (1991); K. Thor Lundgren, *Liability of a Creditor in a Control Relationship with Its Debtor*, 67 Marq. L. Rev. 523 (1984).

arise, the most widely recognized theory involves a creditor's control of a debtor's business which is so dominant that the creditor is characterized as the alter ego of the debtor. A closely related theory in other control cases portrays the debtor as the agent of the lender using classic agency concepts, with resulting lender liability for the acts and transactions of the debtor.

A new theory of liability has developed under which lenders are held liable for the fraudulent practices of dealers providing goods and services to consumers. The most prominent cases include finance companies characterized as controlling the actions of, or being too closely involved in, the practices of home improvement contractors. Secured creditors have been held liable for millions of dollars in punitive damage awards resulting from the purchase or funding of small loans made in contracts for home improvements between homeowners and home improvement contractors. In the transactions, the contractor "arranged" financing for the homeowner, with the lender approving the loan before the work began. Plaintiffs in a number of cases have attempted to apply doctrines such as agency, aiding and abetting, intentional wrongful pattern and practice conduct, and the violation of statutory duties imposed in the lending relationship. These cases are often described under the general heading of "mortgage fraud" and "home equity fraud."

Some commentators cite the explosive growth in the number of these mortgage fraud cases as signaling a resurgence in consumer litigation following the probusiness and politically conservative climate of the 1980's. Also, damage awards in some of the early cases have provided an incentive for private attorneys to take these cases with the hope of recovering more than the minimal damages often available under state and federal consumer protection laws.

3. PROBLEMS WITH DEALERS IN HOME IMPROVEMENT

Contractors in the home improvement industry range from the well-established, financially secure and insured businesses with a long history of excellent work, to the shoddy, almost migrant, no-asset operators who are responsible for many fraudulent practices. Some contractors roam from town to town and even across the country, changing the name of their businesses as they change locations. The practices of the shady operators, pejoratively referred to as the "tin men," have been chronicled in numerous popular magazines and newspapers, even becoming the plot for a major motion picture. Unfortunately, there is no humor in the experience of the homeowners victimized by these con artists who "come through town like locusts, pick it clean and move on to another town."[9]

In 1975 the Federal Trade Commission described deceptive practices in the home improvement indus-

9. Steve Huntley, *Those Home Repairs That Really Aren't*, U.S. News & World Report, July 25, 1983, at 49.

try in support of its development of the FTC Rule. The FTC Rule is discussed in Chapter Nine, at pages 343-360. The home improvement industry and the situation of targeted consumers was described as follows.

Home improvements have long been an area subject to considerable deception and outright fraud. In one especially outrageous scheme, which cost hundreds of homeowners millions of dollars, a few homeowners' suits are finally being heard in the courts. Because the contractor has become bankrupt, however, and because consumers cannot maintain claims or defenses against holders in due course of their negotiable instruments, consumers who are fortunate enough to obtain favorable judgments in court will receive only about five cents on the dollar when the remaining meager assets of the contractor are distributed to satisfy debts and judgments.

A related field of deception is the sale of aluminum siding. The record reflects numerous cases of abuse in siding sales and subsequent collection efforts by third party holders of promissory notes. Such sales occur nationwide, often involve a referral scheme or "model home" ploy and invariably produce substantial indebtedness for the consumer.[10]

10. Trade Regulation Rule Concerning Preservation of Consumers' Claims and Defenses, Statement of Basis and Purpose, 40 Fed. Reg. 53,511 (1975) (footnotes omitted) [hereinafter Statement of Basis and Purpose].

The practices of home improvement contractors and their impact on homeowners described by the FTC in 1975 could be applied to some of the dealings of this industry and other itinerant dealers in the 1990s. Some home improvement contractors who advertise (often through 800 number phone banks using television commercials or through newspaper inserts) are little more than a small office and telephone. The company name often conveys a patriotic or rock-solid impression. The firm may employ only independent contractors who make the sales calls and do the work at the home site. The commissions paid to salespeople in some of the cases exceed the fee paid to the subcontractor for the work on the home. All of these expenses, including a large profit for the home improvement company, are financed at a high interest rate and built into the contract price quoted to the homeowner.

Some subcontractors, who move around the state doing siding or roofing jobs, have little incentive to build a reputation for quality work because such subcontracts are not community-based and will often be there one day and gone the next. The subcontractor simply lives off of the contracts arranged by the home improvement company.

Many home improvement cases cited in the literature provide a good introduction to the practices of some businesses in the industry, but none are more striking than a Texas case and an Alabama case. Perhaps the worst situation for a homeowner was described in *Perez v. Briercroft Service Corp.*, 809

S.W.2d 216 (Tex.1991), where the Texas court noted that shortly after the work was completed on the home, "the siding began to fall off the house, the replacement windows fell apart, the screen doors would not shut completely and the sewer vents terminated in the attic instead of extending through the roof, causing foul odors within the house." *Perez*, 809 S.W.2d at 217.

United States Finance Co. v. Jones, 229 So.2d 495 (Ala.1969), describes the ordeal of an Alabama widow in Baldwin County who could barely read and write. She was visited by two salesmen from a Florida contracting company. The contractor agreed to put aluminum siding on the house and provide a new roof. Instead, the contractor put tar paper on the sides of the house and sprayed it with aluminum paint. The signature of the husband on the mortgage was obviously forged since he was dead at the time the contract was made.

The quality of the work in these cases paints a picture that well illustrates the experiences of some homeowners during the 1990s. Poorly educated, low income homeowners frequently enter into contracts priced at exorbitant levels and have liens placed against their homes. High pressure sales tactics along with the promise of easy financing and other fraudulent inducements, such as the promise of rebates for showing the "model home," are standard operating procedures for some contractors in this industry. Additionally, some of the critical documents are often forged or improperly dated.

As in many industries, the fraudulent practices of a few damage the reputation of those who operate honestly. It is inaccurate to cast all contractors in the home improvement industry as preying on consumers and providing shoddy work. The industry has quality contractors, as well as its defenders. In 1976 at a hearing before the House Subcommittee on Consumer Protection and Finance, Mr. Walter W. Vaughan, Vice Chairman of the Installment Lending Division of the American Bankers Association citation, stated that the home improvement contractor "may be one of the few true craftsmen left."[11] Clearly, a failure in public and self-regulation of the home remodeling industry and some of the associated lending practices that induce homeowners to contract for the work contributed to the increase in recent fraud lawsuits, resulting in millions of dollars in damages against lenders. As a deep pocket, the lender may find itself facing a liability which might be more properly placed on the contractor.

4. FINANCING DEALER CONTRACTS

The availability of easy financing is often heavily promoted in advertisements for aluminum siding and other home improvement work, as well as dealers in other industries. Because many of the contractors have few assets, they rely on placing the

11. Consumer Claims and Defenses: Hearings Before the Subcomm. On Consumer Protection and Finance of the House Comm. on Interstate and Foreign Commerce, 94th Cong., 2nd Sess. 131 (1976) [hereinafter *Hearings*].

paper with a lender in an arrangement much like that of an automobile dealership that arranges financing for its customers. Home improvement contractors place many of their contracts with finance companies, with any particular contractor having four or five finance companies with which it deals. Finance companies often have a separate operating division and separate operating provisions for establishing and maintaining dealer relationships with home improvement contractors. Dealer agreements in home improvement lending are virtually identical to those between a retail seller of goods and a lender that buys the notes or contracts from the dealer.

Often the contract between the homeowner and the contractor reads like a purchase money loan, with the contract containing the homeowner's promise to repay the loan to the contractor, and usually containing a security interest or mortgage to secure the loan. The contractor's rights to payment are then assigned to a lender, with the finance company typically having approved, in advance of the sale, the creditworthiness of the homeowner and having conditionally committed to purchase the paper from the contractor. The most common contract provisions in dealer agreements commit the lender to buy the paper subject to a number of conditions, including completion of the home improvement work to the satisfaction of the homeowner. Dealer agreements may also include a number of protections for the lender, including warranties made by the contractor regarding com-

pliance with required disclosures to the homeowner, indemnification, or reserve account provisions in the event the homeowner defaults or
raises a defense to payment and provisions for
termination of the contractor-lender relationship.
The contract may also indicate that the finance
company is buying the paper with or without recourse against the contractor.

The notes and documents signed by the homeowner often contain assignment provisions and may
indicate the name of the assignee on the contract.
Some have characterized the underlying mortgage
between the homeowner and the contractor as a
sham, given that the loan may be entirely funded by
and assigned to the finance company at the moment
of the execution of the documents by the homeowner. However, the assignment of such lending
contracts should not, by itself, be viewed as a fraudulent or dishonest practice. To do so would be to
indict a long-standing and traditional lending practice recognized as legitimate in many sectors of the
economy, such as the automobile industry and the
retail sale of consumer appliances.

Although the mere assignment of a payment obligation should not be viewed as harmful to the
homeowner or as a deceptive practice, the profit
that is made by the contractor is often taken only at
the time of the assignment and may not be obvious
to the homeowner. For example, although the note
may show an interest rate of eighteen percent to
the consumer, the finance company may purchase
the note at the rate of fifteen or sixteen percent.

The spread between the rates becomes a part of the profit taken by the home improvement contractor. Plaintiffs have argued that this spread or "chop" results in the debtor not receiving the full value of the loan and that the discount should be disclosed to the homeowner. In consumer credit litigation, these are often referred to as "yield spread premium" cases.

The cases discuss whether this type of lending should be characterized as primary or secondary. Traditionally, a primary loan is made directly from the lender to the borrower and does not require an assignment. The terms "indirect" or "secondary" apply to cases in which the lender does not directly lend money to the purchaser, but instead does so by acquiring the contract from the dealer or contractor. The attempt to characterize finance companies as primary lenders in these cases is made by portraying the lender as closely connected with the practices of the contractor. Because the homeowner may never have contact with the lender, the contractor is portrayed as the agent of the lender in securing the loan, setting the stage for a derivative liability argument once the agency relationship is established.

5. UNFAIR LENDING PRACTICES IN DEALER FINANCING

The preceding section described the home improvement industry and detailed the mechanics of common lending arrangements involving the homeowner, the contractor, and the finance company. This part of the chapter builds upon the survey of arrangements and examines the alleged abusive and fraudulent lending practices originating out of the home improvement industry. This section will be followed by an examination of a prominent case where an assignee was held liable for the fraudulent practices of home improvement contractors.

Plaintiffs' lawyers and consumer groups point to a number of factors which they argue contribute to a resurgence of fraudulent consumer lending practices. Some point to the mortgage fraud cases as a legacy of the Reagan administration's 1980's focus on deregulation. Moreover, they point to a general decrease in consumer protection enforcement caused by reductions in funding for consumer protection agencies and legal services to the poor as contributing to the problem.

A review of complaints drawn from litigation occurring across the country involving the cases that are sometimes grouped under the general headings "home equity fraud" or "mortgage fraud" leads one through a maze of legal theories. The common theme is that plaintiffs in low income neighborhoods were targeted by dishonest home improvement contractors whose operations were furthered by the lending practices of finance companies. At the 1992 National Consumer Rights Litigation Conference held in Boston, Massachusetts, the presentation on unfair and deceptive inducements of home improvement contracting and financing, included claims of false advertising, violations of federal truth-in-lending laws, violations of state and federal unfair and deceptive practices acts, fraud, breach of contract, unconscionability, equity theft, violations of state credit regulations, and claims and defenses raised under the FTC Rule.

One of the more novel theories in some of the mortgage fraud cases is what is described as "equity theft." The allegation in support of some fraud claims is that even in poor neighborhoods, increasing land values and repayments in mortgages, particularly among older homeowners, have left a "piggybank" of equity which lenders have taken, through second mortgage loans and subsequent foreclosure. The claim made is that some of the lenders are making loans clearly designed to fail, particularly when the loan stretches repayment capacity beyond any reasonable limit, the debtor's income is poorly documented (if at all), and the loan is made to an individual who brings to the finance company a miserable credit record and repayment history. If there is a low first mortgage balance and a fair amount of equity in the home, the second mortgage loan may be made even though there is little chance that the monthly payment obligation will be met.

Some have also claimed that appraisals have been inflated in order to justify a higher loan amount, with correspondingly high monthly payments that will far exceed the capacity of the debtor, virtually guaranteeing that foreclosure will result. These claims are very difficult to establish except in the most blatant cases, because appraisals are generally viewed as opinions, thereby failing to meet a critical element of fraud as misrepresentation of a material fact. However, some cases have held that expressions of opinion by an expert can form the basis of a fraudulent action. It is only fair to say that appraisers face pressure from both borrowers and lenders to arrive at a figure that will justify a certain amount.

Other lending practices which have been alleged as unfair and predatory include the structuring of loans with large balloon payments—in some cases with no monthly payment but an annual or balloon payment that could not likely be met—causing foreclosure or refinancing with new transaction costs paid by the consumer. Some finance companies dangle small amounts of new money in front of debtors each year, stacking smaller debts on top of one another, and in some cases refinancing the entire balance each time with corresponding transaction costs i.e., various closing fees and prepaid finance charges, that are borne by the consumer each time. Refinancing each year will cause the bulk of each new payment to be interest, with only a minuscule amount going to principal each month. The debtors often pay back only a small amount of principal each year while periodically borrowing a little more in response to a direct mailing from the finance company promoting easy availability. Thus, they remain indebted to the finance company for years for what is initially a modest loan amount. The practice of frequent loan renewals is sometimes called "flipping" and will be discussed further in Chapter Eight, at pages 280-293.

6. A BENCHMARK CASE IN DEALER FINANCING

One of the most important cases involving dealer fraud and financing is *Union Mortgage v. Barlow*, 595 So.2d 1335 (Ala.), *cert. denied*, 506 U.S. 906 (1992). In *Union Mortgage*, the Alabama Supreme Court ruled that an award of $150,000 in compensatory damages in a fraud claim and $6,001,000 in punitive damages was not excessive against a lender which was found to have engaged in a pattern and practice of fraud in funding loans arranged by a home improvement contractor. The home improvement company in this case, American Home, performed home improvement contracts only if Union Mortgage approved credit in advance. No evidence existed that American Home submitted loan applications to any other lenders or performed repairs for any of the applicants for whom Union Mortgage denied credit. American Home had no life of its own, separate from contracts where credit was approved by Union Mortgage.

The loan at issue was secured by a mortgage on the home and was immediately assigned to Union Mortgage in the same document executed by Willie May Barlow and American Home. With a 17.98 percent annual percentage rate on a contract price of $8,000 for the home repairs, the total payments due came to $17,284.80. Union Mortgage paid

American Home only $7,075 for the mortgage. Union Mortgage then resold the mortgage to the Mitsui Bank of Japan for $7,975.93.

It is important to note events which took place prior to the contract in order to show which party instigated the home improvement work and the conditions under which the loan was made. In 1987, the borrower, Willie Mae Barlow, applied for a $2,000 loan from American Home, but the loan was denied. In 1988, a representative of American Home contacted Barlow and told her that Union Mortgage could lend her money but only if American Home could make some repairs on the house. Although the home was not in need of work, the homeowner agreed to have some minor work done and to grant a second mortgage on the home in exchange for receiving $2,000 in cash. At the time, Barlow was delinquent on the first mortgage held by the Farmers Home Administration.

A representative of Union Mortgage called the homeowner to verify that the work on the home had been completed and that all of the loan proceeds had been used to pay for home improvements. The homeowner assured the representative that the proceeds had been used for home improvements, as she had been instructed to by the representative of American Home, despite the fact that $2,000 of the loan proceeds were to be paid to the homeowner.

Other evidence at the trial was offered to show that American Home and Union Mortgage had worked together in similar transactions across the state, resulting in consumers having a mortgage on their homes for inflated repair prices and direct cash payments to borrowers. In several of those earlier transactions, as in this case, the borrowers were in default with other mortgage creditors when the Union Mortgage loan was made. According to the Alabama Supreme Court, in one of its first transactions with American Home, Union Mortgage had clear information that American Home had not left any documents with the mortgagor, that the improvements were not worth the amount of the loan, and that the mortgagor expected to receive cash proceeds from the loan. The court noted that these facts support the plaintiffs' theory that Union Mortgage directly participated in the fraud, if only because it took no direct action of its own to effectively prevent what it now claims to have been a violation of its [own] practices.

Adding to the woes of the creditor in this case was the bankruptcy of Ronald Sellers, doing business as American Home. This resulted in the action against Union Mortgage being severed from the action against American Home and Sellers. The finance company was therefore standing alone before the jury in one more case where a home improvement contractor had defrauded a consumer but could not be held accountable. The lender made a further mistake when it filed a counterclaim against the homeowner for $6,250,000, alleging that the homeowner had committed fraud, conspiracy, and breach of contract.

The Alabama Supreme Court affirmed the fraud and contract claims, but reversed the conspiracy claim, holding that the fraud finding was based on the jury's determination that American Home and its agents were acting as agents of Union Mortgage. In the trial court's charge to the jury, the judge instructed that it is impossible to have a conspiracy between a principal and agent "because they are one [and] the same." The supreme court required the plaintiff to accept a remittitur of the $2,000 conspiracy claim to preserve the fraud award, which was apparently based on the agency analysis.

In examining a number of reported cases from across the country where fraud was alleged in contracts involving home improvement lending, it is hard to find facts as bad as those for the lender in *Union Mortgage*, although arguably most of the extreme facts were caused by decisions and practices of the lender itself. The evidence presented on the long-standing relationship between the contractor and lender, the misrepresentations made by the contractor, and the poor judgment involved in bringing a multimillion dollar counterclaim against a borrower who worked as a maid are just a few of the facts that support the result. Although reasonable minds may differ over the size and effect of punitive damages awards, the actions of the creditor in this case certainly support punitive damages if such are to be awarded in any of these cases.

In *Union Mortgage*, there was conflicting expert testimony over whether the finance company should be considered a primary or a secondary lender. In an apparent attempt to put some distance between the activities of American Home and Union Mortgage, the defendants' expert testified that Union Mortgage should be considered a secondary lender. The term "secondary lender" is often used to describe a lender that comes along after the fact and merely buys paper in the secondary market. This characterization is at odds with the plaintiff's attempt to portray Union Mortgage as the entity directly funding the loan for Barlow, even though the documents reflect a contract between the homeowners and American Home, with an assignment to Union Mortgage. It was in the plaintiff's interest to draw the lender as close as possible to the initial transaction for purposes of establishing knowledge of the fraud and control over the actions of the contractor.

The plaintiff's expert testified that Union Mortgage should be more properly characterized as a primary lender. The Alabama Supreme Court agreed with this characterization in a footnote to the opinion.

Given the rationale in the Alabama Supreme Court opinion, this debate over the correct application of the primary or secondary lender definitions may not be determinative in future litigation. That is, if the basis of *Union Mortgage* is simply the application of agency law with tort liability flowing through to the principal, the application of labels used in basic financial theory is of lesser importance. The outcome does not seem to turn on the application of the "primary" or "secondary" labels.

There is also no need to spend much time resolving the issue in *Union Mortgage*, given the close association between American Home and Union Mortgage. It could be that this attempt to drive the courts to one characterization or the other is simply not a good fit in dealer financing. Although the lender may preapprove and fund the loan, the retail dealer may be the contracting party, with a subsequent, if not concurrent, assignment of the loan to a finance company. However, if litigators feel the need to fit the lender within one category or the other, Union Mortgage could certainly be said to be a lender primarily involved in structuring, approving, and funding loans. It is a vain task in *Union Mortgage* to characterize the lender as merely a disinterested investor looking to buy paper in a secondary market. Although some lenders appear to have been hit in lender liability litigation solely because they are the deep pocket, Union Mortgage can claim no such innocence.

Union Mortgage is a fairly complicated and lengthy decision, with some seemingly contradictory, or at least puzzling language. The lender is at one point described as being not only a primary lender, but also primarily involved in the fraud. At another point, the Alabama Supreme Court appears to uphold the analysis of the trial court based almost exclusively on a derivative or agency theory. Reduced to its simplest form, the facts and behavior of the lender would support either interpretation. The debate over "primary lender" or "secondary lender" labels may be grist for the mill of academics and expert witnesses in finance, but the outcome can be described under a much simpler analysis that juries can understand. That is, the lender was too close to the fraud (primarily liable) or the lender controlled the actions of the contractor engaged in fraud and is thus derivatively liable (under agency theory) for the actions of the agent. Viewed in this way, *Union Mortgage* does not represent a threat to lenders who steer clear of dealers with a bad reputation or whose record of performance in home improvement contracts sounds the alarm. To avoid the sanctions in *Union Mortgage*, lenders must carefully screen dealer applications and police existing relationships so that an agency element is not created when purchasing paper and funding loans. The court in *Union Mortgage* made a special note of the failure of the lender to prevent what it claimed was a violation of its own required practices and procedures.

The attempt to impose liability on a creditor-assignee for the practices of the retail dealer through fraud and agency concepts has spread beyond home improvement financing and has been applied in automobile sales and other areas. And in the event the consumer can establish defenses to payment that could be asserted against the dealer, where the contract still in the hands of the dealer, the assignee-creditor may face those same defenses through the application of a Federal Trade Commission rule, which will be discussed in Chapter Nine.

Although most of the discussion on dealer financing in this chapter has been in the context of home improvement contractors and assignees of home improvement paper, the legal theories discussed would have also been applied to auto dealers and other retailers. Auto dealers have been described as "agents" of financiers or conspirators with lenders in engaging in practices harmful to consumers.

CHAPTER FIVE

CREDIT REPORTS, IDENTITY THEFT, CREDIT REPAIR, AND EQUAL ACCESS TO CREDIT

A. CREDIT REPORTS

1. USE

Before a creditor will extend credit to a consumer, the creditor will often obtain the consumer's credit report. Some creditors may undertake to conduct their own credit investigation of the consumer. Most creditors, however, simply rely on credit reports generated by local or national credit reporting agencies.

Credit bureaus generate reports which are generally used by creditors who want to know whether a consumer is credit worthy. The credit bureau reports are mostly confined to financial information about a consumer. For example, these reports will provide creditors with the amounts and locations of an individual's bank accounts, credit card accounts and other debts, along with information concerning the individual's marital status, income, occupation and any pending or prior lawsuits. Information such as maximum credit limits and the current balance on each account are included in the reports, along with a payment history to reflect the timeliness of payments made.

Nationally, there are three major credit bureaus: Equifax, Experian and TransUnion. These credit bureaus, along with other local and over 600 national bureaus, compile credit information for subscribers. The subscribers not only use the bureaus to obtain credit reports, but they also provide the bureaus with information which may be used by other merchants. Credit reports may also be obtained by non-subscribers at certain higher fees. Of course, an individual's credit report may also be obtained by the individual himself. Generally, if a consumer has been turned down for credit by a merchant, he may obtain a copy of his credit report via one of the three major credit bureaus without paying a fee.

Most bureaus are members of the Associated Credit Bureau of America, Inc. ("ACB, Inc."). ACB, Inc. is an international trade association which represents consumer credit and collection service companies. The ACB, Inc. offers subscribers a "watch service" which monitors public records and the financial transactions of individuals who have been granted credit. This "watch service" keeps creditors immediately informed of indications that the individual will be unable to meet his debt obligations.

When dealing with consumer credit, merchants and consumers are mostly concerned with the credit reports of credit bureaus such as Equifax. In many instances, a bad credit report may cause a consumer to be unable to purchase a car, house or even a television on credit. The spread of consumer reporting agencies are growing in number every day, particularly with the growth of the internet. Just enter a query for credit reports and an array of agencies will pop up on the screen offering to provide credit reports at a low rate in just seconds. For another low fee, some of these agencies also offer to send consumers credit reports once a month. Credit card companies have also gotten involved in the market of offering to provide consumers with monthly credit reports. Because credit reports are so easy to obtain and widely used, consumers should be aware of inaccuracies in their reports.

2.   COMMON LAW PROTECTION

The internet has alleviated one of the major obstacles of common law protection: learning about the error. Today, consumers can get a copy of their credit report simply by logging on to the internet and entering in a query. Before the rise of the internet, consumers had to overcome the practical problem of learning of the existence of the report and the errors therein. Prior to federal legislation in this area, lenders did not even have to disclose the fact that a credit report was obtained or which agency provided the report. Even if a consumer had knowledge of an inaccurate report, his common law remedies were still hindered by other legal obstacles. Particularly, what kind of action can be maintained?

Defamation claims were seldom successful because most jurisdictions regarded credit bureaus as having a "qualified or conditional privilege to fairly publish to its own legitimately interested business customers the information it received in the course of its investigations without being liable for defamatory matter therein, provided it did not exceed or abuse the privilege ..." *Wetherby v. Retail Credit Co.*, 235 Md. 237, 201 A.2d 344, 345 (1964). In jurisdictions which recognize a qualified privilege, a plaintiff can succeed on a defamation claim only if he shows that the credit bureau lost its privilege. A credit bureau may loose its privilege if it (1) made the publication with malice or (2) the recipient of the report lacked the requisite interest therein. Yet, even if the plaintiff can show that the bureau lost its privilege, the plaintiff must also show that he suffered damages. Injury to a consumer's reputation alone may not be a sufficient showing of damages because reputation is not easy to value.

Like defamation, an invasion of privacy claim is also difficult to maintain. First, the plaintiff must be able to show that the bureau made a public disclosure of private facts. Second, the plaintiff must show that the private facts disclosed would be offensive and objectionable to a reasonable man of ordinary sensibilities. The problem here is that much of the information disclosed by a credit bureau such as financial information and marital status is public information.

3. STATE LAWS

A number of states have enacted legislation at-tempting to regulate credit bureaus and protect consumers. However, because of the large size and scope of the operations of credit bureaus, federal regulation has preempted much of the law in this area.

4. FAIR CREDIT REPORTING ACT

In 1970, Congress passed the Fair Credit Report-ing Act (''FCRA''), Title VI of the Consumer Credit Protection Act. This Act was recently amended in 1996 to provide further protection for consumers.[1] The FCRA is ''aimed at protecting consumers from inaccurate information in consumer reports and at the establishment of credit reporting procedures that utilize correct, relevant and up-to-date infor-mation in a confidential and responsible manner.'' *Jones v. Federated Financial Reserve,* 1998 FED App. 0157P (6th Cir.).

a. Scope

The Fair Credit Reporting Act, codified at 15 U. S.C. § 1681, et seq., applies to ''consumer reports'' generated by ''consumer reporting agencies.''

A ''consumer report'' is defined by section 603(d) of the Act as ''any written, oral or other communi-

1. For a thorough background on the history, scope and remedies available under the FCRA, *See* Fair Credit Reporting Act, National Consumer Law Center (3rd ed. 1994 & 1997 Supp.).

cation of any information by a consumer reporting agency bearing on a consumer's credit worthiness, credit standing, credit capacity, character, general reputation, personal characteristics or mode of living which is used or expected to be used or collected in whole or in part for the purpose of serving as a factor in establishing the consumer's eligibility for credit or insurance to be used primarily for personal, family or household purposes; employment purposes; or any other purpose authorized under section 604."

What the definition doesn't tell us is whether reports on individuals compiled for use in commercial transactions are covered by the act. For example, are credit reports compiled by individuals seeking to purchase commercial property included under the Act? Section 603 (c) of the Act defines a "consumer" as an "individual," thereby covering such a transaction. However, the Act, defines "consumer report" as a communication of information for credit to be used "primarily for personal, family or household purposes."

The Act does, however, specifically exclude certain types of reports from the definition of a consumer report. Those reports which are excluded are:

(1) any report by a person or company whose first-hand experience with the consumer is reflected in the report;

(2) any authorization or approval of a specific extension of credit directly or indirectly by the issuer of a credit card or similar device;

(3) any report in which a person who has been requested by a third party to make a specific extension of credit directly or indirectly to a consumer conveys his or her decision with respect to such a request, if the third party advises the consumer of the name and address of the person to whom the request was made, and such person makes the disclosures to the consumer required under section 615.

The first exclusion exists to allow persons doing business with the consumer (such as banks and retail stores) to exchange "trade experience" and to provide information to consumer reporting agencies without becoming consumer reporting agencies under the FCRA.

The second exception applies to the direct or indirect approval, by the issuer of a credit card or similar device, of a specific extension of credit, and would apply to an issuers' denial or disapproval of a specific extension of credit. Yet, if the card issuer's denial is at least in part based on a consumer report, the card issuer must give notice to the consumer of the name of the reporting agency.

The third exception covers attempts by retailers to obtain credit from an entity such as a finance company or other assignee, on behalf of a consumer who wants to buy an item from the dealer. There is no "consumer report" when the potential assignee of the retail installment contract notifies the retail dealer of its decision on whether to buy the paper and finance the deal. Additional issues in dealer-financed sales were discussed in Chapter Four, at pages 83-97.

According to the Act, a "consumer reporting agency" includes "any person which, for monetary fees, dues, or on a cooperative nonprofit basis, regularly engages in whole or in part in the practice of assembling or evaluating consumer credit information or other information on consumers for the purpose of furnishing consumer reports to third parties, and which uses any means or facility of interstate commerce for the purpose of preparing or furnishing consumer reports." § 603(f).

Therefore, credit bureaus, such as Equifax, are credit reporting agencies because they disseminate consumer reports regularly to third parties. Businesses which assemble or evaluate information for its own purposes are not consumer reporting agencies as long as the information is not provided to third parties. Likewise, businesses which assemble or evaluate information which falls outside the definition of a "consumer report" are not consumer reporting agencies.

b. Requirements for Furnishers of Information

In 1996, Congress made some amendments to the FCRA which included, for the first time, rules concerning businesses which furnish information to the credit reporting agencies. Now, not only do credit reporting agencies have the task of ensuring that information is accurate but businesses have the task of ensuring that the information they provide is correct.

Basically, the new law prohibits furnishers of information from providing incorrect information. The downside to the law is that consumers who are victims of incorrect information have no right to relief directly against the furnisher. The enforcement of the law is granted to certain public agencies and state officials.

As set out by the new amendment, furnishers cannot report information they know or consciously avoid knowing is inaccurate. This rule, however, does not apply to furnishers, who provide consumers with an address to notify them of any inaccuracies. This is consistent with the FCRA's "reasonable procedures" defense as to consumer reporting agencies discussed, *infra.* If a consumer claims that information is inaccurate the furnisher must refrain from providing that information to a reporting agency if it is in fact inaccurate. Yet, if the furnisher is unable to determine for a fact that the information is inaccurate, the furnisher may only report the information by noting that it is disputed. The dispute then must also be noted by the credit reporting agency. Additionally, the amendment requires that furnishers, who regularly supply information to reporting agencies, inform the agency of any necessary corrections.

c. Requirements for Consumer Credit Reporting Agencies

There are four main players under the Act: (1) the credit reporting agency; (2) the furnisher of information to the agency; (3) the user of the credit report and (4) the consumer. Each of the players have certain rights and duties under the act and each has a remedy for the other's violations. Therefore, although the FCRA is divided into 25 subchapters, the substantive part of the Act can be grouped into four areas: (1) requirements for consumer reporting agencies, (2) requirements on users of consumer reports, (3) rights of consumers and (4) remedies.

The requirements for consumer reporting agencies can be further divided into two parts: (1) provisions relating to the contents of consumer reports and (2) provisions relating to the use of consumer reports.

Section 607 of the Act, governing compliance procedures, requires that consumer reporting agencies obtain the identity of the party requesting a consumer report and insure that such recipient uses the report only for the permissible purposes listed in the Act. Furthermore, the section mandates consumer reporting agencies to:

(1) use "reasonable procedures" to insure that the reports contain accurate information,

(2) allow users of the report to disclose the contents of the reports to a consumer who has had adverse action taken against him, and

(3) provide notice as required under the act to consumers and businesses who regularly furnish information to an agency of each person's responsibilities under the act. The remaining provision of section 607, subsection (e) deals with the resale of a consumer report.

Aside from section 607's requirement that consumer reporting agencies use reasonable diligence in maintaining accurate reports, section 613 also regulates the accuracy of the reports. Section 613 requires consumer reporting agencies to "maintain strict procedures" to insure that any public information which is reported which may have an adverse effect on a consumer's ability to obtain employment is "complete and up to date."

The other provisions regulating consumer reporting agencies deal with investigative reports. As defined by section 603(e) of the Act, an "investigative consumer report" is the portion of a consumer report which contains information on a consumer's character, general reputation, personal characteristics or mode of living obtained from personal interviews with friends, neighbors or other associates of the consumer.

However, before a consumer reporting agency may conduct an investigative consumer report, certain disclosures must be made to the consumer. Section 606 requires the consumer reporting agency to insure that the party requesting a report has informed the consumer that an investigative report may be made on the consumer in writing three days after the report was requested. The requesting party must also inform the consumer of his right to request that the nature and scope of the investigation be disclosed to him.

Another section of the Act relating to investigative consumer reports is section 614. That section provides that adverse information developed on an investigative consumer report cannot be used again on a subsequent consumer report unless it is less than three months old or is verified again. The purpose here is to purge the reports of dated and inaccurate information that relates to matters beyond the creditworthiness of the consumer.

The major problem with credit reports, aside from the possibility of inaccurate information, is too much information. Credit reporting agencies are at the door step of invading consumers' privacy rights.

In Section 602 of the Act, Congress gave a statement of its findings and purpose of the Act. In this statement Congress recognized a need to protect privacy rights by stating that there is a need to insure that consumer reporting agencies show "a respect for the consumer's right to privacy." Congress also states that the consumer reporting agencies should make sure that all information disclosed is "relevant." However, what Congress failed to include in the Act was any prohibition as to what information could not be included in a consumer report.

One way that Congress chose to achieve the Act's purpose of protecting privacy was by regulating how the consumer reports are to be used. Section 604 limits the uses of consumer reports by third parties to permissible purposes: (1) credit transactions, (2) employment, (3) insurance, (4) eligibility for license, (5) investment transactions and (6) any other legitimate business transaction. A consumer, of course, can request to have his report disclosed to him and government agencies dealing with child support obligations may request a consumer's report.

As discussed above, Section 607 which addresses compliance procedures requires the consumer reporting agency to "maintain reasonable procedures" to insure that the consumer report is only used for the permissible purposes listed under section 604. This requires the consumer reporting agency to deny the request of any party whom it has reasonable grounds to believe will not use the report for a permissible purpose. Therefore, the reporting agency must identify the users and identify the user's purpose.

d. Requirements for Users of Consumer Reports

A user of a consumer report has two primary duties. First, the user must make certain required disclosures to the consumer. Second, the user must make sure that the report is used for a permissible purpose.

Section 615 addresses the requirements placed on users of consumer reports. Specifically, 615(a) provides that users of consumer reports who have taken an adverse action against a consumer based on a consumer report must provide notice to the consumer of the adverse action and the name, address and telephone number of the consumer agency which furnished the report. Furthermore, the user must also provide the consumer with the reason the adverse action was taken and the consumer's rights to obtain a free copy of his report and to dispute the accuracy of the report.

Under 615(b), if a user of information *other than that from a consumer reporting agency* denies a consumer credit in whole or in part based on information obtained by third parties, the user must inform the consumer of his right to request the reason for the adverse action. If a consumer sends the user a written request for the reasons for the adverse action within 60 days of learning of the adverse action, the user must make such a disclosure within a reasonable time.

According to the Act, adverse action includes a denial or rejection in whole or in part against a consumer with regards to insurance, credit, employment or a license. Section 603(k).

Note the differences between 615(a) and 615(b). First, the notification requirement of 615(a) applies whenever the subject of the application is consumer credit, insurance or employment; whereas the notification requirement under 615(b) only applies to credit applications. Second, section 615(b) requires users to disclose to the consumer his right to learn of the reason for the adverse action but does not disclose the source of the information. Yet, when a consumer reporting agency is involved, under 615(a), the user must disclose the source of the report to the consumer.

Employers frequently request consumer reports. Therefore, sections 604, 606 and 615 of the FCRA spell out an employer's responsibilities when using consumer reports for employment purposes. In 1996, Congress amended the FCRA pursuant to the Consumer Credit Reporting Act. The amendments which went into effect September 30, 1997 significantly increased the legal obligations of employers who use consumer reports. For example, before an employer can request a consumer report, the employer must notify the individual in writing that a report is to be used. Then, the employer must get the individual's written authorization before asking for a report.

Once those steps have been taken, and before an employer can use the reports to take an adverse action against the individual, the employer must follow certain steps:

(1) give the individual a pre-adverse action disclosure that includes a copy of the individual's consumer report and a copy of "A Summary of Your Rights Under the FCRA."

(2) after an adverse action has been taken, give the individual notice including the name, address and phone number of the consumer reporting agency; a statement that the agency did not make the decision; and a notice of the

individual's rights to dispute the accuracy of the report.

A final obligation of users is to use the reports only for permissible purposes. It is the consumer reporting agencies duty to identify the user and the user's purpose. However, what if those steps have been taken but the user does not use the report for permissible purposes?

On May 22, 1998, the United States Court of Appeals for the Sixth Circuit decided a case that sends an important message to any business that accesses credit reports. The message is that business can be held vicariously liable under a theory of apparent authority for their employees' misuse of a consumer report. In *Jones v. Federated Financial Reserve Corp.,* the plaintiff learned that an employee of Federated had obtained an on-line credit report on her from TRW (now Experian) at the request of plaintiff s ex-husband so that he could ascertain her whereabouts. 1998 Fed App. 0157P (6th Cir.). The Sixth Circuit reversed the district court's decision and chose to recognize the common law doctrine of apparent authority to hold Federated liable, because the consumer reporting agency, TRW, did identify the user as an employee of Federated and believed that the employee had apparent authority to request and use the report for permissible business related purposes.

In making its holding, the Court held that the doctrine of apparent authority is consistent with Congress's purpose in enacting the Act: protecting the consumer's privacy. The Court noted that companies such as Federated should protect that privacy by maintaining better safeguards and policies.

Also remember that users can become consumer reporting agencies if they regularly furnish such reports or other information constituting consumer reports to third parties. Users should avoid becoming consumer reporting agencies to avoid having to comply with the statutory obligations of those agencies. See page 105, *supra.*

e. Rights of Consumers

Many rights of the consumer have been discussed in the previous pages, i.e., the right to be notified of a user's reliance on adverse information, section 615(a), right to privacy, section 604, and the right to accurate information, section 607. In addition, the consumer also has a right to see the contents of his report and dispute any inaccurate information.

Section 609 allows consumers access to all information in a consumer's file, including the sources of the information, the identification of each person that procured a consumer report, the dates, original payees and amounts of any checks upon which is based any adverse characterization of the consumer and a record of all inquires received by the agency during the one-year period preceding the request. Additionally, the agency must also include a summary of the consumer's rights with the disclosure. What consumer reporting agencies do not have to disclose is information concerning credit scores or any other risk scores or predictors relating to the consumer and sources of information acquired sole-ly for use in preparing an investigative report.

An individual has greater access to his consumer report now more than ever because of the scope of the internet. There are many websites dedicated to furnishing an individual his report in a matter of seconds. The cost of these reports are limited to $8.00 per report and a consumer has a right to a free report if an adverse action has been taken against him with respect to a report within the past sixty days.

After a consumer receives his report, he should check the report for accuracy. If a consumer finds an inaccurate statement, section 611 details the procedures that a consumer reporting agency must take upon receiving notice of a dispute concerning a report. The 1996 amendments also raise stricter standards of what a credit report agency must do to reinvestigate disputed information.

The agency must reinvestigate the subject of the dispute free of charge and record the current status of the disputed information or delete the informa-tion within 30 days of receiving notice of a dispute by a consumer. The 30 day time limit may be extended fifteen days if the agency receives addi-tional information from the consumer requiring ad-ditional consideration. However, the fifteen day ex-tension is inapplicable if the agency has already determined that the information is inaccurate.

The agency can avoid reinvestigation if the agen-cy decides to delete the disputed information. The deletion or correction must be made within three days. To invoke this process, the agency must notify the consumer by telephone of its intended action and provide the consumer with his corrected report within five days after the deletion. As discussed, *infra*, the agency must also provide the consumer with notice of his right to require the agency to notify previous users of his credit report about the deletion.

As part of its reinvestigation, the agency must consider all relevant information provided by the consumer. Additionally, the agency will within five days of receiving notice of a dispute, provide notification of the dispute to the person who provided any item of information in dispute.

Upon notification of a dispute, the furnisher of the information must then investigate the accuracy of the disputed information. If the furnisher does not conduct a proper investigation, it is liable under the Act. Similar to the duties of the agency, the furnisher (1) must conduct an investigation of the disputed information within a reasonable time; (2) review all relevant information furnished to it by the agency and (3) report the results of its investigation to the agency. If the investigation results in the finding of inaccurate information, the furnisher must also report the results to all other reporting agencies to which it had reported the original information. This provides a method of checks and balances between the credit reporting agency and the furnisher. This also provides greater protection for the consumer against inaccurate information.

The agency can refuse to reinvestigate a dispute raised by a consumer if the agency determines that the dispute is frivolous or irrelevant. If, however, a reinvestigation was conducted, at its completion, regardless of the outcome, the agency must provide the consumer with the results within five days. All inaccurate or incomplete information must be promptly deleted or corrected. If a reinvestigation is conducted, but the dispute is left unresolved, the consumer may file a brief statement setting forth the nature of the dispute. The consumer's statement, or the agency's clear and accurate summary of the statement must then be presented in any subsequent consumer report containing the information in dispute.

Furthermore, at the consumer's request, the reporting agency is required to give "notification" that an item has been deleted or that the statement or summary has been added "to any person designated by the consumer" who has received a consumer report within the past two years for employment purposes or within the past six months for any other purpose. The agency must "clearly and conspicuously" disclose to the consumer his right to make such a request.

Once disputed information has been deleted after a reinvestigation, consumers should watch out for their sudden reappearance on the credit report. The disputed information can only be reinserted into a consumers report after certain steps have been taken by the agency. First, the agency must get certification from the furnisher of the information that the information is accurate and complete. Second, the agency must notify the consumer, in writing, within 5 business days after reinsertion that the information was reinserted; the name and address of the furnisher; and that the consumer has a right to add a statement to his file about the disputed information.

Some other "red flags" consumers should watch out for when reviewing their credit reports are:

(1) closed accounts—if information on a closed account is reported, the agency has to categorize it as a closed account;

(2) accounts more than seven years old—a delinquent account can only be reported for seven years beginning 180 days from the date of the delinquency; (prior to the amendment, the seven years began on the date of collection activities or charge-off which could be months or years after the debt became delinquent);

(3) bankruptcy—agencies must report the chapter of bankruptcy filed, whether it is 7 or 13, "if provided by the source of the information" and must report a withdrawal of a bankruptcy petition "upon receipt of documentation certifying the withdrawal."

f. Administrative Remedies

The Federal Trade Commission is invested with the principal responsibility for administrative enforcement of the FCRA. Violations of any requirement of the FCRA are declared to be unfair or deceptive practices under Section 5(a) of the FTC Act. The FTC is also authorized to enforce provisions of the Act through cease and desist orders with respect to consumer reporting agencies, users of reports and others not regulated by federal agencies.

g. Criminal Remedies

Criminal liability exposure is limited to obtaining information under false pretenses. Any person who "knowingly and willfully obtains information on a consumer from a consumer reporting agency under false pretenses" is subject to criminal prosecution and a fine as determined under Title 18 and two years of imprisonment, Section 619.

The person who obtained a consumer report under false pretenses or without a permissible purpose is liable to the consumer for actual damages or $1,000, whichever is greater. Additionally, the person is liable to the consumer reporting agency for actual damages or $1,000, whichever is greater. Section 616.

Officers or employees of consumer reporting agencies who "knowingly and willfully" provide information on a consumer to a person not authorized to receive the information are also open to criminal sanctions of nor more than 2 years imprisonment and a fine.

There are no criminal sanctions against consumer reporting agencies for using inaccurate or obsolete information. However, consumer reporting agencies are not immune from civil liability.

h. Civil Liability

The Act imposes civil liability against any person who "willfully fails to comply with any requirement imposed under the chapter with respect to any consumer." This list of persons includes users and consumer reporting agencies. Remember that users can be held liable for violations by their employees if there is a finding of apparent authority, *see* page 113, *supra*.

Under Section 616, if there is willful noncompliance, a consumer may recover actual damages of not more than $1,000 or less than $100, punitive damages and attorney's fees. Section 617 of the Act deals with negligent compliance. Any person who was negligent in failing to comply the FCRA's requirements is liable to the consumer for actual damages and attorney's fees.

The remedies afforded by the Act may seem generous, but consumers face many problems with private actions. For a consumer to fall under section 616, he must have a "smoking gun" to show willful noncompliance. Section 617's negligent noncompliance remedies seem a little easier to prove. However, looking at section 607 reveals why consumers must overcome a heavy hurdle to show negligence.

Under section 607, a consumer reporting agency can discharge its duties to a consumer by maintaining and following "reasonable procedures" to identify users and their purpose and to insure the accuracy of the report. Likewise, under section 615(c), a user can discharge its duty by maintaining and following "reasonable procedures" to insure compliance with notification requirements. Therefore, if a consumer reporting agency with "reasonable procedures" sends an erroneous report to a user which has reasonable notification procedures but which fails to notify the consumer, neither the consumer reporting agency nor the user of the consumer report is liable.

Thus even under 617's negligent noncompliance, a consumer would have to show that (1) the consumer reporting agency or the user failed to maintain "reasonable procedures" to insure compliance, (2) the failure to maintain such procedures was negligent and (3) the plaintiff was injured. The mere fact that a report was inaccurate and the consumer did not receive notice is not sufficient.

A final observation relating to obtaining civil remedies is that the FCRA preempted most common law actions. Section 610(e) provides that "no consumer may bring an action or proceeding in the nature of defamation, invasion of privacy or negligence with respect to the reporting of information ... against any consumer reporting agency, user of furnisher ... except as to false information furnished with malice or willful intent to injure such consumer." Basically, that provision states that a consumer may sue under common law, but not if the information on which the suit is based was obtained through the Act. The practical problem of obtaining information outside the Act makes any common law claim unlikely.

B. IDENTITY THEFT ACT

As stated earlier in this chapter, consumers should check their credit reports periodically for mistakes. Some of the mistakes found may be inadvertent, while others may be the result of fraud. When a credit card, a social security card or other item of identification is lost, consumers have no method to protect themselves from identify theft. There is generally not much that a consumer can do to ensure that his credit will not be tampered with other than to keep track of his credit history and report any errors. Consumers are not given the chance to obtain a new social security number and there are no red flags placed on the consumer's credit by any reporting agencies that fraud may occur, which results in adverse information on a credit report, due to another who steals the consumer's credit identity.[2]

In cases where a person's credit identity has been assumed by another, the results can be disastrous. In *Patrick v. Union State Bank*, 681 So.2d 1364 (Ala.1996), a bank was held liable for carelessness in opening an account in the name of an individual where the account was opened by an imposter. The imposter used Ms. Patrick's temporary driver's li-

2. For problems encountered by consumers in cases of identity theft and research on how thieves get your "credit identity," *see*, *Are You A Target For Identity Theft?*, Consumer Reports, Sep. 1997 at 10.

cense as identification and opened up a checking account with a deposit of $100.

The bank employee who opened the account testified that the imposter had only one form of identification and told the bank employee that she had no permanent address because, she was currently living at a shelter for abused women, and that she was trying to find a job and a place to live. The bank employee testified that she noticed the imposter did not completely sign her last name on the account signature card and that the signature on the card was different than the signature on Mrs. Patrick's temporary driver's license. The bank employee did not ask the imposter to verify the Social Security Number by presenting a Social Security Card and did not verify either of the telephone numbers given to her by the imposter.

The imposter wrote bad checks, which resulted in the arrest of Mrs. Patrick. The bank was held liable to the impersonated party for opening the account without obtaining satisfactory identification of the account opener. The wrongdoer could not be found. Due to the growing volume of credit identity exchanges through the internet and other sources, problems in identity theft will continue to grow.

In 1998, Congress passed the Identity Theft and Assumption Deterrence Act. This new law is codified in the Fraud and False Statements Chapter of Title 18 of the United States Code. This Act broadens the definition of identity theft and makes it a crime to "knowingly transfer or use, without lawful authority, a means of identification of another person with the intent to commit, or to aid or abet, any unlawful activity that constitutes a violation of Federal law, or that constitutes a felony under any applicable State or local law." 18 U.S.C. § 1028(a)(7). Additionally, the new offense carries with it a fine or imprisonment for not more than 15 years, or both, if the offense involved the transfer or use of one or more means of identification if, as a result of the offense, any individual committing the offense obtains anything of value aggregating $1,000 or more during any one-year period. 18 U.S.C. § 1028(b)(1)(D).

This new law does not protect a consumer's credit report, but it does ensure that any person who attempts to use another's identity to obtain credit will be punished, if found.

C. CREDIT REPAIR ORGANIZATIONS ACT

Aside from the problem of identify theft, consumers should also be aware of credit repair scams. Consumers who are mired in debt often are desperate for a way out. Those are the people towards whom these scams are aimed. The scam is sometimes called "file segregation." As reported from the Federal Trade Commission, these scams promise consumers a chance to hide unfavorable credit information by establishing a new credit identity.

These credit repair scam companies start by warning consumers who have filed for bankruptcy that they will be unable to get credit cards or any loans for 10 years. Then the company promises to help the consumer, for a fee, hide the bankruptcy. There are various mediums through which these credit repair companies reach consumers, such as the internet, mail, classified ads or even infomercials. In some cases, credit repair "kits" are sold to consumers for prices ranging from $25 to $50 dollars.

Not all credit repair agencies are running scams. However, because of the potential for abuse, in 1996 Congress passed the Credit Repair Organizations Act (CROA) to regulate this industry. 15 U.S.C. §§ 1679–1679j. Pub.L. No. 104–208 § 110 Stat. 3009 (Sept. 30, 1996). The Act requires these companies to give consumers three days to rescind a contract for credit repair. This right to cancel must be disclosed to consumers on the contract. Additionally, the Act mandates that the companies make certain required disclosures to the consumer such as "a full and detailed description of the services to be performed." Furthermore, the company must inform the consumer of his right to self-help through the FCRA, allowing the consumer to police and correct inaccuracies.

The Act also prohibits certain types of conduct. Credit repair agencies cannot make any false or misleading statements or statements which in the exercise of reasonable care would be known to be false or misleading, provide misleading advice, engage in any kind of deception or make any statement encouraging consumers to alter their identification.

The following is a list of claims that consumers should watch out for when deciding whether a credit repair agency is running a scam:

(1) You will not be able to get credit for 10 years. FALSE. This is the time period that bankruptcies stay on a credit reports. There are many creditors that are willing to extend credit to consumers with prior bankruptcies. Remember that each lender has its own set of criteria.

(2) The company is affiliated with the government. FALSE.

(3) File segregation is legal. FALSE. Credit repair is legal if it complies with the CROA, but using a false social security number or making false statements to a lender (which is the practice encouraged by these scams) is illegal.

Some of the damages available for consumers who have been a victim of credit repair scams is the greater of actual damages or the amount paid to the organization. Punitive damages may also be allowed, as well as attorney's fees. There is a five year statute of limitations for actions under the Act. The five years begins to run from the date of the occurrence of the violation, or in cases of willful failure to disclose, the limitations period begins from the time the consumer discovered the misrepresentation.

In 1999 the Federal Trade Commission and more than a dozen state attorneys general cracked down on credit repair scams, filing lawsuits against more than 40 credit repair businesses. *See* Katherine Ackley, *'Credit Repair' Businesses Sued By FTC and States*, Wall St.J., Feb. 3, 1999, at A8. The FTC noted that among the fraudulent practices targeted, credit repair companies suggested that consumers trade in their Social Security number for a nine-digit taxpayer-identification number, as well as advising consumers on getting a new driver's license and using a false Social Security number when applying for credit. The FTC noted that the credit repair scams have expanded by virtue of having the internet as a marketing tool.

D. DISCRIMINATION IN ACCESS TO CREDIT

1. SCOPE OF EQUAL CREDIT OPPORTUNITY ACT

Congress enacted the Equal Credit Opportunity Act in 1974 and amended it in 1976 to expand the list of prohibited discriminatory criteria upon which credit cannot be denied. Currently, the Equal Opportunity Act prohibits the discrimination against any credit applicant on the basis of race, color, religion, national origin, sex, marital status, age, the fact that all or part of the applicant's income is derived from public assistance, or the fact that the applicant has in good faith exercised any right under the Consumer Credit Protection Act.

The Equal Opportunity Act is a portion of the Consumer Credit Protection Act which is regulated by the Board of Governors of the Federal Reserve System. The regulations promulgated by this Board are known as Regulation B. Banks, finance companies, retail stores, credit card issuers, and generally, anyone who regularly extends credit is susceptible to the regulations. In addition, the law may apply to those who arrange financing, such as real estate brokers. Also, unlike the Fair Credit Reporting Act, there is no question that the Equal Credit Opportunity Act does apply to business credit. Regulation B, provides for a specialized and more limited treatment of extensions of credit primarily for business or commercial purposes, including agricultural credit. Section 202.3.[3]

2.   DISCRIMINATION IN OBTAINING INFORMATION IN CREDIT APPLICATIONS

Although the Equal Opportunity Act does not regulate the contents of credit applications, Regulation B does. Section 202.5 prohibits creditors from requesting information concerning an applicant's spouse or former spouse, unless the spouse will be liable for the account, will have access to the account, or the applicant is relying on the spouse's income. Information concerning an applicant's sex, marital status, child-bearing, race, color, religion

3.   For a comprehensive treatment of the Equal Credit Opportunity Act, *see Credit Discrimination*, National Consumer Law Center (2nd ed. 1998).

and national origin are also prohibited. This prohibited information, however, may be gathered for monitoring purposes. Section 202.5(b)(2).

There are model application forms available from the Federal Reserve Board. Creditors do not have to use the model forms. However, if a creditor does use the model forms, the creditor is deemed to be acting in compliance with Reg. B's credit application requirements.

3.   DISCRIMINATION IN EVALUATING CREDIT APPLICATIONS

Creditors generally use two methods for evaluating credit applications:

(1) subjective evaluation of the individual applicant, *i.e.*, "judgmental system," or

(2) statistical analysis of the applicant's past credit experience, *i.e.*, "credit scoring."

Credit scoring is used by credit companies which handle a large volume of consumer debt and which screen a large volume of applicants. It is a statistical method of assessing credit risk which rates the likelihood that an individual will pay back the loan considering the consumer's past delinquencies, type of credit, how often credit is applied for and number of inquiries.

How does credit scoring actually work? Creditors use a statistical program to compare the information they receive from one applicant with the credit performance of other consumers with similar profiles. Thus, points are awarded for each factor that serves as an indication that the individual is likely to repay the debt. A total number of points helps creditors predict whether an individual is credit worthy.

Credit scoring came into existence in the 1950's. Today the most well known type of credit risk score is the Fair, Isaac or FICO score. Generally credit bureaus provide risk scores to their subscribers who then use the score to objectively evaluate an applicant's credit worthiness. Each lender uses the scores differently. The scores only become meaningful and useful within the context of a particular lender's own cutoff points and risk guidelines.

Unlike the judgmental method, credit scoring is more reliable because it is based on real data and statistics. It treats all applicants equally, and the Equal Credit Opportunity Act insures that all applicants are treated equally. Credit scoring systems consider many factors, but what it cannot consider are characteristics such as race, sex, marital status, national origin or religion. Section 701.

The consideration of a person's age, however, is a different story. Credit scoring systems can use age as a consideration. However, the system must not assign a negative factor or value to elderly applicants. What may be considered is the fact that the applicant's income may be reduced because of retirement. Creditors are allowed to consider the age of an elderly applicant if such age is used to favor the applicant in extending credit. If the creditor is using a judgmental method, then age can only be considered for the purpose of determining a pertinent element of creditworthiness. Section 202.6.

As seen above, Reg. B, section 202.6 sets out specific rules concerning what can and cannot be considered. Be aware, however, that creditors can follow all of the rules in Reg. B, but still violate the anti-discrimination rules of the Equal Credit Opportunity Act. Practices not specifically mentioned in Reg. B may have a discriminatory effect; legislative history indicates that the Equal Credit Opportunity Act reaches the discriminatory effects of facially neutral actions. *See generally* Baer, *The Equal Credit Opportunity Act and the Effects Test*, 95 Bank.L.J. 241 (1978). The existing case law regarding an effects test is restricted almost entirely to employment discrimination prohibited by Title VII.

4. NOTIFICATION

Section 701 (d) of the Equal Credit Opportunity Act requires creditors to provide applications notification of any action it takes regarding an application for credit.

Regulation B, section 202.9 specifies what must be included in the notification and when notice is required. Basically, the section requires creditors to provide notice (1) within 30 days after receiving a completed application, (2) within 30 days after taking adverse action on an incomplete application; (3) within 30 days after taking adverse action on an existing account or (4) within 90 days after notifying the applicant about a counter offer, if the applicant does not expressly accept or use the credit offered.

If adverse action has been taken then, 202.9(a)(2) governs the content of the notification. The notification must be in writing and include:

(1) a statement of the action taken;

(2) the name and address of the creditor;

(3) a statement of the provisions of section 701 (a) of the Act;

(4) the name and address of the Federal agency that administers compliance with respect to the creditor; and

(5) a statement of the specific reason for the action taken or a disclosure of the applicant's right to a statement of specific reasons within 30 days if a request for such a statement is made within 60 days.

Section 202.9 provides a sample notification form meeting all of the above requirements.

5.   EFFECT OF EQUAL CREDIT OPPORTUNITY ACT ON STATE LAW

The Equal Credit Opportunity Act preempts state credit discrimination statutes which are "inconsistent" with the Act. A state which has laws that are more protective to credit applicants than the Act are not inconsistent with the Act. Section 705(e).

The Federal Reserve Board, along with its other duties, is invested with the power to determine whether a State's law is inconsistent with the Act. This grant of authority, however, does not seem to be exclusive. Courts may make this determination and so may creditors, at their own risk.

Section 705(g) also provides an exemption by Federal Reserve Board regulation from its requirements for transactions subject to "substantially similar" state requirements or more protective state requirements.

Sections 705(a) through (d) of the Act addresses the effect or lack thereof of the Equal Credit Opportunity Act on more general state laws such as usury laws.

6. REMEDIES

Any creditor that fails to comply with a requirement imposed by the Act or Regulation B is subject to civil liability for actual and punitive damages in an individual or class action. Sections 706(a) and (b). Damages, however, are limited to punitive damages of not more than $10,000 in individual actions and the lesser of $500,000 or one percent of the creditor's net worth in class actions. Section 706(b). Equitable and declaratory relief may also be granted, as well as, costs and reasonable attorney's fees. Section 706(c) and (d).

The action may be brought in any United States district court without regard to the amount in controversy or in any other court of competent jurisdiction. Section 706(f). Generally the action must be brought within two years after the date of the occurrence of the violation. There are two minor exceptions when an action must be brought within one year: (1) after the commencement of an administrative enforcement proceeding or (2) after the commencement of a civil action brought by the Attorney General of the United States within two years after the alleged violation. Section 706(f).

The administrative enforcement for the act is delegated to several agencies, depending on the type of credit involved, with the overall enforcement authority given to the Federal Trade Commission.

Although state law remedies may still be available to credit applicants, an applicant cannot recover under both the federal and the state statutes.

CHAPTER SIX

DISCLOSURE OF TERMS IN CONSUMER CREDIT TRANSACTIONS

A. NEED FOR DISCLOSURE LEGISLATION

Congress enacted what is commonly known as the Truth in Lending Act, or "TILA," to require uniform disclosure of the cost of credit in consumer transactions. Prior to the enactment of TILA the disclosures creditors provided consumers varied widely. It was often impossible for consumers to determine the true cost of the credit, and some creditors did not disclose the rate of interest; they only disclosed the number and amount of monthly payments.

Before TILA, those creditors that did disclose the interest rate did so in a variety of ways. Creditors offering a revolving charge plan commonly quoted a monthly rate, generally one and one half percent a month. Other creditors quoted the rate of interest in terms of a dollar add-on. For example, a creditor might explain the finance charge on a new car as $7 per $100 per year for 3 years. Another method of stating the rate of interest was the discount method, where the finance charge was deducted from the face amount of the note at the time the credit was extended.

On January 1, 1967, Massachusetts became the first state to require disclosure of interest rates in consumer credit transactions in a uniform manner. Soon thereafter, Congress adopted the Truth in Lending legislation, which took effect on July 1, 1969.

In 1978, Congress simplified TILA through a complete revision. Congress and the Federal Reserve Board decided that not all of the information then in TILA was useful to consumers in their credit decisions. On March 31, 1980, President Jimmy Carter signed the Depositary Institutions Deregulation and Monetary Control Act, which included the Truth in Lending Simplification and Reform Act of 1980 (Title V of DIDMCA, codified at 15 U.S.C. §§ 1601 et seq.).

In 1988, TILA was amended to add the Fair Credit and Charge Card Disclosure Act, which requires cost disclosures at the time of solicitation and application for a credit card. TILA's 1988 amendment also included the Home Equity Loan Consumer Protection Act, which was aimed at the open-end lines of credit, secured by home equity. In 1994, Congress amended TILA to include the Home Ownership and Equity Protection Act, which was aimed at abuses in home equity lending. And then, in 1995, TILA was again revamped, addressing concerns raised by lenders who made closed-end, nonpurchase money mortgage loans.

B. FEDERAL TRUTH
IN LENDING ACT

1. INTRODUCTION

"Truth in Lending Act," or "TILA," is the popular name for Title I of the Consumer Credit Protection Act of 1968, and is codified at 15 U.S.C. § 1601, *et seq.* TILA is essentially a disclosure statute. It does offer some substantive protection, but the major thrust of TILA remains full disclosure, allowing for meaningful consumer choice. A creditor is free to impose any charges for credit permitted by state or other federal law. Similarly, the legislation does not generally restrict or confine the terms and conditions of the extension of credit. Rather, all that TILA requires is that creditors apprise consumers of the terms, conditions and costs before consumers enter into a consumer credit contract.

2. REGULATION Z AND THE OFFICIAL
STAFF COMMENTARY

Congress empowered the Board of Governors of the Federal Reserve Board to prescribe regulations to carry out the purposes of TILA. In February of 1969, the Federal Reserve Board published a comprehensive set of regulations in 12 CFR 226, commonly known as "Reg. Z". Regulation Z restates many of the TILA sections, but is generally a more thorough statement of the law. There is also an Official Staff Commentary, which is to Regulation Z, what Regulation Z is to TILA. The Official Staff

Commentary makes TILA more user-friendly, with comments and examples that clarify the law and provides even more information than Regulation Z. In analyzing any TILA section, both the Regulation Z provision and the corollary Official Staff Commentary should be reviewed.[1]

3. SCOPE OF APPLICATION OF TRUTH IN LENDING

The Truth in Lending Act has no single, comprehensive scope provision. Congress intended it to apply broadly and to apply to most consumer credit transactions. TILA provides, "Information [about a consumer credit transaction] ... shall be disclosed clearly and conspicuously, in accordance with the regulations of the Board. The terms 'annual percentage rate' and 'finance charge' shall be disclosed more conspicuously than other terms ..." 15 U.S.C. § 1632 (a).

To determine the scope of application of TILA, it is necessary to consider a number of the Act's sections in conjunction with sections from Regulation Z and the Official Staff Commentary. The following discussion considers these sections according to five principal factors that determine the applicability of TILA:

(a) amount of credit,

(b) purpose of credit,

(c) status of debtor,

1. For a thorough treatment of TILA, *see* Truth in Lending, National Consumer Law Center (3rd ed. 1995 & 1998 Supp.).

(d) business of creditor,

(e) imposition of finance charge.

a. Amount of Credit

Large transactions are exempt from TILA requirements, through the operation of 15 U.S.C. § 1603 (3). If more than $25,000 is being financed, TILA does not apply. One major exception to this $25,000 maximum is any extension of credit that is secured either by real property or personal property and that is used or expected to be used as the consumer's principal dwelling. Section 104(3); Reg. Z § 226.3(b). The purpose of the property exception to the large transaction exemption is to make the purchase of a home, trailer, condominium, and so on, also subject to TILA.

b. Purpose of Credit

For TILA to cover the consumer credit transaction, the transaction must be "primarily for personal, family, or household purposes," 15 U.S.C. § 1602 (h).[2] The phrase "personal, family, or household" should be taken at face value. The same phrase also appears in section 9–109(1) of the Uniform Commercial Code.

If a consumer buys an automobile and occasionally uses it for business purposes, the Act still applies. "Cases considering whether a transaction is primarily consumer or commercial in nature look to the

2. 15 U.S.C. § 1602(e) defines "credit" as "the right granted by a creditor to a debtor to defer payment of debt or to incur debt and defer its payment."

transaction as a whole and the purpose for which credit was extended." *Gallegos v. Stokes*, 593 F.2d 372, 375 (10th Cir.1979) (where creditor elicited testimony that the debtor intended to use truck to sell fresh produce as a means of making money). Even if some of the proceeds of the loan are used for a business purpose, TILA may apply. *Semar v. Platte Valley Fed. Sav. & Loan Ass'n*, 791 F.2d 699 (9th Cir.1986) (loan "primarily" for personal purpose even though 10 percent of proceeds used for a business purpose).

c.   Status of Debtor

The Truth in Lending disclosure requirements apply only to transactions involving a debtor who is a "natural person." "Natural person" is not defined in either the statute or the regulations, but the concept is incorporated in the definition of "consumer" in 15 U.S.C. § 1602 (h).

d.   Business of Creditor

The scope of TILA's disclosure requirements are not only limited by the type of debtor–an individual obtaining credit for consumer purposes–but they are also limited by the type of creditor. The creditor must be a person who, in the ordinary course of business *regularly* extends credit. 15 U.S.C. § 1602 (f); Reg. Z § 226.2(a)(17)(i). A natural person or an organization can be a "person" who is a creditor.

In addition, this person must, essentially, be a "professional creditor." This does not mean that the creditor's regular business must be extending credit; it means that whatever the creditor's business, he or she must regularly extend credit in the ordinary course of business. TILA sets forth a general definition of who is a creditor. "Creditor" is defined in 15 U.S.C. § 1602 (f) as:

> a person who both (1) regularly extends, whether in connection with loans, sales of property or services, or otherwise, consumer credit which is payable by agreement in more than four installments or for which the payment of a finance charge is or may be required, and (2) is the person to whom the debt arising from the consumer credit transaction is initially payable on the face of the evidence of indebtedness or, if there is no such evidence of indebtedness, by agreement....

The 1981 Regulation Z revision includes a mathematical test to determine if a person "regularly" extends credit and is, therefore, a creditor. To meet this test, the person must have extended consumer credit more than 25 times in the preceding calendar year. The Commentary explains that if a person extends consumer credit 26 times in 1998, he or she is a creditor for at least the 26th extension of credit in 1998 and for all extensions of consumer credit in 1999. Official Staff Commentary § 226.2(a)(17)(i)(4).

This numerical standard is lower for real estate secured loans. If a person extends credit more than five times in the preceding calendar year and each of those transactions was secured by a dwelling, then that person also "regularly" extends credit within the meaning of Regulation Z. Therefore, if a person extends consumer credit, which is secured by a dwelling, six times in 1998, then the person is a creditor for at least the sixth extension of credit in 1998. And that person is a creditor for all extensions of consumer credit in 1999. Official Staff Commentary § 226.2(a)(17)(i)(6).

The Official Staff Commentary to Regulation Z also addresses the effects of mixing secured real-estate credit with unsecured credit. Extensions of credit that are secured by a dwelling count towards the 25–extensions test. If, in 1998, a person extends unsecured consumer credit 23 times and also extends consumer credit secured by a dwelling twice, then that person becomes a creditor for additional extensions of consumer credit, regardless of whether the other transactions are secured by a dwelling. However, the extensions of credit that were *not* secured by a dwelling do *not* count towards the five-extensions test. Official Staff Commentary § 226.2(a)(17)(i)(5).

In addition, if a person meets either the 25–extensions or five-extensions test, then that person is also a creditor for extending other types of credit. Therefore, a person who extends consumer credit secured by a dwelling in 1998 is also a creditor for all succeeding extensions of credit in 1998 and 1999, regardless of whether those transactions are secured by a dwelling. Official Staff Commentary § 226.2(a)(17)(i)(6).

e. Imposition of Finance Charge

To be a creditor under TILA, not only must a person regularly extend credit, but the credit that that person extends also must meet one of two alternative tests. The credit must either (1) be subject to a finance charge, *or* (2) be payable by written agreement in more than four installments. Although the extended credit must only meet one of these tests, it usually meets both.

Under the first alternative test, if the consumer credit is subject to a finance charge, then the person extending the credit is a creditor. TILA's Official Staff Commentary notes that the obligation to pay the finance charge does not have to be in writing.

Under the second alternative test, if a person extends consumer credit that is payable by a *written* agreement in more than four installments, then that person is a creditor. Any down payment is not included within the meaning of the four install-ments. An oral agreement to pay consumer credit in more than four installments does *not* qualify a person as a creditor. Even a letter that merely confirms an oral agreement does not constitute a written agreement within this definition.

4. ORGANIZATION OF TRUTH IN LENDING ACT AND REGULATION Z

Truth in Lending divides consumer credit trans-actions into two broad categories: open-end credit transactions and other-than-open-end credit transactions (also referred to as closed-end credit transactions). TILA provides different disclosure requirements for each category. So while TILA's disclosure requirements apply to all credit transactions which meet the relevant requirements, the actual requirements will not be the same for all such transactions. After determining that TILA covers a specific transaction, it is then necessary to classify that transaction as open-end or closed-end.

An "open end credit plan" is defined at 15 U.S.C. § 1602(i). It is a plan under which the creditor reasonably contemplates repeated transactions, which prescribes the terms of such transactions, and which provides for a finance charge which may be computed from time to time on the outstanding unpaid balance. If the finance charge is precomputed at the inception of the transaction, it is not an open-end transaction. For most consumers, the most common type of open-end plan is a credit card account.

The other major category of consumer credit in TILA is closed-end credit, which Regulation Z § 226.2(a)(10) defines as "other than open-end credit." Closed-end credit usually involves one transaction and is extended for a specific period of time. The total amounts, number of payments, and due dates are generally agreed upon by the creditor and the customer at the time of the transaction. Common examples of closed credit include a mortgage loan to buy a home and credit sales of large items such as cars, furniture, and major appliances.

5.   GENERAL DISCLOSURE REQUIREMENTS

Precisely what must be disclosed depends on whether the consumer credit transaction is open-end or closed-end and whether it is a loan or credit sale. However, there are some general requirements that apply to all TILA disclosures. Regulation Z § 226.5(a)(1) requires creditors to make disclosures "clearly and conspicuously," "in writing," and "in a form that the consumer may keep." The Findings and Declaration of Purpose of TILA requires a "meaningful disclosure" of credit terms so the consumer may be able to readily compare the various available credit terms. 15 U.S.C. § 1601(a).

The Official Staff Commentary elaborates on the "clear and conspicuous" standard. The clear and conspicuous standard requires that disclosures be in a "reasonably understandable form," and not require that the disclosures be segregated from other material or located in any particular place on the disclosure statement. Official Staff Commentary § 226.5(a)(1).

Regulation Z § 226.5(a)(2) requires that the terms "finance charge" and "annual percentage rate," when required to be disclosed with a number, must be disclosed more conspicuously than other required disclosures, except in a few limited circumstances. A creditor may also choose to disclose these items more conspicuously even when the regulations do not so require.

According to the Official Staff Commentary, "more conspicuous" requires that the actual words "finance charge" and "annual percentage rate" should be accentuated. They can be highlighted by capitalizing the relevant words, when other disclosures are printed in lower case. They can be printed in bold print or contrasting color. They can be underlined, set off with asterisks or printed in larger type. It is fitting that these two terms receive special attention, because they are at the heart of the notion that TILA should provide critical information to consumers who are shopping for credit. The finance charge and APR are the clearest expressions of the true cost of credit.

The standard of "meaningful disclosure" was discussed by the U.S. Supreme Court in *Ford Motor Credit Co. v. Milhollin*, 444 U.S. 555 (1980). In *Mihollin*, the Court described a balance between the competing considerations of complete disclosure, and the need to avoid information overload. *Id.* at 568–569. It does not necessarily mean *more* disclosure. Generally, the disclosure statement should provide the consumer with an easy basis for comparison of terms offered by competing creditors.

Another disclosure requirement is that the disclosures must be in writing. Reg. Z § 226.17(a)(1). And the consumer must be given a copy of the written disclosures. The consumer's written copy is relevant for determining whether required disclosures are "clear and conspicuous." A creditor may give oral disclosures, but they must be consistent with the written disclosures.

TILA's disclosure requirements are detailed and complex. One must first determine the nature of the credit (open-end or closed-end), then examine the statute, Regulation Z and the Official Staff Commentary for guidance. In order to assist creditors who face the daunting task of compliance with TILA, the 1980 amendments required the Federal Reserve Board to publish model disclosure forms and clauses upon which creditors can rely. 15 U.S.C. § 1604(b). Use of the forms is not required, but a creditor who uses one of the forms (and not just the language on the forms) is deemed to be in compliance with the disclosure provisions of TILA, other than the numerical disclosures (where the creditor might make an error). *Id.* However, if a creditor starts to use homemade forms loosely patterned after the model forms, the protection may be lost. And if the creditor uses the wrong form, the protections of 15 U.S.C. § 1604(b) are lost. *In re Melvin*, 75 B.R. 952 (Bankr.E.D.Pa.1987).

6.   CLOSED-END CREDIT DISCLOSURES

a.   Time for Disclosure

TILA requires that closed-end credit disclosures be made "before the credit is extended." 15 U.S.C. §§ 1638(b), 1639(b)(1). Regulation Z uses the phrase "before consumption." Reg. Z. § 226.17(b). Requiring credit disclosures to consumers *before* they enter into credit transactions encourages consumer comparison-shopping. It helps consumers to make careful, rational economic choices and furthers the competition in the consumer credit market. 15 U.S.C. § 1601(a).

Regulation Z § 226.17 sets forth the general disclosure requirements for closed-end credit. Regulation Z § 226.17(b) uses the phrase "before consummation" to describe the time within which creditors or lenders must make closed-end disclosures. "Consummation" is "the time that a consumer becomes contractually obligated on a credit transaction." Reg. Z § 226.2(a)(13). Whether a consumer becomes contractually obligated is a matter of state law. The Official Staff Commentary does note that a contractual commitment agreement that binds the consumer to the credit terms "under applicable law" is considered consummation. Regulation Z does not make this determination. A contractual commitment agreement, for example, that under applicable law binds the consumer to the credit terms would be consummation. Official Staff Commentary § 226.2(a)(13)(1).

Consummation does not occur when the consumer becomes merely contractually committed to buy the goods, unless the consumer also becomes legally obligated to accept a particular credit arrangement. For example, paying a nonrefundable deposit to purchase a car does not constitute "consummation" unless the consumer also contracts for financing at that time. Official Staff Commentary § 226.2(a)(13)2.

b. Disclosure of the Finance Charge

The disclosure of the cost of credit in dollars and cents, as well as a percentage is probably the most important concept in TILA. The finance charge is the cost of credit as a dollar amount, whereas the APR reflects that cost on an annual percentage rate basis. The basic definition of a "finance charge" is broad. A finance charge is: (1) the sum of all charges, (2) payable directly or indirectly by the consumer, (3) imposed directly or indirectly by the creditor, (4) as an incident to or a condition of the extension of credit. 15 U.S.C. § 1605(a). It does not include any charge of a type payable in a comparable cash transaction.

An accurate disclosure of the finance charge (within a slight "tolerance" for error allowed by TILA) is viewed as so critical that a failure to properly disclose the finance charge gives rise to statutory damages as well as actual damages. 15 U.S.C. § 1640(a)(3). Improper disclosure of the amount of the finance charge is also a material violation for purposes of rescission. 15 U.S.C. § 1602(u).

For both the creditor and the consumer, determining the accurate cost of credit for TILA purposes involves breaking down the components of the total obligation into two basic classifications: (1) the amount financed, and (2) the finance charge. The amount financed is comprised of those legitimate components of the obligation which are advanced by the lender directly to the borrower or paid to others on the borrower's behalf. The finance charge is the cost of the credit. These two categories are mutually exclusive.

TILA has an all-inclusive definition of the cost of credit. The term "finance charge" is intended to reflect the true cost of the credit to the borrower and it is often broader than what may be described as the "interest rate." TILA generally reflects an approach that focuses on what the *borrower pays*. TILA's approach, is distinct from the principle underlying most usury laws, which focus on what the *creditor receives* as interest.

Charges that are included in the finance charge are described in 15 U.S.C. § 1605(a) and Regulation Z § 226.4(b). The following charges are included in the finance charge:

(1) interest;

(2) time price differential;

(3) any amount payable under an add-on or discount system of additional charges;

(4) service, transaction, activity and carrying charges;

(5) points;

(6) loan fees;

(7) assumption fees, finder's fees and similar charges;

(8) appraisal, investigation and credit report fees;

(9) premiums or other charges for any guarantee or insurance protecting the creditor against the consumer's default or other credit loss;

(10) charges imposed on a creditor by another person for purchasing or accepting a consumer's obligation, if the consumer is required to pay the charges in cash, as an addition to the obligation, or as a deduction from the proceeds of the obligation;

(11) premiums or other charges for credit life, accident, health, or loss-of-income insurance, written in connection with a credit transaction, except where otherwise treated as part of the finance charge;

(12) premiums or other charges for insurance against loss of or damage to property, or against liability arising out of the ownership or use of property, written in connection with a credit transaction, except where otherwise treated as part of the finance charge;

(13) discounts for the purpose of inducing payment by a means other than the use of credit; and

(14) borrower-paid mortgage broker fees, including fees paid directly to the broker or the lender (for delivery to the broker) whether such fees are paid in cash or financed.

The following charges are not part of the finance charge, if they are itemized and disclosed:

(1) application fees charged to all applicants for credit, whether or not credit is actually extended;

(2) actual unanticipated late payment charges for exceeding a credit limit, or for delinquency, default or a similar occurrence;

(3) overdrawn account charges, unless previously agreed upon;

(4) charges imposed by a financial institution for paying items that overdraw an account, unless the payment of such items and the imposition of the charge were previously agreed upon in writing;

(5) seller's points;

(6) discounts offered to induce payment for a purchase by cash, check or other means, as provided in the Act;

(7) other taxes and fees prescribed by law which actually are or will be paid to public officials for determining the existence of or for perfecting or releasing or satisfying any security related to the credit transaction; and

(8) in transactions secured by real property, fees for, title examination, abstract of title, title insurance, property survey, preparing deeds and mortgages, reconveyance, settlement and similar documents, notary, appraisal, credit reports, and amounts required to be paid into escrow or trustee accounts, if the amounts would not otherwise be included in the finance charge.

7. CREDIT INSURANCE

There are a number of credit insurance products. Their inclusion in consumer credit contracts has always been a point of controversy. Credit life insurance pays off the loan in the event of the death of the borrower. Credit disability insurance, sometimes described as "accident and health" (A & H), typically picks up the monthly payments while a debtor is disabled. Credit property insurance covers the collateral where the loan is secured. Involuntary unemployment insurance covers the monthly payments in the event the debtor loses his job through such things as a lay-off or plant closing. And nonfiling insurance covers the interest of the secured creditor in the event the creditor is unable to retrieve the collateral (after default) due to the creditor's failure to file a financing statement.

The controversy in consumer credit insurance comes from allegations that lenders and credit-sellers use credit insurance as a way to squeeze additional revenue from the borrower, and that the credit insurance premiums should be treated as part of the finance charge, just as interest is included in the finance charge as part of the "cost of credit." Consumer groups also argue that creditors tie the purchase of insurance to the extension of credit as a means of avoiding the limitations on interest under the usury laws. Consumer complaints on credit insurance "packing" were briefly discussed in Chapter Four, in the coverage of the subprime credit market, and will be more thoroughly treated in Chapter Eight.

Industry groups counter that credit insurance serves to protect legitimate interests of consumers and should not be included as a finance charge because the premium is for a product that has value to the consumer and is not like the stated interest on a loan. Creditors hold the view that the charge for insurance has nothing to do with the cost of credit.

TILA's approach is a compromise between these positions. If the creditor complies with all of the following three requirements, credit life, accident and health insurance, and loss-of-income insurance premiums do not need to be included in the finance charge. First, the creditor must not require insurance. Second, the fact that insurance is not required by the creditor must be clearly and conspicuously disclosed in writing to the consumer. Finally, after receiving the "voluntariness" disclosure, the consumer must sign or initial the affirmative written request for insurance. Reg. Z § 226.4(d)(1).

TILA's treatment of property insurance is somewhat different. Charges for premiums for insurance protection against loss or damage to property do not need to be included in the finance charge. However, they can only be excluded if the creditor discloses in a clear, conspicuous, specific written statement: (1) the cost of insurance if obtained through the creditor, and (2) the freedom of the customer to choose the person from whom the insurance is to be obtained. Reg. Z § 226.4(d)(2).

The premium for non-filing insurance may be excluded from the finance charge to the extent that the premium does not exceed the filing cost that would be paid if the creditor chose to record its security interest in the public record. Typically, the charge for non-filing insurance is $10, which is below the cost of filing a financing statement under Article 9 of the Uniform Commercial Code. The validity of non-filing insurance has recently been called into question (separate from TILA disclosure issues) and will be more fully discussed in Chapter Eight.

Credit life or health insurance premiums are a part of the finance charge if the creditor requires the consumer to buy it. Property or liability insurance is a part of the finance charge if the creditor requires the consumer to buy if *from or through the creditor*.

8. BURYING FINANCE CHARGES IN THE CASH PRICE

In addition to claims that creditors often use credit insurance to extract profit from a credit transaction in lieu of charging and disclosing a higher interest rate, it would be entirely contrary to the spirit of full disclosure of the "cost of credit" if creditors were permitted to have one "cash price" for "cash buyers," but a higher "cash price" for credit buyers. That is, in addition to the interest rate that a credit-seller could charge and disclose, if the item has a higher initial price tag for a credit buyer than for the cash buyer, the creditor may be burying a finance charge in the sales price.

Credit sellers of goods and services will often sell their paper (installment sales contract) to a finance company at a discount. An example would be an automobile dealer who might sell a car to Smith for a $10,000 price, and finance the arrangement for Smith, adding on a $3,000 finance charge to be paid off over the life of the installment sales contract. It could also be that a provider of services, such as a health club operator or business that provides karate lessons, signs a contract with a customer for a one-year contract, but also is willing to take the payments over time only if the customer will pay some interest beyond the cash price. That is, the cash price for an annual karate lesson contract might be $600, but if the customer wants to pay it over time and finance the $600 obligation, a finance charge of $120 is added, bringing the stream of payments to $60 per month and $720 per year.

In many cases, dealers (whether they sell cars or karate lessons) do not hold their installment sales contracts, but sell their paper to a finance company at a discount. For example, in the Smith car purchase noted above, the contract may be sold to Acme Finance for $9,500, which is a $500 discount below the $10,000 sales price. The auto dealer will make money if he bought the car at an auto auction for some amount less than $9,500. And Acme finance will make money because it paid $9,500 for an asset that will return $13,000 over the life of the loan; that is, the $10,000 amount financed and the

$3,000 in interest. This so-called "discount financing," is common in used car auto finance, and most particularly in the subprime credit market, previously discussed in Chapter Four at pages 72-75.

The question that has been raised in a considerable amount of litigation in the 1990's is whether the $500 amount should be disclosed to the borrower as a finance charge. Consumer advocates argue that the assignee's total return above the amount it paid for the contract, should be characterized and disclosed as interest because the "true" cash price being realized by the auto dealer is only $9,500. The argument is that the interest rate reflects (in part) the risk on the contract represented by the borrower, and if the assignee has insisted on the discount because the $3,000 finance charge is viewed by the finance company as being inadequate to compensate for the risk, the additional $500 should be lumped together with the $3,000 and disclosed to the borrower as the "true cost of credit."

The question of hidden finance charges in discount financing has caused many problems for courts over time. In addition to disclosure issues under TILA, consumer advocates have used fraud and suppression claims to argue that the credit-seller has a duty to disclose to the buyer that he was willing to take the discounted amount for the item ($9,500 in our automobile example), rather than the $10,000 "cash price" disclosed to the buyer. Although discount financing may be commonly accepted and viewed as a very ordinary practice by those who sell cars and buy paper, experience in litigation has shown that many jurors react very negatively when they discover that a car who claimed that he could not possibly budge below a certain price, after much haggling, had already agreed to sell the contract at less than the "cash price."[3]

In response to some of the fraud and suppression claims that had surfaced under state law, some legislatures responded by amending their consumer credit codes to declare there is no "duty to disclose" the likely sale of paper at a discount.[4] And in some

3. In Johnson v. Mercury Finance Company of Alabama, No. CV–93–052 (Cir. Ct. Barbour County, Ala. Jan. 27, 1995), the jury returned a punitive award of $50 million. The author served as the plaintiff's expert witness in the *Johnson* case, which was settled for less than $2 million. For a discussion of the profits reportedly made by Mercury Finance and other deep discount lenders, *see* Andrew Barry, *Mercury Finance: Steep Incline*, Barron's, Aug. 15, 1994, at 17. For more recent developments detailing the problems at Mercury Finance and the fallout at other deep discount auto lending firms, *see* Jeff Bailey & Carlos Tejada, *Woes Mount for Used–Car Lending Firms*, Wall St. J., Feb. 7, 1997, at A2; Jeff Bailey & Thomas M. Burton, *A Lemon of a Deal: Used–Car Lender Leaves a Sour Taste*, Wall St. J., Feb. 5, 1997, at A1; Jeff Bailey, *Mercury Finance's Controller Denies He Inflated Firm's Profit Statements*, Wall St. J., Jan. 31, 1997, at A3.

4. For example, Ala. Code § 5–19–6(c)(1996) provides: (c) Without limiting the generality of subsection (b), there is no obligation or duty under this chapter to disclose to a debtor any agreement to assign or otherwise transfer a consumer credit transaction contract at a discount or that the assignee of, or person who funded, the consumer credit transaction agreed or may agree to pay the creditor or other person who originated the consumer credit transaction all or a portion of the prepaid finance charges and other fees and/or a portion of the finance charge to be paid by the debtor over the term of the transaction cases, dealers included a disclosure in their contracts to inform consumers that the paper may be sold at a discount.

Whether the amount of the discount which is built into the cash sales price is a finance charge under TILA has not been easy for the courts to resolve. The particular facts of the case must be analyzed, in light of the following passage from § 226.4(a)(2) of the Official Staff Commentary:

Costs of doing business. Charges absorbed by the creditor as a cost of doing business are not finance charges, even though the creditor may take such costs into consideration in determining the interest rate to be charged or the cash price of the property or services sold. However, if the creditor separately imposes a charge on the consumer to cover certain costs, the charge is a finance charge if it otherwise meets the definition. For example, a discount imposed on a credit obligation when it is assigned by a seller-creditor to another party is not a finance charge as long as the discount is not separately imposed on the consumer.

It is important to note that under TILA, the "creditor" in an installment sales contract is the person to whom the debt is initially made payable. 15 U.S.C. § 1602(f). Thus, since the installment sales contract is initially made payable to the car dealer, although later assigned (bought) by the bank or finance company, the car dealer is the creditor who may be absorbing the discount as a

and/or other compensation irrespective of how the compensation is determined or described.

cost of doing business. That is, in the auto example above, the creditor had to give up the $500 in order to get $9,500 cash for the contract, where the car was sold for $10,000.

If the dealer absorbs the loss (discount) as a cost of doing business, the discount may not be viewed as a finance charge. For example, in *April v. Union Mortgage Co.*, 709 F.Supp. 809 (N.D.Ill.1989), a $3,300 discount on a $20,000 contract was not viewed by the court as a "cost imposed on the borrower" because the borrowers had already agreed to pay $20,000 for the work.

More recently, in *Perino v. Mercury Finance*, 912 F.Supp. 313 (N.D.Ill.1995), the judge held that although the buyer of the automobile did not receive a disclosure that the paper would be sold at a discount, the alleged failure to disclose is specifically authorized by TILA and that the discount was not a finance charge but a "cost of doing business" absorbed by the creditor. And the court pointed out that the Official Staff Commentary recognizes that the discount should not be viewed as a finance charge, even though the creditor may take such charges into consideration in the interest rate to be charged or the cash price of the property or services sold. The *Perino* case has been cited favorably in a number of subsequently decided cases where the discount was not held to be a finance charge.[5]

5. *See, e.g.,* Chancellor v. Gateway Lincoln–Mercury, Inc., 233 Ga.App. 38, 502 S.E.2d 799 (1998); Sampson v. Mercury Finance Co.,1996 WL 1057530 (M.D. Ala. 1996); Walker v. Wallace Auto

Although a number of the early deep discount auto cases went in favor of the creditors and assignees, the U.S. Court of Appeals for the Seventh Circuit further analyzed the language in the Official Staff Commentary and noted that a dealer does separately impose a discount on credit buyers (making it a finance charge) when the dealer negotiates "inflated" cash prices with credit customers high enough to cover the discounts, but negotiates lower prices with cash customers. *Walker v. Wallace Auto Sales*, 155 F.3d 927 (7th Cir.1998). The Court noted that a dealer need not disclose the cost of a discount as a finance charge if he recoups the discounts at which he sells the retail installment contracts by negotiating for comparable vehicles the same, relatively high price for *all customers*. This case is the purest application to date of the Truth in Lending concept of providing that there should not be a separate cash and credit price.

Simply put, if a car dealer runs a lot, particularly a subprime lot, where deep discounts are common, he should set a "window price" based on the investment he has in the car, the profit he wants to make and the discount he anticipates he wants to absorb. He should do this across the board and across the lot, *without regard to the nature of the buyers*, and particularly not in regard to whether the buyers will be cash or credit buyers. It would be a TILA violation to have one cash price and another credit price, or to have a "window price" that gets

Sales, Inc., 1997 WL 598149 (N.D.Ill. 1997); Balderos v. Mercury Finance Co., 1998 WL 155912 (N.D.Ill.1998).

bumped up after the individual credit characteristics of a borrower are identified. In any case, if there is a two-tier price system for cash and credit buyers, a TILA violation will likely result because the true cost of the deal changes for the credit buyer and the credit buyer is paying an additional price you do not find in a comparable cash transaction. Recall that under the definition of "finance charge" in 15 U.S.,C. § 1605(a), the finance charge does *not* include charges of a type *payable in a comparable cash transaction.*

It is interesting to note that in open-end credit (credit cards), where the seller is not the card issuer, the card issuer may not prohibit the seller from offering a discount to a cardholder to induce the cardholder to pay by cash, check, or a similar means other than a credit card. 15 U.S.C. § 1666(f)(a). And any discount from the regular price offered by the seller for the purpose of inducing payment by cash or check shall not constitute a finance charge if such discount is offered to all prospective buyers and its availability is disclosed clearly and conspicuously. 15 U.S.C. § 1666(f)(b). Sellers are not required to provide a discount to cash buyers, but they have the option to do so.

9.   ANNUAL PERCENTAGE RATE

The other item that is required to be disclosed more conspicuously than other terminology is the APR, "annual percentage rate." The APR reflects the effective cost of credit when declining balances are taken into account, unlike an add-on rate. Its disclosure must be more conspicuous than any other required disclosure.

Most consumer credit transactions are multiple installment transactions. For example, suppose X and Y both borrow $1,000 for one year. Both agree to pay $100 finance charge. X is to repay the loan at the end of the year. Y is to repay the loan in 12 equal monthly installments. Using $R = I / PT$ to compute the annual percentage rate, the rate in the two transactions would be identical.

The comparison would be misleading in Y's transaction, however. The formula fails to take into account the fact that Y is paying installments over the 12 months of the loan and that each installment payment reduces the amount of credit. Y, unlike X, does not have the use of the entire $1,000 for the entire year. After the first month, Y only has the use of less than the full $1,000. After the second month, Y only has the use of even less. Accordingly, the annual percentage rate disclosed to Y should be higher than the annual percentage rate disclosed to X. Therefore, something more "sophisticated" than $R = I / PT$ must be used to compute the true cost of the credit in transactions in which the debtor pays in installments.

The calculation of APR under TILA recognizes the real cost of the credit, both because of the reduction of principal over time, but also because TILA has a more inclusive definition of "finance charge" than merely the interest on a loan. For example, a state may exclude a certain fee imposed by a lender from the calculation of whether the loan is usurious, but TILA would include the fee in the calculation of the finance charge and APR if the charge is one "imposed by the creditor as a condition to the extension of credit." 15 U.S.C. § 1605(a). Thus, the APR, which uses the more expansive definition of "finance charge," often exceeds the "interest rate" shown on the contract.

The mathematical equation and technical instructions for determining the APR in accordance with the actuarial method are set forth in Reg. Z § 226.22. The Federal Reserve Board has created "Regulation Z Annual Percentage Tables" to supplement Regulation Z. The annual percentage rate disclosed in closed-end credit transactions is considered accurate if it is not more than 1/8 of 1 percentage point above or below the APR determined in accordance with the procedures outlined in the regulation.

The tables are easiest to use when one has a series of evenly spaced payments of an equal amount. However, there are also "irregular" consumer credit transactions. "Irregular" transactions include: multiple advances, irregular payment periods, or irregular payment amounts. Volume II of the Federal Reserve Boards' Annual Percentage Rate Tables can be used to calculate APR's for "irregular" transactions. Reg. Z § 226.22(b)(1). In "irregular" transactions, the first payment may be larger than the others to offset a low down payment. The payment dates may be set to fall near the customer's paydays, so that a transaction entered into on the ninth of the month provides for "monthly" installments due on the first day of each month. Few TILA transactions will use Volume II.

10. OTHER DISCLOSURE REQUIREMENTS

"Finance charge" and "annual percentage rate" are the most critical disclosures available to consumers in comparing the cost of credit, but they are not the only disclosures required by TILA in closed-end consumer credit transaction. Probably the easiest place to read and understand the additional disclosure requirements is in Regulation Z § 226.18. The following are additional disclosure requirements.

(a) The identity of the creditor making the disclosures must be made. Recall that the creditor is the party to whom the obligation is originally made payable.

(b) The "amount financed" used must be disclosed using that term, which shall be the amount of credit of which the consumer has actual use.

(c) A separate written itemization of the amount financed must be made, including:

    (1) the amount of any proceeds distributed directly to the consumer;

    (2) the amount credited to the consumer's account with the creditor;

    (3) any amounts paid to other persons by the creditor on the consumer's behalf.

The creditor does not need to comply with these requirements if the creditor provides a statement that the consumer has the right to receive a written itemization of the amount financed, together with a space for the consumer to indicate whether it is desired, and the consumer does not request it. Reg. Z § 226.18(c)(2).

(d) If the APR may increase after consummation in a transaction not secured by the consumer's principal dwelling, or in a transaction secured by the consumer's principal dwelling with a term of one year or less, the consumer must be informed of the circumstances under which the rate may increase, any limitations on the increase, the effect of any increase and be provided with an example of the payment terms that would result in an increase.

If the annual percentage rate may increase after consummation in a transaction secured by the consumer's principal dwelling with a term greater than one year, the consumer must be informed that the transaction has a variable rate feature and must be provided with a statement that variable rate disclosures have been provided earlier.

(e) The number, amount, and due dates or period of payments scheduled to repay the total of payments must be provided.

(f) The sum of the amount financed and the finance charge, which shall be termed the "total amount of payments" must be disclosed.

(g) The creditor must disclose the demand feature, if the obligation has one.

(h) In a credit sale, the creditor must disclose the "total sale price," using that term, and a descriptive explanation (including the amount of any downpayment), such as "the total price of your purchase on credit, including your downpayment of $_____."

(i) Descriptive explanations of the terms "amount financed," "financed charge," "annual percentage rate," "total of payments," and "total sale price" as specified by the Board, must be provided.

(j) The creditor must disclose whether or not a penalty will be imposed in the event of prepayment, when an obligation includes a finance charge computed from time to time by application of a rate to the unpaid principal balance.

(k) The credit must disclose any dollar or percentage charge that may be imposed before maturity due to a late payment, other than a deferral or extension charge.

(l) The information required in order to exclude credit insurance from the finance charge must be provided.

(m) There must be a contract reference that the consumer should refer to the appropriate contract document for information about nonpayment, default, the right to accelerate the maturity of the obligation, and prepayment rebates and penalties.

(n) In a residential mortgage transaction the creditor must disclose whether a subsequent purchaser of the dwelling from the consumer may be permitted to assume the remaining obligation on its original terms.

(o) The creditor must provide a statement that the APR does not reflect the effect of the required deposit, if the creditor requires the consumer to maintain a deposit as a condition of the specific transaction.

11. ADDITIONAL DISCLOSURES IN CERTAIN RESIDENTIAL MORTGAGE TRANSACTIONS

TILA and Regulation Z § 226.19 also provide for additional disclosures that must be made in certain residential mortgage transactions.

(a) In a residential mortgage transaction subject to the Real Estate Settlement Procedures Act, the creditor must give good faith estimates of the disclosures required by Regulation Z § 226.18 before consummation.

(b) If the APR in the consummated transaction varies from the APR disclosed in Regulation Z

§ 226.18 by more than one eighth of one percentage point in a regular transaction or more than one fourth of one percentage point in an irregular transaction, the creditor shall disclose the changed terms no later than at the time of consummation or settlements.

(c) If the APR may increase after consummation in a transaction secured by the consumer's principal dwelling with a term of greater than one year, then the following must be provided, or information provided in accordance with variable-rate regulations of other federal agencies may be substituted:

  (1) the booklet titled "Consumer Handbook on Adjustable Rate Mortgages" or a suitable substitute, and

  (2) a loan program disclosure for each variable-rate program in which the consumer expresses interest. The following disclosures, as applicable, shall be provided:

    (i) that the interest rate, payment, or term of the loan can change;

    (ii) the index or formula used in making adjustments;

    (iii) an explanation of how the interest rate and payment will be determined;

    (iv) a statement that the consumer should ask about the current margin value and current interest rate;

    (v) that the interest rate will be discounted;

(vi) the frequency of interest rate and payment changes;

(vii) any rules relating to changes in the index, interest rate, payment amount, and outstanding loan balance:

(viii) an historical example, based on $10,000 loan amount, illustrating how payments and the loan balance would have been affected by the interest rate changes implemented according to the terms of the loan program;

(ix) an explanation of how the consumer may calculate the payments for the loan amount to be borrowed;

(x) the maximum interest rate and payment for a $10,000 loan originated at the most recent interest rate;

(xi) that the loan program contains a demand feature;

(xii) the type of information that will be provided in notices of adjustments, and the timing of such notices;

(xiii) a statement that disclosure forms are available for the creditor's other variable-rate loan programs.

12.   ADDITIONAL DISCLOSURE
PROBLEMS

a. **Location of Disclosures**

TILA requires that the disclosures must be "segregated from everything else, and shall not contain any information not directly related" to the disclosures required by Regulation Z § 226.18. Reg. Z § 226.17(a)(1). This requirement is aimed at not loading consumers with so much information that it is difficult for them to understand a lot of it.

There are some exceptions to the segregation rule. First, the itemization of the amount financed may not be included with the segregated disclosures. It must be disclosed separately. Second, the creditor may exclude any or all of the following disclosures from the segregated disclosures: (1) the creditor's identity, (2) variable-rate example, (3) insurance disclosures, and (4) security interest charges. Reg. Z § 226.17(a), fn. 38. Finally, the segregated disclosures may include any or all of the following: (1) acknowledgment of receipt, (2) date of the transaction, and (3) the consumer's name, address, and account number. Reg. Z § 226.17(a), fn. 37.

The disclosures may be grouped together and segregated in a variety of ways. Indeed, the "one-sided of one-page requirement" in prior TILA law has been eliminated. Now the segregated disclosures may appear by themselves, with other information, on the back of documents, or may be con-

tinued from one page to another. Official Staff
Commentary 226.17(a)(1)-(3). The only requirements are that: (1) the disclosures be segregated
together from all other information that is not
"directly related" and (2) are "clear and conspicuous." *See* Official Staff Commentary § 226.17(a).

b. Security Interests

Among other disclosures that creditors must
make, they must disclose whether they have or will
acquire a security interest in the property being
purchased as part of the transaction. 15 U.S.C.
§ 1638(a)(9).

Regulation Z § 226.2(a)(25) provides:

"Security interest" means an interest in property
that secures performance of a consumer credit
obligation and that is recognized by state or federal law. It does not include incidental interests
such as interest in proceeds, accessions, additions,
fixtures, insurance proceeds (whether or not the
creditor is a loss payee or beneficiary), premium
rebates, or interests in after-acquired property.
For purposes of disclosures under sections 226.6
and 226.18, the term does not include an interest
that arises solely by operation of law. However,
for purposes of the right of rescission under sections 226.15 and 226.23, the term does include
interests that arise solely by operation of law.
Reg. Z § 226.2(a)(25).

If creditors err in their disclosures, they should err
on the side of inclusion of disclosed security inter-

ests. Courts strictly enforce creditors' disclosures of whether they have or will acquire a security interest in the property being purchased. In *In re Kenderdine*, the court held that failure to recite in the disclosure statement that the creditor took a security interest in the consumer's home violated Regulation Z § 226.18(m) and 15 U.S.C. § 1638(a)(9). 118 B.R. 258 (Bkrcy. E.D. Pa. 1990). The court imposed statutory damages. *See also Joyce v. Cloverbrook Homes, Inc.*, 344 S.E.2d 58 (N.C.Ct.App.1986) (failure to disclose security interest).

Creditors should also be careful about mingling disclosures required by state law with those required by TILA. Grouping of inconsistent disclosures violates Regulation Z § 226.17(a)(1), which reads, in part: "disclosures shall be grouped together, shall be segregated from everything else, and shall not contain any information not directly related to the disclosures required under section 226.18." *See, e.g., Gresham v. Termplan, Inc., West Bend*, 480 F.Supp. 149 (N.D.Ga.1979).

With respect to security interests, Regulation Z § 226.18(m) also requires creditors to disclose whether they have or will acquire a security interest in other property, identified by item or type. In *Gennuso v. Commercial Bank & Trust Co.*, 566 F.2d 437 (3d Cir. 1977), the creditor violated TILA by failing to properly disclose that he claimed a security interest in "all attachments, accessories and parts used or intended to be used with the above described property ('Collateral') whether now or hereafter installed therein." Creditors, then, must be careful not to misstate security interests or their scope.

13.   OPEN-END CREDIT

a.   Disclosures in Applications and Solicitations

An open-end credit plan is one under which the creditor reasonably contemplates repeated transactions, which prescribes the terms of such transactions, and which provides for a finance charge which may be computed from time to time on the outstanding unpaid balance. 15 U.S.C. § 1602 (i). The most common form of open-end credit in the lives of most consumers is a credit card. In open-end credit, rather than disclosing a total finance charge at the execution of the contract, the creditor applies an interest rate against the unpaid balance to arrive at a monthly finance charge. The growth in open-end credit and credit card debt was previously discussed in Chapter Four, at pages 63-64.

On November 3, 1988, the Fair Credit and Charge Card Disclosure Act was enacted into law. 15 U.S.C. § 1637(c). Under the law, any application to open a credit card account under an open-end consumer credit plan, or a solicitation to open such an account without requiring an application, that is mailed to consumers shall disclose the following information, in tabular format:

(1) the APR;

(2) annual and other fees;

(3) any grace period under which charges must be paid to avoid a finance charge;

(4) the outstanding balance calculation method; and

(5) information on cash advance fees, late fees and over-the-limit fees.

See 15 U.S.C. § 1637(c).

b. Initial Statement

The disclosures noted above, mandated by the Fair Credit and Charge Card Billing Act, must be made at the time of solicitation or application. The next required disclosures are those that must be provided before the first transaction by which the customer becomes obligated in the plan. In a case where a consumer simultaneously opens a plan and makes a purchase, disclosure must be made before that purchase.

Regulation Z § 226.6 lists the required disclosures to be included in the initial statement.

(1) the conditions under which a finance charge may be imposed;

(2) the time period (if any) within which any credit extended may be repaid without incurring a finance charge;

(3) the method of determining the balance upon which a finance charge will be imposed; different creditors use different balances in computing finance charges;

Some creditors look to the balance of the account at the beginning of the billing period. Others look to the closing balance. Some look to the opening balance with adjustments for transactions during the billing cycle.

(4) the method of determining the amount of the finance charge; including any minimum or fixed amount imposed as a finance charge; any service charges, such as those commonly imposed by bank check credit plans, or minimum charges, such as those imposed on some revolving charge accounts, must be disclosed;

(5) where one or more periodic rates may be used to compute the finance charge:

　(a) each such rate,

　(b) the range of balances to which it is applicable, and

　(c) the corresponding nominal APR;

(6) identification of other charges which may be imposed and their method of computation, in accordance with the Federal Reserve Board regulations;

(7) if the indebtedness is or will be secured, a statement to that effect with an appropriate identification of the collateral; and

(8) a statement as to billing error rights and the right to assert claims and defenses in a form prescribed by the Federal Reserve Board (with periodic transmittal of a statement of such rights).

The only required disclosures of terminology for initial open-end disclosures are the terms "finance charge" and "annual percentage rate." These terms must also be more conspicuous than other required disclosures. The initial disclosures must be in writing.

The required disclosures must be made in an "integrated" document. Disclosures may be made on the front and reverse, as long as it is clear that the pages constitute one document. The creditor cannot provide separate pages at different times. The integrated document must be provided all at once to the consumer.

14. PERIODIC STATEMENTS

Creditors must send periodic statements at the end of each "billing cycle" in which there is (1) a closing debit or credit balance in the account of more than $1.00, or (2) any finance charge has been imposed. Reg. Z § 226.5(b)(2)(i). Neither the Act nor the regulations require the use of any particular billing cycle. The most commonly used billing cycle, though, is the calendar month.

Neither TILA nor the regulations specify how soon after the end of the billing cycle the periodic statement must be sent. Yet under Regulation Z § 226.5(b)(2)(ii), periodic statements must be mailed at least 14 days prior to the date that a finance charge may be imposed. A creditor that fails to meet this requirement cannot collect any finance or other charge as a result of such failure.

Creditors must send periodic statements to customers who participate in open-end credit transactions. Under 15 U.S.C. § 1637(b), creditors are required to make the following disclosures.

(1) the beginning balance;

(2) the amount and date of each credit extension with an identification of each;

(3) the amount credited during the billing period;

(4) the amount of the finance charge, itemized to show the application of various rates;

(5) the amount of any minimum finance charges;

(6) each periodic rate, the range of balances to which it applies, and the corresponding APR;

(7) the total finance charge and the range of balances to which it applies;

(8) the balance on which the finance charge is computed and how the balance was determined;

(9) the outstanding balance at the end of the period;

(10) the time within which payment must be made to avoid additional finance charges; and

(11) the creditor's address for billing error purposes.

The periodic statement must also include the amount of any other charges debited to the account. These charges must be itemized and identified by type. "Other charges" are significant charges imposed on the account (other than the finance charges). These "other charges" include:

(1) membership fees, unless such fees are imposed on both cash and credit customers;

(2) late charges;

(3) default or delinquency charges;

(4) charges for exceeding the credit limit on an account;

(5) fees for providing copies of documents in connection with billing error procedures;

(6) taxes imposed on the credit transaction as such;

(7) charges in connection with a real estate transaction which have been excluded from the finance charge;

(8) other charges imposed on credit transactions; and

(9) charges imposed on both cash and credit customers, to the extent that the charge to credit customers exceeds the charge to cash customers.

Creditors must send the periodic statement to customers at the end of each billing cycle if: (1) either a finance charge has been imposed during the cycle, or (2) if there is an outstanding debit or credit balance of more the $1.00 at the end of the cycle. If the consumer owes nothing, then the creditor does not need to send a statement. Reg. Z § 226.7.

15.   RECENT PROBLEMS IN OPEN–
END CREDIT AND MARKETING
OF CONSUMER GOODS

a.   Overview of the Litigation

In the 1980's a considerable amount of litigation developed which involved open-end credit and the sale of big-ticket consumer goods, through door-to-door sales. A great deal of the litigation involved credit card issuers who financed the sale of satellite-TV dishes.[6] The cases include allegations of failure to comply with TILA-mandated disclosures as well as claims that the financing should have been set up as a closed-end transaction, rather than as an open-ended financing. In many of the cases the attempt was made to link the alleged misrepresentations made by dealer and salespersons at the home-owner's door to the credit card issuer through the application of agency law. The attempt to impose liability on the lender or credit card issuer for the fraud of the retail dealer is not a new concept.[7]

Recently, several cases were resolved favorably for the credit card issuers on the agency issue. *Campbell-Salva v. Direct Cable of Mobile/Pensacola, Inc.*, 1997 U.S. Dist. LEXIS 12408, No. 96–0926 BH–M (S.D.Ala. July 14, 1997); *Brooks v. Home*

6. *See generally*, Jeff Bailey, *Lenders Probably Wish They Had Never Heard of Big Satellite Dishes*, Wall St. J., October 15, 1997, at A1.

7. *See generally*, Gene A. Marsh, *Lender Liability for Consumer Fraud Practices of Retail Dealers and Home Improvement Contractors*, 45 Ala. L. Rev. 1 (1993).

Cable Concepts of Tennessee, Inc., 1997 U.S. Dist. LEXIS 12540, No. 96–0757–CB–5 (S.D.Ala. July 29, 1997); *Cosby v. Southeastern Cable Systems*, 1997 U.S. Dist. LEXIS 12407, No. 96–0802–BH–C (S.D.Ala. July 14, 1997). However, there have also been multimillion dollar settlements reported in other cases, particularly where there was evidence of close involvement of the credit card issuer in the marketing of the product or disregard for consumer complaints.[8]

In some cases that settled, the defendants had a good position on the TILA claims, but were shaky on the agency and fraud claims because of specific evidence of aggressive marketing tactics by the dealers, knowledge on the part of the credit card issuers of those practices and a failure to police the dealer-card issuer agreement. In some cases there was a solid compliance program *on paper*, but serious problems in actual practice. Once again, the people in marketing got out on point and in some cases left the compliance people (and compliance manuals) behind.

b.   Marketing Flaws

The following observations are drawn from depositions, credit applications, training manuals and consumer complaints filed with attorney general offices across the country.

The use of revolving credit to provide financing for purchases in this industry allows for minimum monthly payments (usually ranging from $39 to

8.   *See* Bailey, *supra* note 6.

$59) that are low and not out of line with local cable rates, given that the dish is also being purchased. Keeping the minimum monthly payment low in order to compete with cable was a concern in the industry.

Providing the opportunity to consumers to understand the terms of open-end credit is critical and a central concept under TILA. In this industry the credit application included TILA disclosures often attached by a tear-sheet attached to the application. Some credit card issuers gave written instructions to dealers that the *customer* should fill out the credit card application. Filling out the credit application gives the customer a reasonable opportunity to read and understand the nature of the credit.

Many dealers ignored this instruction. Salespersons filled out the credit application and in some cases removed the disclosure tear-sheet before the credit application was signed. It was easy to prove that the instructions of the credit card issuer were being ignored through handwriting analysis and because the credit card applications included such things as misspelling of the customer's name. The credit card issuers never caught the problem because some them contracted to have all documents, including the copies of the three day right of rescission form, warehoused at the dealer. Even a random sample of the contract documents should have alerted the credit card issuer to the fact that the instructions on filling out applications were being ignored and that consumers were merely being asked to sign the forms. In some cases the signatures were obviously forged because the handwriting was the salesperson's who had misspelled the customer's name.

The problem with completion of the contract documents could have been discovered by the credit card issuer with even a cursory review of the completed forms. However, the warehousing of the documents at the dealer's business location left the card issuer in the dark until the complaints started rolling in.

Some of the credit card issuers relied on the dealers to warehouse the loan documents, but the dealers were unable to locate many of the documents when discovery requests were made. Having relied on the dealers to make the required disclosures and execute the forms, the credit card issuers were then embarrassed (at best) by the inability of the dealers to locate the documents. This added to the argument that the credit card issuers failed to police the dealers' agreements, to the detriment of customers.

Some of the credit card issuers got heavily involved in the marketing efforts and some provided sales scripts to aid in closing the deal. Where the alleged misrepresentations related to the *terms of the credit*, rather than the physical product and the reception of certain programs and premium channels, these sales scripts added to the notion that the credit card issuer was not merely an assignee or innocent party. This is particularly true in cases where the credit card issuer continued to work with the dealer after consumer complaints regarding the financing terms started to grow.

The same dangers that exist for assignees who buy dealer paper in the home improvement industry, as discussed in Chapter Four, are found in satellite-TV financing. Some itinerant dealers had no business location and operated out of their homes or the back of a truck. Some of the salespeople flipped burgers during the day and sold satellite-TV systems in the evening. Relying on such dealers and employees to make the appropriate open-end credit disclosures to customers raises all the same issues that are found in home improvement and door-to-door industries.[9]

Some of the satellite-TV arrangements involved another entity standing between the credit card issuer and the dealer. These "distributors" or "wholesalers" facilitated the financing. The presence of this additional entity between the dealer and the credit card issuer made control more difficult to establish, all else being equal.

At least one major credit card issuer that eventually entered this market and got stung, initially expressed great hesitation about serving this industry. All the dangers inherent in home improvement financing were spotted as being present here, particularly the itinerant nature of the dealers. It is clear that people within the company were concerned about losing a new market to the competi-

9. *See generally,* Gene A. Marsh, *Lender Liability for Consumer Fraud Practices of Retail Dealers and Home Improvement Contractors,* 45 Ala. L. Rev. (1993).

tion, and so they launched the program despite the concerns expressed by the people in compliance. In hindsight, following the instincts of the compliance staff would have saved the company millions of dollars.

Using open-end credit and setting the credit limit only pennies above the amount financed in the transaction, where the minimum monthly payment barely covers the accrued finance charge, is an invitation to a claim of "specious open-end credit." Some people who were financed had miserable credit and there was even an acknowledgment in one case that there was a "subprime" market in satellite-TV financing, with higher rates and lower limits. When this information is linked to the alleged misrepresentations regarding the credit terms, the problems multiply.

Allowing itinerant dealers in the hinterlands to warehouse all of the documents, without audits, is an invitation to disaster. In some of the litigation, after complaints started rolling in, some dealers could not find documents but were not cut off from the credit card program.

In some cases the credit card issuers were insensitive to customer complaints about the equipment, television reception and alleged misrepresentations in the terms of the financing. When the nature of the complaints regarding misrepresentation of credit terms were nearly identical across a large geographic area and over time, a red flag should have been raised. In some cases the credit card issuer responded only after the lawsuits started landing.

Door to door sales continue to cause trouble. This is particularly true where the dealers are itinerant and employees work elsewhere during the day, but are door-to-door sales people in the evening. It is not likely that the importance of credit disclosure mandates will ever be grasped, appreciated or observed by these people. And when customers start to complain but are unable to locate the dealer or the sales people, they will go after the assignee. At best, credit card issuers face a write-off because of the operation of TILA in allowing the customer to assert dealer problems against the issuer. At worst, dealers face an agency and fraud claim.

c. "Spurious" Open–End Credit

One of the requirements for the establishment of open-end credit is that the creditor "reasonably contemplates" repeat transactions. In several recent cases consumers have argued that credit card issuers are avoiding the more detailed closed-end disclosures by setting up sales under open-end credit, even though no subsequent transactions are contemplated. The use of private label credit cards to finance door-to-door sales has been at the center of the most recent litigation. For example, "low monthly payments" are at the heart of the marketing of satellite dishes.

At the center of many of the complaints is that salespeople often state that the low payments will last only three to five years, but that the loans in fact amortize for nine or more years. Borrowers claim that the open-end credit transaction is "specious," because no credit card issuer could expect that there would be repeat transactions, where the initial sale is a big ticket item, sold in a door-to-door transaction with an itinerant dealer.

A recent decision by the Seventh Circuit has validated the use of open-end credit in most of these sales. In *Benion v. Bank One*, 144 F.3d 1056 (7th Cir.1998), the circuit court upheld the district court view that Bank One's expectations for repeat transactions were "reasonable," because it produced data for another lender's similar program, showing that repeat sales constituted more than 10 percent of total sales. Judge Posner noted that the Federal Reserve Board had the regulatory expertise, and that courts should be reluctant to plug a loophole, where a regulatory agency had the power and expertise to do so.

16. REAL ESTATE TRANSACTIONS AND TILA

Generally, an extension of credit in which the amount financed exceeds $25,000 is exempt from TILA. However, there is one major exception to this general rule. If the amount financed exceeds $25,-000 and the credit extended is secured by either *real property or by personal property used or expected to be used as the consumer's principal dwelling*, the TILA requires disclosure of the amount financed. 15 U.S.C. § 1603(3).

TILA also gives consumers the right to rescind a credit transaction. TILA rescission rights exist if there is a consumer credit transaction in which a nonpurchase lien or security iterest is or will be placed, on the consumer's principal dwelling.

Section 1635 of TILA is different from most other TILA provisions. It is not primarily a disclosure provision. Instead, it creates an affirmative right to rescind. Rescission under TILA is not a penalty for nondisclosure. Even though a creditor makes all required disclosures, the consumer will have the right to rescind if the transaction comes within 15 U.S.C. § 1635.

To determine whether a consumer credit transaction comes within 15 U.S.C. § 1635, one should ask the following questions:

(1) Will the transaction result in a lien on any property that the consumer uses as his or her dwelling?

The lien may be either a consensual lien, such as a mortgage or deed of trust, or it may be a statutory lien, such as a mechanic's or materialmen's lien. For example, almost all home repair work done on credit gives rise to a right to rescind. Even if the contract waives all of his or her liens, the consumer still has the right to rescind if the contractor's suppliers, subcontractors, employees, etc. might acquire liens for materials that go into the house or work on it.

(2) Is this property that the consumer uses as his or her dwelling also used or expected to be used as the consumer's principal residence?

The right of rescission is restricted to transactions resulting in liens on a "principal residence." The right of rescission would not apply, therefore, if the real property encumbered is a vacation home. A creditor, however, may at times be uncertain as to whether a consumer one day expects to make his or her vacation home the "principal residence." When in doubt, comply with 15 U.S.C. § 1635's requirements.

(3) Is the lien a first lien securing the costs of the dwelling or the construction of the dwelling?

The right of rescission does not extend to first liens to secure the acquisition or construction of the dwelling. If, then, you are able to answer the first two questions "yes" and the third question "no," then the transaction comes within 15 U.S.C. § 1635.

In a contract subject to rescission, the creditor must deliver to each owner two copies of a notice of the right to rescind and one copy of the TILA disclosure statement containing material disclosures. Reg. Z § 226.15(b), § 226.23(b); Official Staff Commentary 226.15(b)–1; 226.23(b)–1. Material disclosures are:

(1) the annual percentage rate;

   (2) the method of determining the finance charge and the balance upon which a finance charge will be imposed;

   (3) the amount of the finance charge; the amount to be financed; the total of payments;

   (4) the number and amount of payments; and

   (5) the due dates or periods of payments scheduled to repay the indebtedness.

Disclosures of the right to rescind must be given "clearly and conspicuously in writing, in a form that the consumer may keep." Reg. Z § 226.5(a)(1).

If the transaction comes within 15 U.S.C. § 1635, the creditor must be reasonably satisfied that the consumer has not elected to rescind before disbursing any money other than in escrow, making any physical changes in the property, performing any work or service for the consumer, or making any deliveries to the consumer's residence. Because the consumer is allowed to cancel by mail, effective at the time of mailing, the creditor should wait for a reasonable time after midnight of the third business day.

The importance of delaying performance is evident by considering the possible consequences of rescission. Upon rescission, the consumer is immediately relieved of all liability for finance or other charges, and the lien retained by the creditor is automatically void. The creditor must, within twenty days after receipt of the notice of rescission, take whatever action is necessary to cancel the lien on the public records. The creditor also has twenty days to return down-payments in cash or by way of trade-in, with charges and fees collected in connection with the transfer.

It is only after the creditor has fulfilled these obligations that the consumer is required to tender property that the creditor has previously delivered. At the consumer's option, the tender may be made at the site of the property or at the consumer's residence. If the creditor fails to take possession of the property within twenty days after tender, then the property becomes the consumer's, without obligation on his or her part to pay for it.

A consumer may waive the right to rescind under 15 U.S.C. § 1635(d) in "emergency" situations. Reg Z § 226.23(e)(1). To modify or waive the right, the consumer must give the creditor a dated, written statement that describes the emergency, that specifically modifies or waives the right to rescind, and that bears the signature of all the consumers entitled to rescind. An emergency situation is where the extension of credit is needed in order to meet a bona fide personal family emergency.

17.   FEDERAL ENFORCEMENT OF TILA

a.   Administrative Enforcement

No single agency is charged with administrative enforcement of TILA. Instead, the following agencies are examples of those charged with enforcement of Truth In Lending in the areas which they regulate:

(1) Comptroller of the Currency (national banks);

(2) Federal Reserve Board (non-national member banks);

(3) Federal Deposit Insurance Corporation (insured banks not members of the Reserve System);

(4) Federal Home Loan Bank Board (savings institutions not insured by FDIC);

(5) Bureau of Federal Credit Unions (federal credit unions);

All other Truth in Lending activities of creditors are administered by the Federal Trade Commission. Thus, the vast bulk of administrative enforcement activities against retailers who sell on credit and commercial lenders other than banks is left to the FTC.

Under Section 1607(b), a violation of any requirement of Truth in Lending (including Reg. Z) is also a violation of the Act under which the agency exercises power over creditors regulated by it. Thus, for example, any powers which the FTC can exercise against a violator of the Federal Trade Commission Act can also be exercised against a violator of Truth in Lending. Section 1607 TILA also lists the various federal agencies charged with monitoring compliance with Truth in Lending. Upon discovering a creditor violation, the agency can take a number of steps. Section 1607(e) allows the agency to order creditors in serious violation to adjust accounts of consumers so that they do not have to pay a higher finance charge (or APR) than was disclosed to them. If the adjustment is less that $1 per account, the agency may require that the amount be paid into the U.S. Treasury (but only after a year has passed, so that the statute of limitations on possible civil actions will have run). Section 1607(e)(3).

b. Criminal Actions

Section 1611 makes it a crime for a creditor to "willfully and knowingly" give false or inaccurate information or to fail to make disclosures required by the Act. Violators are subject to a fine of not more than $5,000 or imprisonment for not more than one year, or both, for each violation of the Act. The Department of Justice is responsible for enforcement of these criminal sanctions.

As a practical matter, 15 U.S.C. § 1611 is unlikely to lead to many criminal convictions of creditors in violation of the Act. Federal district attorneys are generally faced with a heavy enough caseload that ferreting out Truth in Lending violators does not rank high on their list of priorities.

Arguably, however, the provisions of § 1611 may have significance to the borrower-litigant in a civil suit. This is due to the common law rule that an illegal contract is void because it is against public policy. Under that rule, a creditor would not only be stripped of their right to sue on a contract for a borrower's refusal to pay, but they would be deprived of quasi-contractual relief as well. Since Congress thought "willful and knowing" noncompliance with TILA was serious enough to be labeled criminal, a borrower-litigant might point to such noncompliance as justification for failure to pay the excessive loan amount, thereby barring any judicial relief being awarded the creditor. Furthermore, the majority rule holds that a consumer retains his or her Truth in Lending claim with regard to a contract which is found to be unenforceable under state law.[10]

18.   CONSUMER REMEDIES

a.   Introduction

Private consumer actions under § 1640 have been the most effective method of enforcing the disclosure requirements of Truth in Lending. To recover, a consumer must establish: (1) the transaction comes within Truth in Lending; and (2) the creditor failed to comply with the Act or Regulation Z. The consumer need not show that the creditor's violation resulted in any injury or that it led to the consumer's decision to enter into the credit transaction. Nor must the consumer show that the creditor intended or knew about the violation or that the

10.   *See, e.g.*, Dryden v. Lou Budke's Arrow Finance Co., 630 F.2d 641 (8th Cir.1980); Williams v. Public Fin. Corp. 598 F.2d 349 (5th Cir.1979), *reh'g denied*, 609 F.2d 1179 (5th Cir.1980); Lawrence v. Credithrift of America, Inc., 622 F.2d 1207 (5th Cir.1980). For a contrary holding, *see* Jensen v. Ray Kim Ford, Inc., 920 F.2d 3 (7th Cir.1990) (holding that consumer may not sue for disclosure violations contained in contract on which consumer's signature was forged since forged contract is of no effect); Fairley v. Turan–Foley Imports, Inc. 864 F.Supp. 4 (S.D.Miss.1994) (following Jenson).

consumer was deceived. Furthermore, even the slightest, technical violation may be actionable. Violations give rise to several remedies: actual damages, individual statutory damages, class action statutory damages, and attorney fees.

b. Standing to Bring Claims for Damages

Section 1640(a) provides that creditor liability arises when a creditor fails to comply with disclosure requirements "with respect to any person." Usually, the person seeking remedies is a "consumer" who is the primary obligor in the credit transaction.[11] However, the definition of "person" includes a natural individual or an organization. 15 U.S.C. § 1602(d). Courts have held that the phrase "with respect to any person" need not be limited to consumers or primary obligors.[12]

A person's standing is measured as of the date of the contract. Thus, a person who is not a party to a mortgage, but is subsequently deeded the subject property, does not have standing to raise Truth in Lending. *First Trust Nat'l Ass'n v. Daruka*, 1991 WL 100855 (Conn.Super.Ct.1991). The standing issue may also arise in situations where the creditor has died and the estate seeks to pursue the Truth in

11. A "consumer" is a cardholder or a natural person to who consumer credit is offered or extended. (For purposes of the right to rescind, the definition is expanded.) 15 U.S.C. § 1602(h); Reg. Z § 226.2(a)(11).

12. *See, e.g.*, Barash v. Gale Employees Credit Union, 659 F.2d 765 (7th Cir.1981); McCullough v. Bank of Stamford, Inc., L. Trib. 35, Clearinghouse No. 44,553 (D. Conn. Feb. 10, 1988); Maddox v. St. Joe Papermakers Federal Credit Union, 572 So.2d 961 (Fla.Dist.Ct.App.1990).

Lending claim. Generally, the claim survives the death of its holder.[13]

Finally, a consumer who has discharged an underlying debt in bankruptcy may pursue a Truth in Lending claim if the trustee has abandoned the claim and the debtor has scheduled the TILA claim as an asset. *Johnson v. Rutherford Hospital*, 13 B.R. 185 (Bankr.M.D.Tenn.1981). If the creditor's debt has been discharged, that debt may not be set-off against any potential TILA recovery by the debtor. *Id.*

c. Measure and Purpose of Damages

Under Section 1640, the measure of damages in an individual action is actual damages plus a statutory penalty. The statutory penalty is twice the amount of the finance charge so long as the amount is not less than $100 or more than $1,000. However, under the Truth in Lending Act Amendment of 1995, these amounts are increased to $200 and $2,000 if the transaction giving rise to the claim is closed end and real property or a dwelling is secured. In addition to these "statutory damages," a claimant may recover actual damages, costs, and "reasonable attorney's fees as determined by the court." 15 U.S.C. § 1640(a)(2)(A) and (3).

The inclusion of the statutory damage provision is to provide an economic spur for creditor compli-

---

13. *See, e.g.*, James v. Home Constr. Co., 621 F.2d 727 (5th Cir.1980). To claim on behalf of an estate, claimant probably must be officially appointed to represent the estate under state law. *In re* Evans, 114 B.R. 434, further proceedings, 120 B.R. 817 (Bankr.E.D.Pa.1990).

ance with the Act's requirements,[14] and to encourage consumers to act as "private attorneys general" to promote enforcement. *See, e.g., Rodash v. AIB Mortgage Co.*, 16 F.3d 1142 (11th Cir.1994). Once liability is established, damages are mandatory.

Since these statutory damages are unrelated to any harm suffered by the consumer, they are frequently referred to as civil "penalties." This common use of the term "penalties," taken with the Act's provision for criminal liability, has given rise to arguments that these damages are penal and should be construed narrowly. The Supreme Court, however, silenced most of these arguments in *Mourning v. Family Publications Service*, 411 U.S. 356, holding that "since the civil penalty described is modest ... we need not construe this section narrowly as a criminal statute." Indeed, the leading cases conclude that these damages are not a penalty, but serve a remedial purpose.[15] Indeed, since the statute on its face avoids mentioning punitive damages,[16] courts should construe statutory damages as merely remedial.[17]

14. *In re* Marshall, 121 B.R. 814 (Bankr.C.D.Ill.1990)(statutory damages are to deter future violations), *aff'd* 132 B.R. 904 (C.D.Ill.1991), *aff'd* 970 F.2d 383 (7th Cir.1992).

15. *See, e.g.*, Murphy v. Household Fin. Corp., 560 F.2d 206 (6th Cir.1977); Barrett v. Stamford Motors, Inc., No. B–85–49 (D. Conn. Dec. 10, 1986)(TILA damages are remedial and a TILA claim survives the death of the plaintiff debtor).

16. Compare the liability portions of the Equal Credit Opportunity, another Title of the Consumer Credit Protection Act, which characterizes non-actual damages as punitive. 15 U.S.C. § 1691e(b).

17. For a fuller exploration of the measure and purpose of TILA's statutory damages provisions, *see* Truth in Lending, *supra* note 1, pp. 413–414.

d. Multiple TILA Statutory Damages

(1) Multiple Violations Generally

Section 1640(g) provides for only a single statutory recovery even for multiple disclosure violations in a single transaction or open-end account. However, Section 1640(g) provides that a creditor's "continued failure to disclose after a recovery has been granted shall give rise to rights to additional recoveries." Furthermore, in *Hemauer v. ITT Financial Services*, 751 F.Supp. 1241 (W.D.Ky.1990), the court allowed double recovery of the statutory penalty where a creditor had split a single transaction into two separate contracts. The court found the defendant violated TILA requirements that disclosures be clear, conspicuous and grouped together. The court refused to allow the creditor to then argue that it was a single transaction when damages were being awarded. Thus, the court awarded statutory damages as if there were two contracts.

(2) Refinancings

In refinancing situations, an apparently single transaction may in fact be a series of separate transactions with statutory damages available for each. For example, in *Dennis v. Handley,* 453 F.Supp. 833 (N.D.Ala.1978), a consumer pawned a ring for $200, renewable each month upon payment of $20 accrued interest. A missed payment would allow the pawnbroker to hold the property free and clear. The court found this arrangement to be a series of separate transactions rather than an account payable in installments. Since each renewal was a new transaction, the consumer was allowed five recoveries, one for the original loan and one for each of four renewals.

Refinancing, or "flipping," of consumer credit transactions, discussed in Chapter Eight, generally gives rise to multiple statutory damages to the extent there are TILA violations in both the original transaction and the refinancing, even if the violations in the separate transactions are identical.[18] A consumer may recover more than two times the statutory damages if there a more than two refinancings with a TILA violation. This is so because a refinancing is by definition a new and separate transaction under Regulation Z.[19]

(3) Multiple Obligors

Assume that a husband and wife both sign a note in a consumer credit transaction. In such a case, both are consider debtors or obligors. If the creditor violates TILA, these obligors are limited to one recovery of statutory damages. 15 U.S.C. § 1640(d). However, this limitation does not extend to actual damage claims or class actions. In such a case, each obligor may recover separate actual damages. The limitation was incorporated into the statute by the 1980 TILA Simplification Act. Prior to that Act, the

18. *See, e.g.*, Abele v. Mid–Penn Consumer Discount, 77 B.R. 460 (E.D.Pa.1987); Simpson v. Termplan of Georgia, Inc., 535 F.Supp. 36 (N.D.Ga.1981).

19. Reg. Z § 226.20(a).

circuits were split on whether multiple obligors could receive separate recoveries of statutory damages. Thus, depending on which circuit court adjudges a claim, multiple obligors who assert TILA damage claims on loans subject to pre-Simplification TILA—such as a long-term mortgages—may recover multiple damages.

(4) Multiple Creditors: Assignee Liability

Consumer credit sales frequently involve the assignment of a credit seller's rights against the consumer to a financial institution. Under Regulation Z, Reg. Z § 226.2(a)(17)(i)(B), only the party "to whom credit is initially payable on the face of the note or contract" has the obligation to make disclosures. Therefore, as a general rule, the consumer may only recover against the credit seller.

On the other hand, the section on "Liability of Assignees", 15 U.S.C. § 1641(a), provides that an action for a TILA violation which may be brought against a creditor may also be brought against an assignee, but only if the violation is evident on the face of the loan documents.[20] The rationale behind this provision is that a purchaser of loan paper should at least be expected to read the terms of the documents purchased. However, this provision does not entitle a consumer to separate statutory damages from both the creditor and the assignee. Indeed, in *Greenlee v. Steering Wheel, Inc.*, 693

20. Rescission is available against assignees regardless of whether the violations were apparent on the face of the documents.

F.Supp. 1396 (D.Conn.1988), where the plaintiff sought damages from both the creditor and assignee, the court held that this provision did not alter the rule that assignees and creditors are jointly and severally liable.

Consumers have also attempted to argue that assignees are liable for damages under the so-called FTC "Holder Rule," officially entitled Preservation of Consumers' Claims and Defenses, discussed fully in Chapter Nine. FTC Trade Reg. Rule, 16 C.F.R. Part 433. The argument for the consumer is that the rule insures that any legal rights that the buyer has against the seller arising out of the transaction are also valid against subsequent holders. However, the courts who have addressed this question have held that to the extent the "Holder Rule" conflicts with TILA's "Liability of Assignees," TILA takes precedence.[21] Thus, the assignee is only subject to liability to the extent the violation is evident on the face of the loan documents.

e. Violations Giving Rise to Statutory Damages

(1) Generally

Statutory and actual damages are generally available for any violation of TILA Part B (credit transaction), with some exceptions for certain disclosure items.[22] In addition, they are available for viola-

---

21. Taylor v. Quality Hyundai, Inc. 150 F.3d 689 (7th Cir.).

22. 15 U.S.C. §§ 1631–1647. The exceptions are for some specific open-end disclosures (§ 1637) and some of the closed-end disclosure requirements (§ 1638).

tions of Part D (credit billing) and Part E (consumer leases). For instance, violations of the general requirements that disclosures must be clear and conspicuous and timely given result in statutory damages claims, as do violations of the rescission requirements. On the other hand, there is no liability for either actual or statutory damages for violations of Part C (advertising).

(2) Specific "Disclosure" Violations: What Is a Penalty Violation And What Is Not

While much of the rhetoric surrounding the passage of the Simplification Act, suggested that statutory damages were limited to the violations itemized in Section 1640(a)(3), that has not proved to be the case. Indeed, a careful reading of the statute and subsequent case law show that statutory damages are applicable for many additional TILA violations.

Section 1640(a)(3) specifically provides statutory damages for failure to disclose the items listed there. In addition, Section 1638(a) makes statutory damages available in closed-end transactions for failure to disclose the following:

(1) the amount financed;

(2) the unitemized finance charge;

(3) the annual percentage rate;

(4) the total payments;

(5) the number, amount, and due dates or periods of payments; and

(6) a statement that a security interest has been retained.

On the other hand, statutory damages are not available under Section 1638 for failure to disclose the following:

(1) the identity of the creditor;

(2) itemization of the amount financed and the right to obtain an itemization of the amount financed;

(3) the total sales price;

(4) explanations of the amount financed, finance charges, annual percentage rate, total of payments, and total sales price;

(5) late payment charges;

(6) prepayment rebates and penalties;

(7) reference to other contract documents; and

(8) the assumption policy notice in residual mortgages.

Section 1637 deals with open-end disclosures. Section 1637(a) makes statutory damages unequivocally available for the failure to disclose any information required to be in the initial disclosure, and requires that those disclosures be made in a timely manner. Section 1637(b), which governs periodic statements, allows statutory damages for the failure to disclose:

(1) the amount of the finance charge, itemized if appropriate;

(2) periodic rates;

(3) the annual percentage rate;

(4) the balance upon which serves as the bases for computing the finance charge;

(5) the new balance;

(6) the free-ride period; and

(7) the address for billing errors.

These are the only "disclosure violations" which give rise to statutory damages under the section. Statutory damages do not arise if the creditor fails to disclose the beginning balance, the total amount credited, or to describe any credit extensions.

f. Recovering Both TILA Damages and State Law Damages

The Truth in Lending Act does not prevent a consumer from recovering damages under both TILA and state law for similar violations. The applicable state law usually governs the issue.

Several states have their own truth in lending laws, and nearly all have some sort of disclosure statute. Some state disclosure laws require the consumer to choose between federal TILA claims and state disclosure claims. Where the state statute does not require such a choice, courts apply state law principles to determine whether a choice is required or a double recovery allowed. The majority of courts allow double recoveries.[23]

23. *See, e.g.,* Hemauer v. ITT Financial Services, 751 F.Supp. 1241 (W.D.Ky.1990); Public Fin. Corp. v. Riddle, 403 N.E.2d 1316 (1980); Cantrell v. First Nat'l Bank, 560 S.W.2d 721 (Tex. Civ.App.1977).

Courts generally allow recovery under both state law and TILA claims where the state law violation is a violation of state usury or state UDAP statutes. Only by allowing dual recovery may the purposes of each law be served. An award of only TILA damages does not deter a creditor from violating state law and fails to serve the state's interest in gaining compliance with the state law. Courts have gone so far as permitting TILA damages even where the contract has been held void under state law.[24]

Given the interplay between state consumer laws and TILA, consumer attorneys should always consider a possible UDAP claim in addition to a TILA claim. For instance, a consumer will likely be able to recover TILA damages for disclosure violations and UDAP damages for unfair or deceptive practices in a sales fraud claim. Furthermore, the TILA violation may constitute a UDAP violation, giving rise to a dual claim. Indeed, in some states, failure to comply with TILA may be a per se UDAP violation. *See, e.g.*, *Massachusetts Consumer Protection Regulations*, 940 Mass. Reg. § 3.16C. For instance, in *Commonwealth ex rel. Zimmerman v. Nickel*, 26 Pa. D. & C. 3d 115 (C.P. Mercer Ct. 1983), the court found that a failure to provide a TILA rescission notice was a UDAP violation. Finally, the fact that state UDAP statutes may grant superior remedies

24. *See, e.g.*, Lawrence v. Credithrift of America, Inc., 622 F.2d 1207 (5th Cir.1980); Dryden v. Lou Budke's Arrow Fin. Co., 630 F.2d 641 (8th Cir.1980) Williams v. Public Fin. Corp., 598 F.2d 349 (5th Cir.1979); *reh'g denied*, 609 F.2d 1179 (5th Cir. 1980).

to TILA claims makes it even more incumbent upon the consumer lawyer to consider joint claims.

g. Recoupment and Set-off

Section 1640 specifically provides that a consumer in default on a debt is not barred from asserting a creditor violation of the Act as an original action or as a defense or counterclaim to a collection action brought by the creditor. Indeed, Section 1640(e) goes so far as providing that notwithstanding the one-year statute of limitations governing affirmative enforcement actions, a consumer may assert "a violation of this title in an action to collect the debt ... as a matter of defense by recoupment or set-off in such action, except as otherwise provided by State law." Thus, while a consumer may not sue for recovery once the statute of limitations has run, he or she may use this provision to negate or reduce the creditor's award in a collection action. This can sometimes involve a significant amount. For example, in *In re Steinbrecher*, 110 B.R. 155 (Bankr. E.D. Pa 1990), the consumer was awarded $3,000 in statutory damages as recoupment on three refinanced loans in a creditor collection action. Furthermore, the consumer may also recover attorney fees in such an action upon a showing of the creditor's TILA violation.

h. Statutory Damages and Rescission

After the Simplification Act, Section 1640(a) provides actual and statutory damages, attorney fees, and costs for failing to comply with any requirement of the section on rescission. Thus, if a consumer successfully brings an action to rescind, he or she may also recover attorney fees and costs.

Furthermore, Section 1635(g) was amended so that "in addition to rescission the court may award relief under [Section 1640] for violations ... not relating to the right to rescind." When taken together, these changes in TILA made it clear that one may recover statutory damages for a disclosure violation and rescind the transaction as well, and that he or she may recover statutory damages for a creditor's failure to follow appropriate procedures for rescinding a contract.

i. Rescission Generally

Section 1635(a) provides that a consumer has a right to rescind a credit transaction in which a lien attaches to "any property which is used as [the consumer's] principal dwelling." Thus, a person whose principal dwelling is a mobile home or trailer has the same right to rescind as the conventional homeowner. This right to rescind runs until midnight of the third business day following the consummation of the transaction or the delivery of the TILA-required information, disclosures, and rescission forms, whichever is later. Once the consumer exercises his or her right to rescind, the creditor has twenty days to return to the consumer any money or property given to the creditor as down payment or otherwise. Furthermore, any liability for a finance or other charge dissolves upon rescission by the consumer.

j. Actual Damages

(1) Background

There was no provision for actual damages in the civil liability clauses of the TILA prior to 1974. However, in 1974, Congress amended the Act to add liability for actual damages in both individual and class actions. Moreover, in contrast to the Section 1640(d) provision limiting damage awards to one recovery of statutory damages, actual damages which arise from a single transaction may be awarded to more than one person. Indeed, the single recovery rule of Section 1640(d) refers to statutory damages under (a)(2). There is no similar limitation upon actual damages authorized under (a)(1), so the creditor remains liable to "any person" who sustains actual damages. However, the meaning of actual damages was left to the determination by courts on a case-by-case basis.

(2) Standards For Proving TILA Actual Damages

Unfortunately, there is a paucity of case law to provide guidance in interpreting TILA's actual damages clause. However, since creative financing calculations frequently understate the finance charge, consumer attorneys should nevertheless explore possible claims for actual damages.

A likely source for actual damages lies in any difference between a creditor's misstated financial disclosure and the hidden, correct amount owed by the debtor. There has been some division of opinion over whether a consumer seeking actual damages must demonstrate detrimental reliance upon an inaccurate financial disclosure to obtain relief or whether a less stringent, more objective standard of liability should apply.

Perhaps the most detailed judicial analysis of TILA actual damages to date appeared in *In re Russell,* 72 B.R. 855 (Bankr.E.D.Pa.1987). The court held that where a disclosure statement contains a substantial TILA violation, as opposed to a simple technical violation, a consumer is entitled to actual damages measured by the difference between the misstated financial charge and the actual amount charged. Thus, the consumer's showing that the creditor materially understated the finance charge by $1,490 (by hiding a $1,190 "origination fee" and a $300 "commission") entitled the consumer to $1,490 actual damages.[25] The court refused to apply a detrimental reliance standard on the ground that TILA is a remedial statute, and that Section 1640(b) implies that consumers should be awarded as actual damages a reduction of the debt owed in an amount equal to the undisclosed finance charges or the dollar equivalent of the disclosed APR, whichever is less.

The Russell court's rejection of the common law barriers to liability under federal remedial statutes seemingly applies to both proof of damage and proof of the extent of damages. Indeed, the great degree of difficulty in proving actual damages under reme-

25. *See also In re* Stewart, 93 B.R. 878, 883, 886 (Bankr.E.D.Pa.1988)(inflated sales prices of goods sold on credit contained hidden finance charge; the excess price and excess interest thereon held actual damages under TILA).

dial statutes like TILA argues against common law reliance standards of proof before awarding damages.[26] As noted by the Supreme Court in *Story Parchment Co. v. Paterson Parchment Paper Co.*, 282 U.S. 555, 563 (1931): "the risk of uncertainty [in damage calculations] should be thrown upon the wrongdoer instead of upon the injured party." Instead of using the subjective detrimental reliance standard, then, courts may test whether a disclosure violation is material to an informed use of credit by use of one of two familiar objective standards: a "reasonable credit consumer" standard or a "least sophisticated consumer" standard.[27] By using either of these objective standards, courts avoid thwarting the remedial purposes of TILA.

A contrasting standard for measuring actual damages to that applied in *Russell* is the common law detrimental reliance standard. This standard requires a consumer to prove reliance upon an inaccurate disclosure and that this reliance caused the consumer to choose a less favorable financial arrangement than they would have otherwise chosen. To a large extent, this standard requires the consumer to make a common law fraud or misrepresentation showing. The one difference is that when applied to a TILA claim, the consumer need not

26. *See, e.g.*, Zenith Radio Corp. v. Hazeltine Research Inc., 395 U.S. 100 (1969); Bigelow v. RKO Pictures, 327 U.S. 251 (1946).

27. *See, e.g.*, Jeter v. Credit Bureau, Inc., 760 F.2d 1168 (11th Cir.1985)(FTC's "least sophisticated consumer" standard applied to the Fair Debt Collection Practices Act, a later title of federal Consumer Credit Protection Act).

show the creditor's bad faith, intent, or negligence. Even so, the standard requires a higher burden of proof of the consumer than the "remedial" standard applied in *Russell*.

Two early TILA class action cases are sometimes cited as support for application of the higher detrimental reliance standard before actual damages may be awarded. In both *McCoy v. Salem Mortgage Co.*, 74 F.R.D. 8 (E.D.Mich.1976), and *Vickers v. Home Federal Savings & Loan Ass'n*, 404 N.Y.S.2d 201 (App. Div. 1978), the courts held that to recover actual damages in TILA action, a consumer must show that they relied upon inaccurate disclosures which prevented them from obtaining a better deal elsewhere. However, *McCoy* and *Vickers* have generally not been followed,[28] and on at least one occasion, they were explicitly rejected. *In re Russell*, 72 B.R. 855 (Bankr.E.D.Pa.1987). Significantly, each case was decided before the establishment of subsequent federal financial regulatory agency restitution enforcement policies, and before congressional reports equated restitution with actual damages (without any reliance test).[29] In addition, they were

28.   *See, e.g.*, Iuteri v. Branhaven Motors, Inc., Clearinghouse No. 41,259 (D. Conn. Nov. 14, 1985); Sutliff v. County Savings & Loan Co., 533 F.Supp. 1307 (N.D.Ohio 1982); Ransom v. S & S Food Center, Inc., Clearinghouse No. 27,682 (S.D. Ala. Sept. 11, 1979), *aff'd* 700 F.2d 670 (11th Cir.1983); *In re* Russell, 72 B.R. 855 (Bankr.E.D.Pa.1987); Preston v. First Bank of Marietta, 473 N.E.2d 1210 (Ohio Ct. App. 1983). *But see* Adiel v. Chase Federal S & L Ass'n, 630 F.Supp. 131 (S.D.Fla.1986), *aff'd* 810 F.2d 1051 (11th Cir.1987).

29.   S. Rep. No 720 95th Cong., 2d Sess. 12 (1978) and S. Rep. No. 73. 96th Cong., 1st Sess 13 (1979).

decided prior to the decision of the Supreme Court in *Ford Motor Credit Co. v. Milhollin*, 444 U.S. 555 (1980), making the rules of the Federal Reserve interpreting TILA virtually binding and conclusive on the courts. Ultimately, *McCoy* and *Vickers* may simply reflect a judicial bias against class actions for TILA damages rather than a reasonable rule for individual claims for actual damages.

On balance, there is a strong argument that a reliance standard ignores the broad thrust of the Truth in Lending Act. There is no mention in the Act of a reliance standard. Nor does the legislative history indicate that Congress had reliance in mind when it added actual damages to the Act. Finally, the remedial nature of the Act argues strongly for a liberal, rather than a restrictive, application of the actual damages remedy.

(3) Practical Approaches to Obtaining Actual Damages

(A) GENERALLY

It is impossible to list all the possible claims for TILA actual damages. Since many disclosure violations can result in actual damages to the debtor, consumer attorneys must consider creative approaches consistent with TILA's remedial purposes. This subsection addresses possible approaches a consumer attorney might use to obtain restitutionary damages, damages for missed opportunity, and consequential damages in claims for actual damages. However, some of the approaches discussed may be effectively limited if a court applies a detrimental reliance standard.

(B) RESTITUTIONARY DAMAGES

As Russell demonstrated, one approach to computing TILA actual damages is to measure the difference between the cost of credit actually charged the consumer and the disclosed charges. In addition, if the disclosure document is internally inconsistent, actual damages might be measured as the amount of the difference between the inconsistent disclosures. The rationale for calling such damages restitutionary is that creditors should not be allowed to claim amounts greater than those disclosed to consumers.

The most helpful characteristic of restitutionary damages from the point of view of the consumer attorney is that they may be determined from disclosure documents themselves, without an investigation into the intent of either creditor or consumer. While not an exhaustive list, the following are examples of restitutionary claims an attorney might extrapolate from loan documents.[30]

(1) *Understated APR:* Claim the difference between the disclosed APR and the disclosed finance charge.

(2) *Understated Finance Charge:* Claim the difference between the finance charge as disclosed and

30. It should be noted that the 1995 amendments require that the degree of error in the finance charge and affected disclosures, such as APR and amount financed, must surpass certain tolerance levels before they are actionable.

the actual finance charge (See *In re Russell, supra*, at p. 209).

(3) *Improper Credit Life, Accident, Health or Loss of Income Insurance Disclosures:* Failure to disclose that the insurance is optional or to disclose the insurance price may be treated as a finance charge or APR violation.

(4) *Excess Late Charges and Prepayment Penalties:* Claim charges in excess of those disclosed as actual damages.

(5) *Service Charges Omitted from Finance Charge:* Such charges may be actual damages.

(C) DAMAGES FOR CONSUMER'S MISSED OPPORTUNITY

Missed opportunity damages require a higher burden of proof than restitutionary damages. To recover, the consumer must prove that absent a TILA disclosure violation, he or she might have acted to obtain better terms or to avoid unwanted charges. If the court determines that there was in fact a TILA violation, it may apply one of two tests to determine missed opportunity damages.

Under the less restrictive of these tests the debtor is required to show that had appropriate disclosure been made, he or she could have secured a better financial arrangement. For example, if the APR was improperly disclosed, the consumer could show that transactions with a lower APR was available in the marketplace. Thus, the test merely requires a showing that the debtor could have obtained more favorable terms, not necessarily that he or she would have opted for those more favorable terms. The rationale behind this test is that it is often impossible to prove exactly what the consumer would have done if disclosures had been properly made. Thus, in keeping with TILA's remedial purposes, it should be enough to show the missed opportunity and to measure damages against the violating creditor accordingly.

The second test places an increased burden on the consumer by requiring a showing that both an opportunity existed to enter into a more favorable arrangement and that the consumer likely would have acted differently if accurate disclosures had been made. As a practical matter then, the consumer would have to present evidence regarding the probability that he or she would have taken a better alternative had the creditor given proper disclosure. Clearly, this is a much more difficult burden for the consumer to meet in seeking missed opportunity damages.

(D) CONSEQUENTIAL DAMAGES: EMOTIONAL DISTRESS

Actual damages may include a claim for consequential damages. To seek and recover consequential damages, the consumer attorney must carefully interview his or her debtor-client to ascertain all the consequences suffered as a result of the disclosure violation. Humiliation, harm to one's reputation, and mental or emotional distress have been held to be a proper basis for awarding actual damages under TILA. For instance, in *Iuteri v. Branhaven Motors, Inc.*, No. N–81–254, Clearinghouse No.

41,259 (D. Conn. Nov. 14 1985), the court found
that the forgery of the debtor's signature on a retail
contract and the creditor's failure to accurately
disclose financing terms had caused actual damages
in the form of "emotional trauma and unnecessary
aggravation." Thus, the court awarded the plaintiff
$2,000 in damages. *Iuteri* makes it clear that the
consumer attorney is well advised not to overlook
emotional distress as a possibility when computing
actual damages.

19. DEFENSES

a. Statute of Limitations

Section 1640 provides that TILA claims may be
raised "within one year from the date of the occurrence of the violation." A significant amount of
litigation arose over the meaning of this phrase.
The cases indicate that its meaning is, in part,
dependent upon whether the underlying transaction
is an open or closed-end transaction. Early cases
involving closed-end transactions raised the question of whether the relevant date was the date when
the contract was made for the extension of credit or
the date when credit was actually extended. The
general rule that emerged is that the statute of
limitations begins to run at the time the contract is
entered into. *See, e.g., Rust v. Quality Car Corral,
Inc.*, 614 F.2d 1118 (6th Cir.1980); *Bartholomew v.
Northampton Nat'l Bank*, 584 F.2d 1288 (3d Cir.
1978). In open-end transactions, however, the limitations period does not begin to run until a finance

charge has been imposed. *See Goldman v. First Nat'l Bank of Chicago*, 532 F.2d 10 (7th Cir.1976).

As noted in Section 18g., *supra* at p. 206, the one-year limitation does not bar an obligor from alleging a TILA violation when a creditor brings a collection action. This is explicitly allowed under Section 1640(e): "This subsection does not bar a person from asserting a violation of this title in an action to collect the debt which was brought more than one year from the date of the occurrence of the violation as a matter of defense by way of recoupment or set-off in such action, except as otherwise provided by State law."

b. Bona Fide Error

Section 1640(c) provides a defense to the creditor that bars liability if the preponderance of the evidence shows that the violation was unintentional and "resulted from a bona fide error notwithstanding the maintenance of procedures reasonably adapted to avoid any such error." Examples of such errors include clerical, calculation, computer malfunction, computer programming, and printing errors. However, an error of legal judgment with regard to one's TILA obligations is not a bona fide error.

c. Correction of Error

Finally, Section 1640(b) allows a creditor to escape liability for a TILA disclosure violation if that creditor makes a timely correction of the error. The creditor must act to correct the mistake within 60 days after first discovering the error and before the consumer gives notice of the error or brings an action for a TILA violation.

C. TRUTH IN SAVINGS ACT

While Congress enacted TILA in order to provide consumers with the real cost of credit, the Truth in Savings Act (TISA) was enacted in 1991 in order to provide consumers with essential information about accounts at depositary institutions. TISA (12 U.S.C. § 4301 et seq.) covers checking, savings and time accounts held by an individual primarily for a personal, family or household purpose. A depositary institution is one that is either federally insured or is eligible to apply for such insurance.

The implementing regulation for TISA is Regulation DD. The disclosure requirements under TISA and Regulation DD aid comparison shopping on the savings side, just as TILA and Regulation Z do on the borrowing side. However, TISA applies only to banks and thrifts, while TILA applies to all lenders. The essential disclosures TISA requires includes fees, the "annual percentage yield" (APY), the interest rate and other terms. Interest must be paid on the full balance in the account each day, based on one of two methods for calculating the balance.

Banks and thrift institutions must adopt policies and procedures to implement the required disclosures and full documentation must be kept for all compliance efforts. The National Credit Union Administration must adopt regulations "substantially similar" to those prescribed by the Federal Reserve Board, within 90 days of Federal Reserve Board adoption. The NCUA is permitted some leeway in crafting the regulations in order to recognize the unique nature of credit unions.

The disclosures required by TISA include:

1. A description of all the charges that can be assessed against an account holder and the circumstances under which each charge can be imposed;

2. The amount of such charges, or the method by which the amount is calculated; and

3. Minimum balance requirements, including how the balance is calculated and the consequences of falling below the minimum.

Depositary institutions must maintain a current schedule of the terms and conditions applicable to each class of accounts that is offered. These account schedules must be written in clear and plain language, and be available upon request to any person.

The account schedules must include:

1. The annual percentage yield (APY);

2. The period during which the APY will be in effect;

3. The annual rate of simple interest;

4. The frequency with which interest is compounded and credited;

5. The method used to arrive at the account balance;

6. Any minimum account balance requirements; to realize yields;

7. Any minimum time requirements to realize yields;

8. Any early-withdrawal penalties; and

9. Any other occurrence which can cause a reduced payment.

In addition to the recovery of actual costs and reasonable, the consumer can recover actual damages and statutory damages of $100 to $1,000. TILA also recognizes a bona fide error defense and the institution can avoid liability if it corrects errors within 60 days of discovery. The correction must include reimbursement for fees that were improper and the crediting of interest that should have been paid.

D. THE CONSUMER LEASING ACT

1. INTRODUCTION

Chapter Five of the Truth in Lending Act is the Consumer Leasing Act (CLA). The CLA mandates the clear disclosure of a number of lease terms and provides for an award of actual damages, statutory damages, plus attorney fees for failure to comply with the disclosure requirements. As is true with other parts of TILA, the CLA is supplemented by a regulation (Regulation M), and an Official Staff Commentary.

In 1996 the Federal Reserve Board amended Regulation M. The amendments added new substantive requirements for lease advertisements, as well as lease disclosures. The Commentary was updated and new model disclosure forms were produced.

The CLA applies to leases of greater than four months duration. If the lease is terminable without penalty during the first four months, the CLA does not apply. Because rent-to-own transactions are terminable without penalty at any time, they are not subject to the CLA.

The CLA does not apply to leases where the total contractual obligation exceeds $25,000. The total contract obligation includes the total of payments due under the lease, plus any trade-in or initial payment. It does not include an option price stated in the contract, for a consumer to purchase the item, or the residual value at the end of the term, which is what the item is expected to be worth.

The CLA applies only to "consumer leases," defined as being primarily for personal, family or household purposes. Lessees are not covered where they are a corporation or other business organization. For most consumers the most important application of the CLA is in automobile leases. Only personal property leases are covered by the CLA. Real property leases are not covered by the CLA.

2.   REQUIRED LEASE DISCLOSURES

One of the most significant changes in the new regulation is the requirement that enumerated disclosures be segregated from other required disclosures. The requirements are detailed in 12 C.F.R.

§ 213. The segregated disclosures must be separate from other information and shall contain only the following information:

a.   The amount due at lease signing;

b.   The payment schedule and total of periodic payments;

c.   Other charges;

d.   Total of payments;

e.   An eleven-step payment calculation;

f.   A notice that the charge for early termination may be substantial;

g.   The warning and amount or method of determining the charges for excessive wear and tear; and

h.   The end of term purchase option price.

Separate from the segregated disclosures, the required disclosures are:

a.   A Description of the Leased Property;

b.   The Payments to Be Made at Lease Consummation;

c.   The Schedule and Amount of Lease Payments;

d.   Official Fees and Taxes;

e.   Other Charges Not Included in the Lease Payment or Due at Consummation;

f.   Any Required Insurance;

g.   Any Express Warranties Given;

h.   The Party Responsible for Maintenance;

i.   Any Security Interest;

j.   Late Payment and Default Charges;

k.   Whether or Not the Consumer Has the Option to Purchase the Leased Property;

l.   The Consumer's Liability for the Difference Between the Property's Estimated Value and Its Realized Value if the Lease So Provides;

m.   A Series of Eleven Disclosures That Show the Derivation of the Monthly Payment Amount; and

n.   The Total of Payments.

3.   REMEDIES FOR CLA DISCLOSURES

With the exception of advertising violations where the consumer is not damaged, the lessor's liability for violation of the CLA is:

a.   Actual damages; plus

b.   Twenty-five percent of the total periodic lease payments, except that this statutory liability shall be no less than $100 or greater than $1,000; plus

c.   Costs and reasonable attorney fees.

E. THE INTERSTATE LAND SALES FULL DISCLOSURE ACT

The Interstate Land Sales Full Disclosure Act is patterned after the Securities Act of 1933. It requires that anyone selling or leasing 100 or more lots of unimproved land as part of a common promotional plan in interstate commerce must first file a "statement of record" with the Office of Interstate Land Sales Registration. The Office of Interstate Land Sales Registration is a division of the Department of Housing and Urban Development. The requirements for the statement of record are set out in 24 C.F.R. 1710.100 (1998). The statement of record contains very detailed information about the land and the developer. Preparing the statement is similar to preparing a registration statement for the Securities and Exchange Commission. Section 1702 of the Act and 1710.10–1710.13 of the regulations lists the transactions that are exempt from the application of the Act. The most important exemption is intrastate land offerings (as the title of the Act indicates).

After the statement of record is approved by HUD as being accurate on its face and as containing the required information, a developer may then offer land for sale or lease. The developer must also furnish each purchaser a "property report" before signing any contract or agreement. The requirements for the property report are in 24 C.F.R. 1710.29 (1998).

Section 1709 provides the right for relief in an action at law or in equity against a developer or agent if the sale or lease was made in violation of the Act. The amount of such penalties may not exceed $1,000 for each violation, and the maximum penalty for all violations by a particular person during any one-year period shall not exceed $1,000,-000. Criminal penalties are set forth in Section 1717 for willful violations of the Act. Upon conviction, a person shall not be fined more than $10,000 nor be imprisoned for more than five years, but a person may receive both of these punishments.

The most important remedy under the Act is a purchaser's right of rescission. Three different provisions of the Act create this right. First, a purchaser who did not receive the property report required by the Act *prior to* signing a contract has a right to rescind for two years from the date of signing the contract. The land sale contract must clearly disclose this right of rescission.

Second, there is also a two-year rescission period if the sales contract does not contain the disclosures required by Section 1703(d). The purchaser loses this right of rescission if he/she receives a warranty deed within 180 days of signing the contract.

Third, there is an absolute seven-day right of rescission that exists regardless of the disclosures that the seller makes. During this limited time period, the right to rescind is absolute. The sales contract must clearly disclose this right of rescission.

In addition to these rescission rights under the Interstate Land Sales Full Disclosure Act, consumers also have the right to rescind under Section 125 of TILA, to the extent that it applies.

There is nothing in either statute that precludes or preempts the operation of the other. A number of transactions will be covered by both Acts. If an individual is acquiring land in an "interstate land sale" on credit for consumer purposes, both Acts will cover the transaction. As always, Section 125 of TILA will only apply if the property so acquired is used or is to be used as the consumer's principal residence.

F.   REAL ESTATE SETTLEMENTS PROCEDURE ACT

Since 1975, some real estate transactions have been governed by yet a third federal disclosure statute: the Real Estate Settlement Procedures Act ("RESPA"). This Act applies to all "federally related mortgage loans." The definition of "federally related" focuses on: (1) the lender and (2) the nature of the property encumbered.

Virtually all mortgage lenders taking a first lien on residential real property are covered: banks, savings and loan associations, and other lenders insured or regulated by a federal agency. State chartered lenders who make more than $1 million in "residential real estate loans each year" are also covered.

The property must be a one to four family residential dwelling (which can include a mobile home). The Act is much broader than TILA in that there is no inquiry into the nature of the debtor or the debtor's use of the residential dwelling. For example, the Real Estate Settlement Procedures Act would apply, given the proper lender, to a purchase money mortgage obtained by a corporation to buy a one to four family dwelling from another corporation as an investment.

Although the Act simply uses the term "mortgage loan," regulations promulgated by HUD translate this term into purchase money order to buy real property. 24 C.F.R. 3500.2(b) (1998). Accordingly, home improvement loans are not covered by this third disclosure provision.

The primary burden of complying with the requirements of RESPA falls on lenders. When someone applies for a "federally regulated mortgage loan," the lender must deliver to the applicant a copy of the HUD Special Information Booklet prepared by the Secretary of HUD to explain the nature and costs of real estate settlement services. The lender must supply the Booklet by delivering it or placing it in the mail to the applicant not later than three days after the borrower's loan application is received. 24 C.F.R. 3500.6(a) (1998).

The lender must include with the Booklet a good faith estimate of the amount or range of charges for specific settlement services the borrower is likely to incur in connection with the settlement.

The lender must make available to the borrower an accurate Uniform Settlement Statement.

The statement must

conspicuously and clearly itemize all charges imposed upon the borrower and all charges imposed upon the seller in connection with the settlement and shall indicate whether any title insurance premium included in such charges covers or insures the lender's interest in the property, the borrower's interest, or both. 12 U.S.C. § 2603(a).

The borrower may, however, request to inspect the statement the day before settlement, and he/she must be allowed to inspect the items known on that day by the person who will conduct the settlement.

The Real Estate Settlements Procedure Act is not a pure disclosure statute. The Act contains a number of substantive regulations. A seller may not require a buyer to purchase title insurance from any particular company. Kickbacks and unearned fees are prohibited. For example, a title insurance company may not pay a referral commission to the lender's attorneys. Advance deposits in escrow accounts are limited. In addition, RESPA prohibits lenders from charging fees for the preparation of disclosure statements that it and TILA require.

G.   THE HOME OWNERSHIP AND EQUITY PROTECTION ACT OF 1994

1.   INTRODUCTION

The Home Ownership and Equity Protection Act of 1994 (HOEPA),[31] became effective on October 1, 1995. *See* 15 U.S.C. § 1604(d). The law is designed to prevent a number of the predatory lending practices found in mortgage lending, particularly in the subprime credit market (discussed in Chapter Four), where interest rates are very high and transactions are often packed with credit insurance products and other add-ons.

Some lenders, particularly in the subprime credit market, employ a strategy of moving consumers from an initial installment credit sale (purchasing an appliance on credit), to a loan secured by goods, and then to a real estate loan. Training manuals and material produced in discovery reflect a strategy to move borrowers from smaller to larger loan amounts, and with the nature of the credit moving along a continuum from unsecured, secured by goods, and then secured by real estate. The predatory lending practices commonly found in mortgage lending are what caused Congress to enact HOEPA, and most particularly abuses found in refinancings and home equity loans triggered by promises of "debt consolidation."

31. Subtitle B of Title I of the Riegle Community Development and Regulatory Improvement Act, Pub. L. No. 103–325 (Sept. 23, 1994).

Borrowers who are overextended, with a number of credit card and finance company accounts are given a hard-sell on debt consolidation, with the promise of lower interest rates and lower monthly payments. What is not appreciated by most consumers is that converting these "junk" consumer debts into a mortgage loan is particularly dangerous, because the collateral has now moved away from charcoal grills and weedeaters, to the home. The ramifications of default are great. There are not many experiences more traumatic than losing a home. And again, creditors who claim to be helping consumers in debt consolidation, who then turn around and load-up the transaction with credit insurance products, high points, fees and other add-ons, are then creating a lot of unnecessary debt among a group of people who were already living on the edge. As noted in Chapter Four in the discussion of subprime lending, the people who can least afford it often end up with the largest amounts of unproductive debt, due to high fees and the packing of credit insurance products.

"Residential Mortgage Transactions" are exempt from the provisions of HOEPA. 15 U.S.C.§ 1602(aa)(1). A "residential mortgage transaction" means a transaction in which a mortgage, deed of trust, purchase money security interest arising under an installment sales contract, or equivalent consensual security interest is created or retained against the consumer's dwelling to finance the acquisition or initial construction of the dwelling. 15 U.S.C. § 1602(w). The residential mortgage transaction exemption will result in refinancings and home equity loans being subject to HOEPA, but purchase and construction loans are exempt. But not all refinancings and home equity loans will be covered. The two triggers for the special protection provided by HOEPA are based on the annual percentage rate (APR) and points and fees charged on the loan.

2. THE APR TRIGGER

A loan will be subject to HOEPA if the APR at the time of consummation exceeds by more than ten percentage points the yield on treasury securities having comparable maturities at the time the loan is made. 15 U.S.C. § 1602(aa)(1)(A). All of the provisions under TILA for the calculation of the APR and the tolerance levels will apply. For mortgage loans with adjustable interest rate provisions, coverage will be determined based on the APR on the date of consummation of the loan.

3. POINT AND FEES TRIGGER

Where the total charge for points and fees exceed 8 percent of the total loan amount, HOEPA will be triggered if the total loan and fees equal $400. 15 U.S.C.§ 1602(aa)(1)(B). Points and fees include:

(a) all items included in the finance charge for the loan, other than interest and any time-price differential;

(b) all compensation paid to mortgage brokers; and

(c) real estate charges included in 15 U.S.C. § 1605(e), other than escrow charges for future payment of such items as taxes.

4. DISCLOSURE REQUIREMENTS

If HOEPA is triggered, there are certain disclosures that must be made. These disclosure requirements are in addition to disclosures that are mandated by other provisions of TILA.

The following disclosures must be made in conspicuous type:

(a) "You are not required to complete this agreement merely because you received these disclosures or have signed a loan application."

(b) "If you obtain this loan, the lender will have a mortgage on your home. You could lose your home and any money you have put into it, if you do not meet your obligations under the loan."

15 U.S.C. § 1639(a)(1).

The creditor must also disclose the APR and the amount of the regular monthly payment for fixed-rate loans. 15 U.S.C. § 1339(a)(2)(A). For adjustable rate loans, the creditor must disclose the APR, the regular monthly payment, a statement that the monthly payment may increase and the amount of the maximum potential monthly payment. 15 U.S.C. § 1639(a)(2)(B). The disclosures must be given not less than three business days prior to consummation of the transaction. 15 U.S.C. § 1639(b)(1). New disclosures are required if the terms of the loan change, making the old disclosure inaccurate. 15 U.S.C. § 1639(b)(2)(A). For adjustable rate loans, the creditor must disclose the APR, the regular monthly payment, a statement that the monthly payment may increase and the amount of the maximum potential monthly payment. 15 U.S.C. § 1639(a)(2)(B). The disclosures must be given not less than three business days prior to consummation of the transaction. 15 U.S.C. § 1639(b)(1). New disclosures are required if the terms of the loan change, making the old disclosure inaccurate. 15 U.S.C. § 1639(b)(2)(A).

5. ADDITIONAL SUBSTANTIVE PROTECTIONS AND PENALTIES

In a transaction covered by HOEPA, prepayment penalties are prohibited, with a five-part exception. The most important outcome of this provision is the elimination of the use of the Rule of 78's, discussed in Chapter Eight, at pages 287-289, unless the exception applies. 15 U.S.C. § 1639(c)(2).

There are special provisions in HOEPA dealing with payments to home improvement contractors. Abuses in the financing of home improvement contracts were detailed in Chapter Four, at pages 79-83.[32] Under 15 U.S.C. § 1639(i), when a creditor finances a home improvement contract, payments

---

32. For a discussion of problems in home improvement lending, *see* Gene A. Marsh, *Lender Liability for Consumer Fraud Practices of Retail Dealers and Home Improvement Contractors*, 45 Ala. L. Rev. 1 (1993).

in covered loans may not be made in an instrument payable directly to the contractor alone. The payment must be made either to the consumer only or in a jointly payable instrument.

Violations of HOEPA can lead to actual damages, statutory damages, and the payment of attorneys fees and costs. Failure to make the required disclosures constitutes a failure to make a "material disclosure" under TILA, and gives a right to rescind the transaction up to three years from the date of consummation. 15 U.S.C. § 1640(a)(3).

CHAPTER SEVEN

REGULATING THE COST OF CREDIT

A. HISTORY OF RATE REGULATION

Although it may be difficult for some people to embrace, the making of a loan is really just the sale of dollars, for a price. The price is generally referred to as the "interest" on a loan. Lenders note that they are in the business of selling and "moving" money, and that sales volume is as critical to them as it is to any retailer of goods. In many ways, selling money is no different than selling beer, where some people are willing to pay an exaggerated price, in what is becoming an increasingly deregulated market for the cost of credit. A six-pack purchased at a convenience store or ski resort grocery may sell for twice as much as it does at a large grocery store in the suburbs, but people pay the price because the convenience outweighs the cost, or no other alternative is available. Some people shop for credit facing similar constraints.

However, people do not view money and beer in the same way. Were the sale of money viewed by most people as the sale of six-packs, we would not have the mountain of consumer credit regulations we have today, including some of the usury laws that regulate the cost of credit. When it comes to money, people generally do not like high rates and are tolerant of more regulation. However, although it is true that today there are more disclosure requirements in consumer credit than at any other time in our history, many of the laws regulating the cost of that credit have been swept away or preempted by federal laws that moved us to a more deregulated market.

But some usury laws remain with us today and are as controversial now as they were long ago. The issue of whether to impose usury laws has long been debated. A detailed history of usury laws, however, is beyond the scope of this nutshell. Nonetheless, there are two important influences on usury laws that aid in understanding the status of usury laws today.

One part of the history which is of practical significance is the influence of the Bible. Phrases such as "Take thou no usury of him, or increase: but fear thy God; that thy brother may live with thee," teaches us that extracting interest is wrong. Also, as early as 2000 B.C. the law limited the rate of interest that could be charged on loans of money.

The other important influence on our usury laws is from Europe. In 1545, Henry VII allowed taking interest legally for the first time in England. Following that path, Massachusetts enacted the first usury statute in the colonies in 1661.

Consumer credit, however, has a much shorter history; it became common only at about the turn of this century. A jeweler started it all. Frank Macker began offering unsecured personal loans to average income consumers in order to support the purchase of his jewelry. Soon after, in 1878, Household Finance Company started as the first of many companies to tap this credit market.

Until that time, most people were farmers rather than wage earners. But in the late 19th century, the United States economy began to see a change from a purely agrarian society to an industrialized society. With industry and the mass production of consumer goods, the average citizen needed some sort of credit system to purchase the goods being produced. In some cases, banks and finance companies provided the flow of credit needed to support a consumer economy.

Still, there were impediments to consumer finance companies. The usury laws in many places prohibited lenders from charging more than 6% per annum. There was no way profit could be made at that rate. These artificially low rates caused people to look elsewhere, including illegal loan shark markets.

The rise of loan sharks who charged abusive interest rates and the lack of legitimate consumer credit prompted a study by the Russell Sage Foundation in 1907. This led to the adoption of the Uniform Small Loan Law, which was drafted in 1916. The effect of this law was to mandate an all inclusive fee to prevent hidden charges and raise the usury ceiling to make small lending more profitable. Small loans were defined as loans of $300 or less and the maximum charge for such loans was set at no more than 3 ½ percent per month.

The Uniform Small Loan Law is only one of the exceptions to general usury statutes that have been created for consumer credit transactions, allowing higher rates for smaller loans. As other lenders entered into the consumer credit market, other statutory exceptions developed. For example, the regulation of retail sales where the seller provided credit resulted in still more statutes regulating the amount of finance charges a seller can impose when goods are purchased "on time." In 1928, the National City Bank of New York became the first large commercial bank with a committed consumer loan program. Then in the 1950's finance companies became affiliated with automobile manufacturers, where auto dealer paper was purchased and serviced by affiliated finance entities.

Effectively, the Uniform Small Loan Law legitimized the consumer finance industry. This led to a host of other regulations at both the local and national level. The National Commission on Consumer finance used the word "hodgepodge" to describe the array of usury laws in place. Thus, as creditors got more creative in the lending policies, the legislator responded with further regulation.

B. SHOULD THERE BE
RATE CEILINGS?

The consumer finance industry is one of the most heavily regulated industries today. Aside from federal regulations, such as TILA (discussed in Chapter Six), most states have consumer credit laws, some of which set ceilings on the cost of consumer credit. Most of the ceilings are on small loans and credit sales.

Critics of rate regulation make a two-fold argument: (1) let basic principles of the free market control, and (2) regulation decreases many consumer's ability to get credit. The first argument is that in the United States, government price control is resorted to only in abnormal or emergency situations. The market, not the state, controls the cost of beer; therefore, the market, not the state, should control the cost of cash. There is nothing inherent in the consumer credit market that makes it any less competitive than any other market. Second, critics argue that present usury statutes hurt, rather than help consumers. The effect of regulating the finance charge in loans is to determine which consumers can obtain cash from legitimate lenders i.e., only consumers with favorable credit.

State legislatures have generally favored usury laws because these laws gave them power over the credit industry, and voters tend to favor usury laws that keep rates low. High interest rates are easy to hate. Thus, access to affordable credit will always be a popular political platform. In addition, like other advocates of usury laws, legislatures feel that regulation is necessary to prevent economic disaster and consumer exploitation. These laws are necessary to prevent lenders from engaging in such evils as discriminating or overcharging.[1] The need for some regulation may be particularly strong where many of the consumers are poor, illiterate and without political power.[2]

Rate control advocates argue that it is essential to ensure that a "fair" cost of money will be charged to the borrower and a "fair" rate of return given to the creditor. Additionally, setting maximum interest rates determines what types of people have access to legitimate lenders. Because of the importance of such a determination, leaving the decision to the industry itself is too dangerous. Lenders want profit so they are prone to accept loans at any rates to justify the risk. The problem is that at some point, many people think the rates are too high and far higher than is needed to compensate for the risk. As the legislators contend, this can result in severe injury to the economic community. When too many people are allowed to borrow money at elevated rates, some portion of that group will be unable to repay the loan. The greater the risk of default, the higher the interest rate may be, and this can only

1. *See* Paul Hayeck, *An Economic Analysis of the Justifications for Usury Laws*, 15 Ann. Rev. Banking L. 253, 1996.

2. *See* Gene A. Marsh, *A Practitioner's Guide to the New Alabama Mini–Code*, 48 Ala.L.Rev. 957 (1997) (noting that low income and high illiteracy rates lead to the need to protect the public in consumer credit markets).

result in more insolvencies. Because of the economic consequences to the community, the state has ample justification for determining at what point a person can no longer borrow money.

This economic argument is used by both advocates and critics of usury laws. Advocates argue that usury laws are necessary to create a competitive market. On the other hand, critics argue that the competitive market will set a fair interest rate without legislative involvement. One group, the National Commission on Consumer Finance, seemed to support arguments in both camps.

First, the Commission stated that: "Rate ceilings in many states restrict the supply of credit and eliminate creditworthy borrowers from the consumer credit market. Some seek out less desirable alternatives, such as low quality credit sellers and illegal lenders. Furthermore, many borrowers who are not rejected pay rates higher than they would be charged in workably competitive markets." This occurs when interest rates rise above low usury ceilings, set below the equilibrium, causing quantity demanded to exceed quantity supplied. Hence, the short credit supply excludes many potential consumers from the consumer finance market. Those excluded are consumers who are more credit risky than credit worthy and for whom lenders must charge rates above the rate ceiling."

However, the Commission also stated that:

"This situation could be changed by eliminating rate ceilings and relying on competition to ensure that borrowers pay reasonable rates for the use of credit. However, the statistical evidence considered here indicates that competition cannot be relied upon at this point in time to establish rates at reasonably competitive levels in many states. Raising rate ceilings in some areas where markets are highly concentrated would merely allow suppliers to raise prices, accept somewhat higher risks, but remain secure within the legal or other barriers which assure them that their market power and monopoly profits will not be diluted."

And, finally, the Commission concluded that:

"Clearly, then, rate ceilings cannot be eliminated until workably competitive markets exist. But reasonably competitive markets cannot be expected to exist where low rate ceilings have driven many competitors from markets. In some instances, higher rate ceilings must be accompanied by policies to ensure that new competitors enter the market."

Hence, the Commission asserted that credit markets are noncompetitive and usury statutes are necessary to keep interest rates at a competitive level. Additionally, the usury statutes also work as a regulatory tool and promote economic growth.

C. PROBLEMS IN PROVING USURY

Although the cost of consumer credit has been significantly deregulated, usury laws continue to govern many consumer credit transactions, particularly for small loans and credit sales. So, how are usury laws applied?

Interest is the price of using someone else's capital. This price is dependent on such factors as the term of the loan, the cost to the creditor of servicing the loan, the risk that the creditor will not be repaid, the amount of the loan and the credit rating of the individual borrower. As discussed at the beginning of this chapter, usury was defined during Biblical times as *any* interest. Today, however, usury is "the exaction of a greater sum for use of money than the highest rate of interest allowed by law." *Foreign Commerce v. Tonn*, 789 F.2d 221 (3d Cir. 1986).

There are generally four elements of usury:

(1) a loan of money or forbearance of debt;

(2) an agreement between the parties that the principle shall be repayable absolutely;

(3) the exaction of a greater amount of interest or profit than is allowed by law and

(4) the presence of an intention to evade the law at the inception of the transaction.

Several matters related to the elements of usury are discussed below, beginning with the element that is often the most difficult to prove.

1.   INTENT

The intent element of usury does not require the plaintiff to show that the defendant lender had a specific intent to commit usury. The lender's subjective intent is often viewed as irrelevant in a usury case. If the loan is usurious on its face then the courts will impute a usurious intent on the parties. This presumption or inference of intent as explained in *Cochran v. American Sav. & Loan Ass'n,* 586 S.W.2d 849 (Tex.1979), was recently reaffirmed. "Intent in usury cases does not mean intent to charge a usurious rate of interest. Rather, it means intent to make the bargain made. The subjective intent of the lender is irrelevant if, in fact, the lender has contracted for, charged or received interest on a loan in excess of the maximum permitted by law." *Najarro v. SASI Int'l, Ltd.,* 904 F.2d 1002 (5th Cir.1990). In other words, the intent of the parties is presumed to be reflected in the documents which they signed.

An inference of usurious intent, however, does not end the case. The lender may escape liability in some states if he can show that the "receipt of usury was a result of an accidental and bona fide error." *Id.* Some other defenses available to creditors are (1) mistake of fact or mathematical error; (2) miscalculation; (3) de minimus damages; (4) rectification of the situation upon discovery and (5) evidence that the parties did not intend to make the bargain they made. On the other hand, a mistake of law is not sufficient, *i.e.,* "I thought that the maximum rate was five per cent more than that."

2.   SHOULD LOANS AND CREDIT SALES RECEIVE DIFFERENT TREATMENT?

Traditionally, general usury statutes have been applied only to loans. In the past, credit sales were sometimes viewed as exempt from provisions of general usury statutes because of a judicially created rule, commonly referred to as the time-price doctrine.

Essentially, the time-price agreement depends on the presentation of two prices to the purchaser: (1) a cash price and (2) a time-price. Under the time-price doctrine payments are to be made over a period of time, but the difference in amounts between the two prices was not considered as interest. *Whitaker v. Spiegel, Inc.*, 95 Wash.2d 408, 623 P.2d 1147 (Wash. 1981). This judicially created exception to the usury law applies to bona fide installment sales.

The time-price doctrine was originally formulated on a series of English land sales cases holding that (1) a seller may have two prices—a cash price and a credit or "time-price" and (2) it is immaterial if the time-price exceeds the cash price by more than the statutory allowance for interest on a loan in the amount of the cash price.

The first American statement of the time-price rule, *Hogg v. Ruffner*, 66 U.S. 115 (1861), was also a land sale case. The land involved was agreed to be worth only $20,000. The time-price was nineteen promissory notes of $2000 each. The Court held that usury laws did not apply, saying:

"A vendor may prefer $100 in hand to double the sum in expectancy, and a purchaser may prefer the greater price with the longer credit; and one who will not distinguish between things that differ must say, with apparent truth, that B (purchaser) pays a hundred per cent for forbearance, and may assert that such a contract is usurious; but whatever truth there may be the premises, the conclusion is manifestly erroneous. Such a contract has none of the characteristics of usury; it is not for the loan of money, or forbearance of a debt."

This is the usual justification of the time-price doctrine: that usury only applies where there is a loan or forbearance of money, and that a sale of property does not involve such a loan or forbearance. That is a narrow construction of the loan or forbearance language in usury statutes. Courts and commentators have, however, offered other explanations for the time-price doctrine. The Minnesota Supreme Court explained the doctrine as originating from the laissez-faire mercantilism of the nineteenth century. "These cases usually involved items of high price which the buyer ordinarily could not afford to purchase with cash and a buyer and seller substantially on equal footing in bargaining over price and credit charges." *Rathbun v. W.T. Grant,* 300 Minn. 223, 219 N.W.2d 641 (Minn. 1974). This view suggests that buyers on time do not need the same protection that borrowers do—"a purchaser is not like a needy borrower, a victim of a rapacious lender, since he can refrain from the purchase if he does not choose to pay the price asked by the seller." *Id.*

Another explanation which has been offered is more historical in context. When usury laws were first enacted credit buying was virtually unknown and since usury laws ran counter to freedom of contract, they should not be extended absent a clear-cut legislative mandate. Finally, it is argued that national competition among sellers in the marketplace will protect buyers from exorbitant credit charges.

In modern times, the time-price doctrine is generally viewed as a legal fiction and most jurisdictions no longer apply the doctrine to consumer credit transactions for usury purposes. Thus, since courts have recognized that a modern credit sale is not logically distinguishable from a loan by the seller to the buyer, the usury laws applied to the difference between the cash price and the total of payments over time. However, a *few* states cling to the fiction that a loan and credit sale are different, when measuring the difference between a cash price and time-price transaction.

3. HAS THE MAXIMUM LEGAL RATE BEEN EXCEEDED?

Determining whether a creditor is charging more than the legal rate of interest is often a complex process involving a number of separate issues and problems.[3] Lawyers working in these cases are wise to employ accountants who may do the "credit math" analysis to see if the creditor's compensation exceeds the legal limit. The process becomes even

3. For the most comprehensive treatment available on all issues relating to credit math, *see* The Cost of Credit, National Consumer Law Center (1995 and 1998 Supp.).

more complex as creditors' lending practices become more and more diverse. Not only is a borrower unsure whether the maximum legal rate has been exceeded, but courts have to decide whether interest has been charged at all. Only some of the most obvious and important issues are discussed here.

D. TYPES OF LENDERS AND CREDIT

Most states have statutes which establish numerous exemptions or exceptions to general usury rates and provide special ceilings with respect to finance charges. These exceptional or special rates vary depending on who the lender is or what type of credit is being extended. The most common statutes are based on the size and type of credit.

For example, virtually every state has a specific regulation for "small" loans. These "small" loans are consumer loans which in some states may be as large as $5000 while in other states as small as $2000. Also, with the resurgence of pay-day loans, discussed infra, some states have excepted the payday loans from their small loan acts and provide for a separate, much higher set of usury limitations.[4] It is also very common to have separate statutes which permit very high rates on pawnshop transactions, including auto-title-pawns.

In some states there are exceptions to general usury statutes which establish maximum rates of

4. Some examples of rates on payday loans established by some states for a 14 day loan are: California—625%, Iowa—391%, Florida—261%.

interest on loans secured by real estate, especially home mortgages. Additionally, most states have special legislation regulating interest charges on loans to be repaid in installments and finance charges imposed in connection with the retail installment sales, with automobiles occasionally treated separately.

E. FEDERAL PREEMPTION

State law is not the only regulator of interest rates. Federal law may preempt state usury laws in several different ways and areas. Under the National Bank Act, 12 U.S.C. § 85,[5] a national bank may charge "interest at the rate allowed by the laws of the State ... where the bank is located, or at a rate of one per centum in excess of the discount rate on ninety-day commercial paper in effect at the Federal reserve bank in the Federal reserve district where the bank is located, whichever may be greater. . . . "

A determination of the rate of interest allowed by state law is accomplished by "reference to the state

5. There is no comparable provision for federally chartered savings and loan institutions. Federal credit unions can make loans "at rates of interest not exceeding 1 per centum per month on unpaid balances, inclusive of all charges incident to making the loan." 12 U.S.C. § 1757(5). Therefore, a state law prescribing a lower interest rate is preempted. *See McAnally v. Ideal Fed. Credit Union*, 428 P.2d 322 (Okl.1967). This provision may also mean, however, that federal credit unions cannot charge as much for loans as state institutions where the allowable rate exceeds 12 per cent per year. *Cf. Brown v. Austin Area Teachers Fed. Credit Union* , 588 S.W.2d 629 (Tex.Civ.App.1979).

court's interpretation of the state's constitution and statutes. As such 12 U.S.C. § 85 does not merely incorporate the numerical rates established by the state, but adopts and encompasses the entire body of case law interpreting the state's limitation of usury." *Roper v. Consurve, Inc.*, 777 F.Supp. 508 (S.D.Miss.1990), *aff'd*. 932 F.2d 965 (Wash. 1991).

Because the rate allowed by the state has been interpreted by the courts to allow a national bank to charge the highest rate charged by any person or entity in the state under like conditions, the national banks have a favored lender status. Under this interpretation national banks are not limited to the rates applicable to state banks and therefore, have a minor advantage over state banks.

Federal law may also preempt state usury laws by allowing state chartered institutions as well as national ones to charge on certain types of loans an interest rate which exceeds local ceilings. For example, the Veterans Housing Amendments Act of 1976 rendered inapplicable to certain federally insured loans and mortgages any state constitutional provision "expressly limiting the rate of interest which may be charged, taken, received or reserved by certain classes of lenders." 12 U.S.C. § 1709–1a.

Another good example of federal preemption is Title V of the Depository Institutions Deregulation and Monetary Control Act of 1980. That Act exempts mortgages or loans "secured by a first lien on residential real property" from state laws "expressly limiting the rate or amount of interest, discount points, finance charges or other charges." 12 U.S.C. § 1735f–7a(a)(2). Although the Act was enacted to promote the stability and viability of financial institutions by allowing them to charge market rate on mortgage loans, states may opt out of the Act and enact its own usury limits. *Brown v. Investors Mortgage Co.,* 121 F.3d 472 (9th Cir.1997). The DIDM-CA allows a State to reassert a usury limitation if the State adopts a law which states explicitly and by its terms that the State does not want the provisions of subsection (a)(1) to apply. The State must act to reassert its usury limitation within three years.

The patchwork quilt of usury laws in place across the country may require a search of state and federal law, and in some cases several state statutes may need to be consulted. Although lids may be established in a general state usury law provision, those provisions may not operate and be overridden by separate statutory provisions that deal with pawnshops, payday loan shops, rent-to-own stores and even finance companies. The search for the appropriate usury law rarely lends itself to one-stop-shopping among the various provisions of state law.

F.   COMPUTING THE MAXIMUM AMOUNT THAT CAN BE CHARGED

Interest rates are not quoted under state law with any degree of uniformity. Most state usury statutes provide for a maximum "add-on" rate. Under the add-on method, interest is computed by using a I = PRT formula (Interest = Principal x Rate x Time) which figures interest on the full original term, disregarding the fact that repayments will be made in monthly installments.

To illustrate, C lends B $100 for 1 year at 8%. At the end of the year C will collect the entire principal of $100 plus $8.00 of interest. Now, if C required B to pay in monthly installments, the computation is a little different. The same formula is used, but now the $8.00 is "added on" to the $100, making the amount owed $108 payable over 12 months or $9 per month.

Clearly, C receives more by selling on time because now C is charging interest on the principal already paid back in each month's installment. To determine C's annual percentage rate of return on the $100 extended to B, first determine the average life of the loan. Let's assume that the average life of the loan is 12 months plus 1 month, divided by 2, or 6 ½ months. If C is getting $8 for $100 for 6 ½ months, then he is getting about:

8 x 12/6 ½ or 14.77% per year of B's money.

This use of an average term produce a rough figure. Precise measures of the real interest rate can be found by using available software programs and tables that are produced by the Federal Reserve Board, discussed in Chapter Six at pages 162–165.

Here is a brief table of the Annual Percentage Rates for various add-on rates and terms.[6]

ANNUAL PERCENTAGE RATE					
Add On Rate	6 Mos.	12 Mos.	24 Mos.	36 Mos.	60 Mos.	120 Mos.
6	10.21	10.90	11.13	11.08	10.85	10.21
8	13.59	14.45	14.68	14.55	14.13	13.12
10	16.94	17.97	18.16	17.92	17.27	15.86
12	20.29	21.46	21.57	21.20	20.31	18.49

A number of state statutes regulate the rate of interest as a discounted amount per year rather than as an add-on. Discount means that something is taken away—in this case the interest. Thus, if C gets a note from a B for $100 due in a single payment at the end of a year and C charges 8% discount, the charge is still the interest which is $8 but it is discounted or taken away when B gets the money. So that, rather than getting $100, B only gets $92. Clearly, on a discount transaction, C will earn $8 on the $92 B actually receives, which is 8.70% and not 8%. This is true even without installment payments.

6. Note that the APR goes up then down as the term increases. This is difficult to explain, but there are two influences at work. The first influence is the installment payment effect. At 6% add-on for 1 month the rate is 6% because there are no installment payments. At 2 months the charge is doubled but the average term goes from 1 month to 1 1/2 months (2 + 1, divided by 2), which is far from doubling, and the APR jumps from 6% up to 7.99%.

The other effect is the charge. The charge is always simple interest for the term: double the term, you double the charge. But at compound interest, if you double this term you more than double the charge. So gradually this effect takes over and the APR starts down and keeps on going down as the term increases.

When a creditor charges a discount for the full term and then requires installment payments, the effect is as the following table illustrates:

ANNUAL PERCENTAGE RATE

Discount Rate	6 Mos.	12 Mos.	24 Mos.	36 Mos.	60 Mos.	120 Mos.
6	10.53	11.58	12.59	13.38	15.04	22.24
8	14.15	15.68	17.33	18.79	22.28	49.60
10	17.83	19.91	22.42	24.85	31.58	——
12	21.56	24.28	27.87	31.73	44.33	——

The use of the APR (computed in the manner required by the Truth in Lending Act, considered in Chapter Six at pages 162–165, *supra*) in connection with add-on and discount statutes in the preceding paragraphs is instructive in two ways. First, it shows the assistance the federal Truth-in-Lending Act provides to a consumer who wants to compare different rates in the marketplace. Second, it shows the confusion that Truth in Lending causes in determining whether a creditor is charging more than the legal rate of interest. Merely looking at the disclosed APR may not tell you whether the usury law has been violated. To illustrate, assume that the Truth-in-Lending disclosure statement sets the APR at 14% and the applicable statute sets the maximum rate of interest allowable at 8%. At first glance, this seems to be a usurious transaction. However, as seen above, if the state statute is an "add-on" statute, there's no usury, for a loan with a six month maturity.

Computing the finance charge on an open end credit card account may also be a tricky process.

Consumers are told that a credit charge has an APR of 19.8% computed periodically. But what exactly does that mean, *i.e.*, how is the periodic balance determined?

The complexity with finance charges begins with the fact that there are at least four different methods of calculation. The methods are: (1) ending or closing balance; (2) previous balance; (3) average daily balance and (4) adjusted balance. Under the Truth in Lending Act, creditors are required to disclose to consumers the method used in determining the balance on which the finance charge is imposed. There is, however, no requirement that any certain method be used. The most common method is the average daily balance and many arguments can be and have been made as to the legally proper method. Some states have statutes mandating that a certain method be used.

G.   OTHER COMPUTATION PROBLEMS

Most usury statutes, which affect consumers, regulate interest at per annum or per year. Some state statutes define "year" or "per annum" but many do not. So, is a year 360 days, 365 days or 366 days for leap year?

Assuming that a creditor uses 360 days (whether because the state statute requires such or because the state statute provides no definition), the interest rate is divided by 360 to create a daily factor. Then the actual number of days that a loan is outstanding is then multiplied by the daily factor. Thus, interest charged for months of different lengths is different and interest for a calendar year is greater (using 360) than if a 365 day year had been used. (The lower the denominator, the higher the daily interest factor.) For example, if the APR is 21%, 365 days is used, and the number of days in the billing cycle is 30 days (days in the billing month) and the outstanding balance is $1,045.11, the interest that month is $18.03. The daily factor is 0.0575%. If, however, the days used is 360 days, the daily factor is 0.058% the interest would be $18.29.

The practice of computing interest on the basis of a 360 day year results in the collection of addition interest of 1/12 per cent of the rate of interest agreed to by the parties, regardless of the agreed upon interest rate, amount or maturity of the loan. The authorities are split on the issue of whether or not usury results from interest on the basis of 360 day per year which produces in a single calendar year more interest than is produced by applying the maximum rates to a calendar year of 365 days.

There is another problem which results from regulating interest on a per annum or yearly basis. Since consumer loans are often for more than a one year term, does the per annum language in the usury statutes refer to the amount that can legally be charged during any one year of a loan or to the aggregate amount that can be charged over the entire term of the loan?

Aside from the annual percentage rate, lenders frequently impose front-end fees that amount to interest (*see* pages 263–265, *infra*) or require advance payments of interest. As a result, the total interest which the borrower pays during the first year of a loan may be at a rate which exceeds the legal maximum even though the total interest paid over the life of the loan is within the usury limits. Thus, can a conceptualization which "spreads" the interest over the entire term of the loan protect a lender, who, in fact, collected interest during the first year at a rate above the legal maximum?

The cases are divided on this issue and are often hard to reconcile, but authorities in a number of jurisdictions support the "spreading" of interest. One of the leading cases is *Nevels v. Harris*, 129 Tex. 190, 102 S.W.2d 1046 (1937). There the true principal of the note amounted to $6080 payable in five years at an interest rate of eight per cent per annum. In addition, the lender charged the borrower a $320 fee for making the loan. The front-end fee added to the first year's eight per cent rendered that year's interest payments usurious. The court, however, looked to the full term of the note, spread the interest over the five year term of the contract and found that the note was not usurious.

According to the *Nevels* doctrine, "if the contract for the use and detention of the principal debt is not a sum greater than such debt would produce at [the maximum legal rate of interest] from the time the borrower had the use of the money until it is repaid, it is not usurious."[7] This doctrine was reaffirmed by the Texas Supreme Court in 1977 in *Tanner Development Co. v. Ferguson*, 561 S.W.2d 777 (Tex.1977) and has been reaffirmed many times by lower courts. The most recent case dealing with the "spreading doctrine" is *Pentico v. Mad–Wayler, Inc.*, 964 S.W.2d 708 (Tx.Ct App. Corpus Christi 1998). In that case, the court held that the spreading doctrine could be applied before a loan is paid off. *But compare*, *In re Brummer*, 147 B.R. 552, (Bankr.D.Mont.1992), where the court interpreted Tanner as applying only to loans which are facially usurious.

A lender may also seek the protection of the interest spreading doctrine when the interest rate paid by the borrower exceeds the legal maximum under a variable rate provision in a credit contract. Using the spreading doctrine, creditors argue that a loan is not usurious if "the total compensation to the creditor included some charges on account of the total loan period which, when spread throughout such period, did not produce a total return in excess of the maximum rate but, by reason of the debtor's voluntary shortening of the term, did produce such excess." *Arneill Ranch v. Petit*, 64 Cal. App.3d 277, 134 Cal.Rptr. 456 (1976).

7. "The term 'spreading' is defined as a method of allocating the total interest provided for in a loan agreement over the full term of the loan." *Groseclose v. Rum*, 860 S.W.2d 554, 558 (Tex.App.Dallas 1993). For a thorough analysis of the spreading doctrine in Texas *see* St. Claire, *The Spreading of Interest Under the Actuarial Method*, 10 St. Mary's L.J. 753 (1979).

Unlike a fixed rate of interest, a variable rate clause allows the interest rate to change during the term of the loan depending on the movement of some external index or factor such as the prime interest rate or the consumer price index. Because whether variable rate will exceed the maximum legal rate is dependent on a contingency, in addition to the spreading doctrine, the *Arneill* court also adopted the interest contingency rule.

The creditor in *Arneill Ranch v. Petit* charged an interest rate of "7 ½ percent per annum, or at the prime rate plus 2 percent ...whichever is greater." The maximum legal interest rate was 10 percent. Hence, the interest on the loan would only exceed the maximum legal interest rate if the prime rate exceeded 8 percent. The prime rate did eventually rise above 8 percent causing the interest rate to be 10.08 percent one period and 11.46 percent for another period. So, the debtor sued claiming the loan was usurious.

Applying the interest contingency rule, the appellate court, disagreed with the debtor and held that a variable interest rate agreement, although it provides under certain conditions for interest charges in excess of 10 percent, does not violate the prohibition of excessive interest if the parties contracted in good faith and without intent to avoid usury laws. The court stated that "[w]hen payment of full legal interest is subject to a contingency, so that the lender's profit is wholly or partially put in hazard, the interest so contingently payable need not be limited to the legal rate, providing the parties are contracting in good faith without the intent to avoid the statute against usury." *Id.* at 462. Whether creditors use the spreading doctrine or the interest contingency rule to justify a transaction which is alleged to be usurious, the key issue is whether the transaction was conducted in good faith. The determinative question is whether the variable interest rate was used "as a colorable device to obtain greater profit than was permissible under (the usury) laws." *Id.* The majority of courts will avoid "unfairly transforming an innocent transaction into a usurious one."

Another device which some courts have accepted to keep a transaction from being usurious is a "savings clause." A savings clause, when clearly written, overrides the regular interest provision if that provision would result in a usurious rate. Following the precedence of the *Arneill* Court the court in *In re Dominguez*, 995 F.2d 883 (9th Cir.1993), held that a "savings clause created 'at the very least, an ambiguity' that precluded a ruling that the agreement was usurious on its face." The court recognized that such clauses could be used as a "subterfuge or sham, designed to permit the collection of a usurious rate of interest without an appearance of violation of the law." *Id.* Therefore, the court did not consider the savings clause as making non-usurious an interest rate that exceeded the maximum legal rate. Rather, the court considered the clause as evidence of "what the parties entering the agreement intended the actual interest rate to be." *Id.*

Several states have enacted statutes which regulate variable rate loans, or at least, their use in some types of transactions. For example, Pennsylvania law governing residential mortgage interest rates permits variable rate mortgages contingent upon "the Monthly Index of Long Term United States Government Bond Yields for the second preceding calendar month plus an additional 2 ½ percent per annum rounded off to the nearest quarter of one per cent per annum." 41 P.S. § 301(b). The statute also contains a number of provisions which are intended to protect the consumer. Among them is the requirement that what goes up must go down. Specifically the statute provides "that when an increase in the interest rate is required by a movement in a particular direction of the prescribed standard, an identical decrease is required in the interest rate by a movement in the opposite direction of the prescribed standard." 41 P.S. § 301(e)(2). So that if the variable rate goes up when the Monthly Index goes up then, the variable rate must go down when the Monthly Index goes down. A similar provision can be found in California. Ca.Civil. § 1916.5(a)(1).

Variable rate loans are one way a lender can contend with an inflationary economy. Lenders do this by tying interest rates to economic indicators. Another way a lender can beat inflation is by indexing the principal instead of the interest rate. This is done by including in the loan contract a provision for adjusting the principal which the debtor must repay proportionately to the change in the cost of living over the term of the loan. The important usury issue associated with an indexed principal loan is this: is the additional principal which a borrower must pay when the cost of living increases considered interest when deciding whether or not the rate of interest exacted by the lender is usurious? The answer was "yes" according to a 1976 case. This case is still valid today, but the issue has not been addressed more recently.

In *Aztec Properties, Inc. v. Union Planters Nat'l Bank*, 530 S.W.2d 756 (Tenn.1975), cert. denied 425 U.S. 975 (1976), the debtor borrowed $50,000 and agreed to repay the lender " 'in constant United States Dollars adjusted for inflation (deflation)' with interest at ten percent per annum." A formula in the note adjusted the principal for any changes in inflation measured by the Department of Labor's Consumer Price Index. The borrower repaid the lender $50,000 when the note matured plus the accrued ten percent interest; but the borrower refused to pay an additional $500 of the indexed principal based on the inflation adjustment formula. The lender sued and the defense was usury.

The bank argued that the indexed principal was just that, *i.e.*, "principal," not interest. Its precise argument was that the $500 equaled the difference in value (or purchasing power) between the principal lent and returned. The court disagreed, however. Observing that Tennessee lenders have long borne the risk of inflation and noting the absence of cases to the contrary, the court held that "indexed principal" constitutes interest. The next section discusses the other charges which may be considered interest.

H. WHAT CHARGES ARE CONSIDERED INTEREST?

Regardless of what type of rate regulation a state imposes, before a debtor, attorney or court can determine if a transaction is usurious, he must be able to determine the amount of the interest rate. But what charges are considered interest?

Generally, any compensation, remuneration or other benefit exacted by the lender will be deemed interest unless the charge is to reimburse or compensate the seller for a specific expenditure or service other than extending credit. (Some state statutes enumerate and regulate specific types of charges. Delinquency or late charges and attorney's fees are examples.) The reimbursement may be for external expenses such as charges for house counsel, appraiser or preparing loan documentation. The fee must be for a separate expense and cannot be compensation for the use of the money loaned. Any such service charge must be reasonably related to the expense and service of the lender. And, the reimbursement must be for *specific* charges. A charge to compensate the lender for part of its overhead i.e., rents, salaries or loan losses, is generally held to be an additional interest charge. However, a charge for services directly related to the loan rendered by salaried employees are not interest.

But, see Tenn. Code Ann. § 45–15–111(a), (b); *In re Henley*, 228 B.R. 425 (Bankr.E.D.Ark.), where the legislature statutorily authorizes auto pawnbroker lenders to charge consumers a "customary fee" to defray ordinary costs of operating a title pledge office. In addition the statute authorizes lenders to recover the costs of repossession and attorney's fees.

1. LOAN ORIGINATION AND CLOSING EXPENSES

These are expenses generally charged by banks or mortgage companies to do an appraisal, obtain a credit report and record the mortgage. Absent a specific statute providing otherwise, most jurisdictions consider these to be reasonable expenses incurred by the lender in preparing a loan, and therefore are not interest. Loan origination fees, however, which are expressed as points (a point is one percent of the principal) are often considered interest in the usury test because the charge for points varies with the size of the principal.

2. COMMITMENT FEES

These are charges paid to a lender in exchange for a promise to make a loan in the future. Courts disagree as to the treatment of these fees. Some courts consider a commitment fee to be interest because it is nothing more than an overhead cost or the lender passing off the risk to the borrower that interest rates might go up, after the lender has committed to a fixed rate. Therefore, the commitment fee serves as a discount or the taking of interest in advance. *See Henslee v. Madison Guaranty Savings and Loan Association*, 297 Ark. 183, 760 S.W.2d 842 (1989). In *Henslee* the court held that a commitment fee was interest regardless of whether it was charged on every loan or was paid out of the principal. Other courts decide whether a commitment fee is interest by determining whether the fee is a legitimate "reasonable" cost to the buyer. *See First American Bank & Trust v. Windjammer Time Sharing Resort, Inc..*, 483 So.2d 732 (Fla.App.1986). The determination of what is reasonable is answered by looking to customary and acceptable practices in the trade on a case by case basis.

3. CHARGES PAYABLE BY THE DEBTOR ON DEFAULT

These charges are generally foreclosure costs or other types of expenses incurred in the collection of the debt. Courts generally do not consider these charges to be interest. But what about unaccrued or unearned interest or finance charges which may be included when the maturity of an obligation is accelerated[8] by the lender because of the debtor's default? The consequences of a lender claiming unaccrued interest in this type of case vary from state to state because of differing judicial attitudes

8. Example of an acceleration clause: in the event of default the entire unpaid balance of the Total of Payments shall at the option of the seller become immediately due and payable.

and statutory provisions. In one state, for example, even if the creditor sues for unearned interest, the court simply deducts it from any final damage award. In another state, however, a claim for unearned interest might result in a usury penalty or invalidation of the credit contract. *See Palace Industries, Inc. v. Craig*, 177 Ga.App. 338, 339 S.E.2d 313 (1985); *Bell v. Loosier of Albany*, 237 Ga. 585, 229 S.E.2d 374 (1976), where lenders lost their claims and attorney's fees by accelerating a loan under a contract and filing a complaint against a debtor seeking recovery of the balance due, without first rebating or deducting the unearned interest that would have been earned except for the acceleration. A contract may be usurious or invalid from its very inception simply for failing to deal clearly with the problem of acceleration and unearned interest. *See, e.g., Brookshire v. Longhorn Chevrolet Co.*, 788 S.W.2d 209 (Tex.Civ.App. 1990); *In re DeBlase*, 577 F.2d 994 (5th Cir.1978); *In re Sprouse*, 577 F.2d 989 (5th Cir.1978); *Commercial Credit Corp. v. Chasteen*, 565 S.W.2d 342 (Tex.Civ.App. 1978). In any event, a debtor is not liable for unaccrued interest when the lender accelerates a note or other credit contract because of the debtor's default, regardless of what penalty the lender suffers by claiming unearned interest.

4. PREPAYMENT PENALTIES

According to common law, a lender is not obligated to accept prepayment of a loan prior to its maturity date. By paying the loan off early, the debtor is able to stop the running of interest and the lender loses money. So, in addition to having a "no prepayment" clause, lenders may also include prepayment penalties. Generally, these penalties will not be considered as interest because they are viewed as consideration given in exchange for an early termination of the loan or other credit agreement. A lender, however, may lose its right to a prepayment penalty by accelerating the maturity date of the debt due to debtor's default, as discussed above. *Rodgers v. Rainier National Bank*, 111 Wash.2d 232, 757 P.2d 976 (1988). "This is so because acceleration, by definition, advances the maturity date of the debt so that payment thereafter is not prepayment but instead is a payment made after maturity." *Id.*

A requirement by the creditor that the debtor take out insurance as a condition of obtaining the loan presents special problems. Credit life and property insurance are separately considered in the material on Federal Truth In Lending, *infra* at pages 153-155, and again at pages 294-322.

5. IS IT REALLY A CREDIT TRANSACTION?

As stated earlier, categorizing charges as either interest or not interest is not easy. In many instances courts, creditors, consumers and the experts in the industry all disagree. Determining what is or is not an interest charge is further complicated by new financial schemes. Many of these schemes hide interest charges beneath the surface of legitimate names. These new financial arrangements attempt to elude any remaining usury regulation to shelter effective rates of return which are far higher than permitted under small loan acts.

Most of these schemes surfaced in the 1980s and 1990s. Some of them merely put life back into ways of making money that were here at the turn of the century. For example, rent-to-own operations have charged consumers up to 300 percent annual interest, rapid refund companies have reached charges of 520 percent per annum and auto pawn transactions have charged effective annual rates of up to 900 percent. Then there are the payday loans and other similar check cashing services.[9] Payday loans were discussed previously in Chapter Four, at page 67.

6. WHICH STATE RATE LAW APPLIES?

Maximum rates of interest differ from state to state.[10] Therefore, when a transaction involves a contract with more than one state, conflicts of laws questions may arise. Suppose, for example, that a buyer who resides in State A (where the maximum rate of interest is 10 per cent) finances the purchase of an automobile with a seller in State B (where the

9. *See* Steven W. Bender, *Rate Regulation at the Crossroads of Usury and Unconscionability: The Case for Regulating Abusive Commercial and Consumer Interest Rates under the Unconscionability Standard,* 31 Hous.L.Rev. 721 (1994).

10. For a comprehensive review of legal interest rates on a state-by-state basis, *see* Appendix A, The Cost of Credit, National Consumer Law Center (1995 & 1998 Supp.).

maximum rate of interest is 15 percent). Which state's interest applies? Can the seller charge 15 percent interest without violating any usury laws?

The general rule is the same as the rule under contract law, *e.g.*, the rights and duties of the contracting parties are governed by the law of the state with the most significant relationship to the transaction and the parties. Restatement (Second) Contracts § 188. When addressing usury, specifically, the court should consider (1) the place of the contracting, (2) the place of any negotiations which occurred, (3) the place of performance, (4) the location of the subject matter and (5) the domicile of residence of the parties. Restatement (Second) Conflict of Laws § 203 (1971). By applying these factors, the courts generally look to the law of the state with the most significant relationship to the transaction that would favor the agreement. In the above example, without more facts, the answer would most likely be "yes."

Some contracts include a choice of law provision specifying by which state's laws the parties want the transaction to be governed. However, the inclusion of such a clause does not always mean that the court's will apply the law of the state chosen by the parties. In *State ex. rel. Meierhenry v. Spiegel, Inc.*, 277 N.W.2d 298 (S.D.1979), the court applied the law of the customer's state where the customer bought merchandise on a revolving credit plan from a mail order company located in another state, despite an agreement between the parties to be bound by the company's state. *See also, Cook v.*

Frazier, 765 S.W.2d 546 (Tex. Civ. App. 1989), where the court applied Texas law to a contract for the purchase of time-share investment property located in Arkansas even though the parties agreed to be bound by Utah's law. Although the sellers formed a Utah business partnership to purchase the property, the court found the choice of law provision to be a sham and subterfuge to avoid the usury laws of Texas. The court pointed out that the contracts were negotiated and executed in Texas by Texas residents and all payments under the contract were made in Texas.

Another issue regarding conflicts of laws and usury is the use of general bank credit cards by customers of national banks. Courts do not have to delve into a traditional contract or conflict of laws analysis to determine which state's law applies because the Supreme Court and Congress has already provided an answer. A national bank can charge the highest rate of interest allowed by the laws of the state where it is located. *See* 12 U.S.C. § 85; *Marquette Nat'l Bank of Minneapolis v. First of Omaha Service Corp.,* 439 U.S. 299 (1978) and discussions at pages 249–251, *supra.* That means that a bank located in Nebraska may charge its cardholders the highest maximum rate of interest under Nebraska law even if its cardholders live in Minnesota and are dealing with Minnesota merchants, and even if the maximum interest is Nebraska is higher than the maximum interest in Minnesota. Thus, interest rates may be "exported" to other states. The term "interest" under the National Bank Act includes flat-rate fees charged on credit cards such as annual fees, late payment fees, returned check charges and over-the-limit fees, as well as, percentage-based charges. 12 C.F.R. § 7.4001(a); *Smiley v. Citibank* (South Dakota), N.A.,517 U.S. 735, 116 S.Ct. 1730, 135 L.Ed.2d 25 (1996); *Richardson v. Citibank*, 908 P.2d 532 (Colo.1995) (the court held that the charge of a late fee was not prohibited where the bank was a national bank and the fee was an interest charge under 12 U.S.C. § 85 despite the fact that Colorado's law prohibited such fees.) The National Bank Act is important because "if the location of the Bank were to depend on the whereabouts of each credit transaction, the meaning of the term 'located' would be so stretched as to throw into confusion the complex system of modern interstate banking. A national bank could never be certain whether its contracts with residents of a foreign state were sufficient to alter its location for purposes of § 85." *Marquette*, 439 U.S. at 312.

I. REMEDIES

The remedies available to a debtor for violations of usury statutes are determined by state law. The penalties vary widely. For example, in many states, there is a forfeiture of all interest, while in other states the lender forfeits either a multiple of all interest or the excess of interest. In several states, there is a forfeiture of a percentage of the principal plus interest. Finally, in some states, the entire loan may be voided and made uncollectible.

Federal law sets the penalties for national banks that violate state usury laws. Although state rate regulations are incorporated by the National Banking Act, state sanctions are not. The only penalties for a bank exacting usurious interest are those set out in Section 86 of the Act: (1) forfeiture of the entire interest and (2) liability for twice the interest received where the bank has actually received usurious interest.

CHAPTER EIGHT

REGULATION OF OTHER TERMS IN CONSUMER TRANSACTIONS

A. FTC CREDIT PRACTICE RULE

1. INTRODUCTION

The FTC Trade Regulation Rule Concerning Credit Practices became effective on March 1, 1985, and can be found at 16 C.F.R. 444. The Rule prohibits six practices in consumer credit that are considered an unfair act or practice within Section 5 of the FTC Act. Finance companies, retailers and other creditors within the jurisdiction of the FTC are subject to the Rule. Although the FTC Rule does not apply to banks, the Federal Reserve Board, the Office of Thrift Supervision and the National Credit Union Administration have enacted analogous rules for banks, thrifts and credit unions. The rules promulgated by these regulating agencies do not prohibit financial institutions from purchasing consumer credit contracts containing these prohibited terms, as long as the institutions do not enforce the prohibited creditor remedy.

273

2.   REMEDIES FOR VIOLATIONS
OF THE FTC RULE

As noted previously in Chapter Two, there is generally no private right of action under the FTC Act for violation of an FTC Rule. However, state UDAP provisions that prohibit unfair or deceptive acts and practices could be used to challenge violations of the FTC Act Rule. A violation of an FTC Rule is treated as a *per se* violation of some state UDAP statutes.

In some cases, violations of the FTC Credit Practices Rule are used by plaintiff's lawyers to provide "heat" in a case, where the focus of the case is on credit insurance sales, packing and flipping of consumer credit transactions. And where a creditor uses a false threat to enforce a remedy that is prohibited under the FTC Credit Practices Rule, state law and the Fair Debt Collection Practices Act (Chapter Nine, pages 398–406) may come into play, depending on the nature of the action taken and whether the party dealing with the consumer is the actual creditor or a debt collector. In any case, there are a number of ways to assert a violation of the FTC Credit Practices Rule on behalf of consumers, either offensively or defensively. The Federal Trade Commission staff has stated that it is also an unfair and deceptive practice to include a prohibited provision in a consumer credit contract, and then later disclaim the enforceability of the provision.

Despite the relative clarity of the FTC Credit Practices Rule and the alternatives available to consumers to affirmatively assert violations of the Rule or to assert violations of the Rule defensively, many creditors continue to include provisions in their contracts that are prohibited. Spotting violations of the FTC Credit Practices Rule, particularly among subprime lenders and credit sellers, is not uncommon. This is particularly true in the areas of confessions of judgments, waiver of exemptions and the taking of nonpurchase money security interests in certain household goods, discussed below.

3.   PROHIBITED PRACTICES UNDER THE FTC RULE

Listed below are the practices prohibited by the FTC Rule.

(a) Cosigner Provision

The failure to provide cosigners with the following warning, indicating the potential obligations of a cosigner. The required notice is as follows:

Notice to Cosigner

You are being asked to guarantee this debt. Think carefully before you do. If the borrower doesn't pay the debt, you will have to. Be sure you can afford to pay if you have to, and that you want to accept this responsibility.

You may have to pay up to the full amount of the debt if the borrower does not pay. You may also have to pay late fees or collection costs, which increase this amount.

The creditor can collect this debt from you without first trying to collect from the borrower.

The creditor can use the same collection methods against you that can be used against the borrower, such as suing you, garnishing your wages, etc. If this debt is ever in default, that fact may become a part of *your* credit record.

This notice is not the contract that makes you liable for the debt.

This disclosure must be made on a separate document and be given to the cosigner prior to their becoming obligated. A person is not considered a cosigner if they are a joint applicant who is entitled to receive the proceeds or will be the co-owner of property purchased in the transaction. The FTC has issued a number of informal staff opinion letters governing this and the other portions of the FTC Credit Practices Rule. The informal staff opinion letters are not binding on the courts or the FTC itself, but could certainly provide some cover to creditors, particularly where the plaintiff is asserting fraud. Some courts are unwilling to allow findings of "intentional conduct" where regulatory agencies have provided an opinion, even though the opinion may not be viewed as binding on the court.

(b) Pyramiding Late Charges

It is a violation of the rule to pyramid (stack) late charges by assessing more than one delinquency charge for one late payment. Thus, if a debtor was late with a payment and was assessed a late fee on that payment, but failed to include the late fee, a second late fee could not be added to the account if the next monthly payment arrive on time. It would be appropriate to add and carry the first late fee on the account, but not to add a second late fee unless the consumer was again late in making a subsequent payment.

(c) Confession of Judgment

The consumer credit obligation must not contain a cognovit or confession of judgment, warrant of attorney or other waiver of the right to notice and the opportunity to be heard in the event of suit.

(d) Waiver of Exemptions

The consumer credit contract must not contain a waiver of exemptions concerning property exempt from attachment or execution, unless the waiver applies solely to the property that is subject to a security interest granted in the transaction.

(e) Assignment of Wages

It is an unfair act or practice for the consumer credit contract to include a provision for the assignment of wages, unless:

(1) the assignment by its terms is revocable at the will of the debtor, or

(2) the assignment is a payroll deduction plan or preauthorized payment plan, commencing at the time of the transaction, in which the

> consumer authorizes a series of wage deductions as a method of making each payment, or

(3) the assignment applies only to wages or other earnings already earned at the time of the assignment.

Mandatory wage assignments are allowed in the context of payroll deduction plans of the type used in credit union loans, as long as only a part of the debtor's paycheck is taken. Employers do not violate the Rule by complying with a wage assignment, regardless of its legality under the Rule.

(f) Non–Purchase Money Security Interests in Certain Household Goods

It is an unfair act or practice to take a non-purchase money security interest in certain household goods. The futility and predatory nature of taking a security interest in existing household goods has long been attacked by consumer advocates. In many cases, creditors had no intention of foreclosing on collateral, but merely took the security interest to exert leverage over the debtor, through the threat of repossession and the embarrassment it would cause. Most household goods have little resale value. It would cost more to repossess them than they would bring in resale. And it adds insult to injury to the consumer where the creditor seeks a security interest in what is known to be "junk" collateral, and then be told that credit property insurance must be in place to "cover the creditor's interest." In such cases, the creditor's only real interest is to realize an additional profit through the retention (often undisclosed) of some of the premium paid for the credit property insurance. The point is that collateral, where taken, should be real. If the only collateral taken is close to worthless at the time the credit contract is executed, the *economic reality* is that it is an unsecured credit transaction, although we may treat it *legally* as a secured transaction.

Recognizing that some household goods do have value and could appropriately serve a legitimate legal and economic interest as collateral for the credit transaction, the Rule allows for nonpurchase money security interests in works of art, electronic entertainment equipment (except one television and one radio), items acquired as antiques and jewelry (except wedding rings).

Through informal staff opinion letters, the FTC includes within the definition of "household goods," such items as vacuum cleaners, air conditioners, freezers, ovens, microwaves, fans, clocks and other items that are ordinary and more essential items in daily living. Thus, through inclusion in the definition of "household goods," these items are intended to be protected from a nonpurchase money security interest. But excluded from the definition of "household goods," and therefore subject to a security interest are such items as luggage, hot tubs, boats, snowmobiles, tape players, barbeque grills, and VCR's. Without regard to the validity of the security interest, it is a good question whether collateral such as a used barbeque grill is of any economic value to the creditor. Taking the FTC

Rule to the limit, as some creditors are inclined to do, it is not uncommon to find items such as charcoal grills, weedeaters, socket and wrench sets, and other such items on the list of collateral. In depositions, creditors freely admit that they rarely, if ever, go after such collateral when the debtor defaults. It is more trouble than it is worth to repossess a used barbeque grill, a fish aquarium (who keeps the fish?) and a socket wrench set.

Related to the taking of this "junk" collateral is the question of whether nonfiling insurance is legitimate where a creditor admits that it never goes after the collateral when the debtor defaults. Recall from the discussion of nonfiling insurance in the TILA section on credit insurance (Chapter Six), that nonfiling insurance is a peculiar product that covers loss a creditor might suffer in the event that it is unable to realize on the collateral *because of its failure to file*. If you choose to avoid going after junk collateral, are you ever suffering a loss for your inability to realize on the collateral *due to your failure to file*? In such circumstances, is nonfiling insurance legitimate in anyway? Why sell insurance (where you are allegedly covering something at "risk") if you know out front you are never going after such collateral? What is "at risk" in such a case? This question will be discussed in Part C of this chapter.

B. FLIPPING

Creditors and credit sellers make money on the interest and other charges they impose on consumer credit transactions. They also make money through the workings of credit math, when loans are renewed early in their term, and are not permitted to run to their full maturity. Both the workings of credit math and the performance benchmarks that are often in place for employees in the consumer credit industry create an incentive to keep loans "fresh" and to renew existing accounts, particularly when the account works its way through the amortization schedule. The phenomenon of frequent loan renewals in consumer credit, particularly as it is practices by finance companies, is often referred to as "flipping."[1]

1. THE INCREASE OF LOAN RENEWALS

Lawyers representing consumer debtors with finance company loans are often surprised to find that new loans are made and existing loans refinanced several times each year. Although we live in a world of "easy credit terms" and are surrounded by examples of the improvident use of credit, consumer finance company lending practices often sur-

1. On March 16, 1998, the author testified on subprime lending, flipping and packing, before The U.S. Senate Special Committee on Aging, Senator Charles E. Grassley, Chairman. At that hearing, flipping was defined as:

the practice of inducing a borrower into signing several successive loans where each refinances the previous loan. The predatory lender profits from this scam through prepayment penalties, new points, other charges, and an ever-increasing loan balance. The loan balance increases as the principal of the subsequent refinance loan is used to pay off the previous loan, the fees and costs of the previous loan, and the fees and costs of the new loan.

prise even the most hardened advocates of E–Z credit. These lending practices are particularly noteworthy when one considers that many of their borrowers started out as credit risks, having come to the finance company after being bounced by a bank or other depositary institution.

Finance companies frequently will contact existing customers, offering a few hundred additional dollars. Some training manuals urge the employees to make solicitations every time the customer comes in to make a payment. If the debtor bites at the apple, the existing loan will be "paid off" and a new loan will start, but with a great deal of the balance being "old money." That is, after rebates (most likely credits on the account) for unearned interest and insurance premiums, the new amount financed will be comprised of the unpaid principal balance from the old loan, the few hundred additional dollars given to the debtor in the new loan, and new credit insurance products (credit life, credit property, nonfiling, credit disability, etc.) that were sold and financed by the creditor.[2]

These frequent loan renewals are rabidly marketed through telephone and mail solicitations. Most of us would stop dealing with a bank or other lender that solicited us for new money nearly every time

2. Observations on flipping are drawn from training manuals, branch operations manuals, training videos, and depositions of former employees of finance companies, on file with the author. These observations on flipping are largely drawn from Gene A. Marsh, *Limitations on Flipping*, 4 Cons. Adv. 4 (1998). Consumer Advocate is a publication of the National Association of Consumer Advocates.

we made a car payment. However, finance companies are not timid in offering new money to debtors. The mechanics and incentives in establishing the flipping system are described below. The system is a product of several forces at work, including the compensation system for finance company employees, state law which favors creditors in the amounts rebated for unearned interest and insurance premiums, very slick (and at times deceptive) marketing practices, *and* some borrowers who have no credit discipline. The problems are magnified when a borrower is poorly educated and even illiterate. Many finance company borrowers come to the table with little formal education.

All of us are familiar with the advantages, disadvantages, and the reality of refinancing home mortgages, and even car loans. However, most people are surprised by the system that has been implemented by the consumer finance company lending industry, where debtors often send in regular payments, but make little progress against loan principal. The system resembles the nightmare where one is running hard but making little progress against the tiger that is about to pounce. Finance company loan renewals establish a pattern which makes people indentured servants, working hard but never making progress against debts.

The flipping system also magnifies the harm done in the sale of consumer credit insurance products that are so prevalent in finance company lending. Consumer credit insurance, which is generally a bad bargain by any measure, is especially costly where the rebates for unearned insurance premiums are credited under the Rule of 78's. The use of the Rule of 78's works to the creditor's advantage when loans are renewed early in the term.[3]

2. EMPLOYEE INCENTIVES AND MARKETING STRATEGIES IN LOAN RENEWALS

Commercial banks have never been known for paying overly generous salaries to consumer lending officers who are in the trenches. Finance companies pay even less, and sometimes a great deal less. Additional financial incentives are sometimes offered in a bonus point system that is based on loan volume, with point subtractions for loans made that are late or delinquent. The bonus system may be based on individual branch performance.

In some companies, loan volume is double-counted. That is, monthly loan volume is measured without regard to whether the most recent loan includes a large block that is merely a renewal of an earlier loan. In depositions, some employees have reported that they renew loans in order to increase their loan volume. This is close to the system of "churning" accounts in the securities industry. Some employees have stated that as the end of the month approaches, the pressure to turn loan volume increases and the "quality" of new loans diminishes.

3. *See* James H. Hunt, *The Rule of 78: Hidden Penalty for Prepayment in Consumer Credit Transactions*, 55 B.U. L. Rev. 331 (1975) (providing the most comprehensive treatment available on the workings of the Rule of 78's).

Deposition testimony also includes frank admissions that some loans are renewed in order to remedy the problem of loan delinquency. Thus, a loan looks current for the bonus system, even though the borrower has been having trouble making payments *before* the loan renewal. Not only testimony, but also training films, include passages encouraging renewals for existing delinquent accounts, particularly if new collateral or a cosigner can be added to the loan. The same training video offers advice to employees, encouraging them to use loan renewals to cure delinquent accounts. Loan renewals or refinancings which extend the term and lower the monthly payments may be defensible, but the cost of loan extension in precomputed add-on transactions is significant. The pressure to sell credit insurance products is also magnified in such a system because the insurance premiums are financed, thus raising loan volume.

Training manuals and video training tapes also include passages encouraging employees to use expressions such as "line of credit" in soliciting renewals. However, a complete refinancing of an existing loan and a restarting of the clock on the old money is hardly what you get in a true line of credit. A true line of credit—even a home equity loan with an established line—allows for draws without much in the way of transactions costs. However, it is the operation of the Rule of 78's, new prepaid finance charges, and the other transactions cost that are so expensive for borrowers whose loans are flipped by finance companies.

Other passages in lending manuals include directives that "all efforts are devoted toward motivating individuals to make contact with our office." One manual states that "the bulk of our business is repeat business," and that "renewals are SOLD NOT BOUGHT." Another noteworthy passage is one that reminds lenders that "the alert employee will map out an effective game plan," and "sell eligible applicants to his maximum worth or high credit." However, a study of loan documents and admissions by employees suggest that high credit limits are sometimes exceeded in order to make a delinquent account look current. As is often the case in commercial and corporate loans, some of the loans become problems because the lender ignores internal directives on approval ratios.

In fairness to lenders, it is a fact of life that financial institutions are in the business of selling money and sales volume is critical in any business. In many ways, selling money is no different than selling shirts. However, the lender-borrower relationship has never been viewed as a place where all bets are off relating to disclosures, sales practices, and complications after the sale is made. Thus, the exceptionally aggressive lending practice of finance companies will not be viewed simply as the sale of the next shirt. When it comes to consumer lending, the dynamic changes, and people expect more than the law of the jungle to prevail.

3. ADD-ON INTEREST AND
THE RULE OF 78'S

The most common methods utilized in the calculation of interest in consumer finance loans are the
add-on and actuarial methods. Actuarial interest is
calculated by applying a periodic interest rate to the
outstanding balance of the loan principal for each
period for the term of the loan. This is the method
that is used to amortize real estate mortgage loans.
In order to calculate actuarial interest and payments for installment transactions, one generally
must resort to formulas or tables which are widely
available.

Computing interest by the add-on method is easy
and is the method most commonly utilized by consumer finance companies. Add-on interest is a
method for calculating precomputed interest, where
the consumer agrees to pay the total of payments,
which includes both principal and the full amount
of precomputed interest. Thus, if a consumer agreed
to borrow $1,000 at twenty percent interest, to be
paid over a twenty-four month period, the calculation for payments would be as follows:

(1) $1,000 x .20 x 2 yrs. = $400 interest

(2) $1,000 principal plus $400 interest =
     $1,400/24 mos. = $58.33/mo.

With the add-on system, interest is calculated as
though the borrower had full use of the principal
for the full period of the loan, but because some

principal is being repaid with each installment, the debtor pays a fixed amount of interest on a diminishing principal. thus, the add-on method understates the true simple interest rate and the real cost of the loan.

It is the actuarial method—not the add-on method—that most closely approximates and will in some cases match (if there are no prepaid finance charges or other complications) the annual percentage rate (APR) that most of us know under the mandates of TILA. Because TILA requires a common method for reporting the true interest rate on loans based on an annual percentage rate (APR), the add-on rates dramatically understate the effective "simple" or actuarial rate on a loan.

Because interest on add-on loans is precomputed, the lender must have some system in place to rebate or credit the account for unearned interest in the event the loan is paid off early or refinanced. The most common method for rebating unearned interest charges (and unearned credit insurance premiums) is under the Rule of 78's, or the Sum of the Digits Method. State law follows a federal mandate requiring the use of some method other than the Rule of 78's for loan with terms longer than sixty months. However, because most consumer finance companies make loans with maturities of five years or less, the Rule of 78's is widely used to rebate unearned interest and unearned insurance premiums.

Although the Rule of 78's is easy to use, it carries a disadvantage for the borrower. The method used by the Rule of 78's weighs the early months too heavily and the latter months too lightly in calculating interest earned by the creditor. Thus, if a loan is prepaid (or started over, in the case of a refinancing), the creditor would be credited with more interest earned (and not rebated) than if the interest calculation were made on the actuarial method.

It is readily established mathematically and accepted beyond dispute that the higher the APR for a given indebtedness, the greater is the error in the Rule of 78's in calculating interest earned by the creditor at certain points in the loan, when compared to the actuarial method. Further, with many consumer loans, the point at which there will be the greatest divergence (error) between the Rule of 78's and the actuarial method is roughly one-third of the way through the loan term. At any point in the loan, the difference between an actuarial rebate and a Rule of 78's rebate on any given precomputed loan will vary with loan size, the interest rate on the loan, the loan term, and the time of prepayment.

4.   OBSERVATIONS ON FLIPPING

With regard to both car loans and home mortgages, most of the early payments are largely interest and little is principal. It is only later in the loan that a borrower starts to make serious progress against the principal. Conversely, most of the interest income for lenders is made early in the loan. In depositions, finance company employees and executives readily admit that the companies make more money on "new" loans and that old loans are not profitable. This is no great revelation and holds true whether interest is calculated on an actuarial basis or in a precomputed, add-on arrangement. There is no real "fault" or devious practice here. It is merely mathematics at work.

Many borrowers can grasp the ramification of restarting an old loan (such as home mortgage refinancing) and know the costs and benefits of doing so. These borrowers can read and write. They also do not receive solicitations for "new money" every time they make a payment or receive a monthly statement. Additionally, they are not met with pitches for credit insurance products at every turn.

The same cannot be said for consumer finance company borrowers, many of whom do not bring much formal education to the table. Among the many consumer finance company loan documents and depositions the author has read over the past several years, only a few borrowers were college graduates and many were people who did not finish high school. Others could not read or write. The data on educational levels, dropout rates and illiteracy in some states makes none of this a surprise. When some of these borrowers are matched against very polished, rehearsed, and high pressure promotional practices, with use of terms such as "line

of credit'' and representations regarding the value
(and even the necessity) of credit insurance products, it is not much of a contest in the negotiation
process.

Many finance companies include advertisements
for more money in each monthly statement they
send to the borrower. Seasonal pitches are common,
offering a few hundred additional dollars for Christ-
mas money or a summer vacation. Other pitches
included on the monthly statement will congratu-
late the borrower for making a few timely payments, and offer several hundred more dollars if the
debtor will visit the office. However, rather than
making a new and second small loan, which is the
impression created by the advertising, the creditor
will restart the clock on the old money in a consolidation.

When pressed on why the finance company could
not make a second, small loan, particularly when
the loan request was triggered by the lender's solicitation, the standard answer is "it's company policy." No further explanation is offered.

Accounting firms hired to work in consumer finance litigation have developed excellent models to
compare the costs to the borrower of the refinancing (flipping) system that is in place and the costs to
the borrower if payments on the old loan were
allowed to continue, while a new, second small loan
was made. The differences in costs are dramatic in
most cases and have not be refuted. Even if the
APR on the renewal loan is lower than the APR on

the old loan, the actual out of pocket costs for the new refinanced loan may be greater than those that would be paid if a second small loan were made available, while payments on the old loan were continued.

The extra costs to the borrower are in part the result of the operation of the Rule of 78's (as it is applied to interest and unearned credit insurance premiums). In order to induce the borrower to take on more debt, some finance companies extend the loan maturity to a new term. Thus, what was once an initial loan with a twenty-four-or thirty-month maturity will often turn into a new loan at forty-eight or even sixty months. Although the debtor may take this arrangement because the monthly payment stays the same, the mountain of interest builds, particularly in a precomputed, add-on loan scenario. And because the creditor will most likely make a new pitch for a loan renewal (and a few hundred more dollars) several months down the road, the principal amount remains largely undiminished or grows.

To see an illiterate borrower who has had a loan "renewed" five, six, or even eight times in two years, and who is sometimes sold as many as three or four credit insurance products (credit life, credit property, credit disability, "involuntary unemployment insurance," and nonfiling may appear individually or all together in one loan), is enough to make most traditional lenders shake their heads. And in some cases, because of the dismal credit record of the borrower *before the first loan was made*, the expression "throwing good money after bad" appears to be unknown in selected consumer finance company branches, where loan volume dictates incentives and policies.

The frequency of loan renewals in consumer finance company lending is *not* merely the result of borrowers who voluntarily go to the well too many times. This practice is designed and encouraged by finance companies, without question. A recent opinion from the Seventh Circuit United States Court of Appeals is highly critical, as is the growing body of literature examining the economic incentives and strategies involved in the process. In *Emery v. American General Finance*, 71 F.3d 1343 (7th Cir. 1995), Chief Judge Richard Posner, was highly critical of the practice of flipping. Judge Posner pointed out that in one loan renewal where the borrower received an additional $200, the monthly payments jumped from $89 to $108, and the incremental additional cost was $1,200, for transactions that were packed with credit life and disability, property and nonfiling insurance. Judge Posner wrote: "So much for the Truth in Lending Act as a protection for borrowers." 71 F.3d at 1346. The case has a complicated history on remand, but Judge Posner's comments on flipping caught the attention of consumer advocates and creditors.

C. CREDIT INSURANCE

1. INTRODUCTION

In addition to the profits earned through finance charges on credit contracts, the sale of credit insurance and other add-ons can be extremely profitable for lenders and credit sellers. Lenders and retailers who are able to sell credit insurance to consumers receive significant compensation through retention of a part of the premiums. For example, in *Spears v. Colonial Bank of Alabama*, 514 So.2d 814 (Ala. 1987), the car dealer retained fifty percent of the premiums. This is not an uncommon arrangement. The credit insurance industry is often described as a place where there is "reverse competition," because insurers can offer the highest commissions through the sale of the most expensive products.

It is not uncommon to find a consumer finance company loan which includes credit life, credit disability, involuntary unemployment insurance, credit property insurance and even nonfiling insurance. The borrowers comes in to get a loan, but walks away with the loan and a great deal of dead weight added to the amount financed, having included the credit insurance premiums. "Packing" is the term that is used to describe the creditor's practice of loading up the loan with credit insurance.[4] Credi-

4. At the March 16, 1998, hearing of the U.S. Senate Special Committee on Aging, Senator Charles E. Grassley, Chair, packing was described as:

tors often use expressions such as the "payment protection plan," rather than use the word "insurance" in the sales pitches. And some sales training videos stress the importance of breaking down the costs as "cents per day," rather than focusing on the total cost of the credit insurance products. In the deposition of a former employee of a national consumer finance company, employees talked among themselves as having sold to the customer "the full-meal-deal" when the loan was packed with all the insurance products. In other depositions, employees were told not to complete the loan documents and calculate monthly payments until the customer had turned down insurance at least three times.

2. REGULATION OF CREDIT INSURANCE

As was discussed in Chapter Six, the federal Truth in Lending Act (TILA) largely regulates the disclosure requirements related to credit insurance products and dictates the process for consumers to indicate their decision to buy credit insurance products. For example, TILA allows the premium for credit life insurance to be placed in the amount

the practice of adding unnecessary credit insurance, other loan add-on products, and fees to a loan. The lender rolls the price of the insurance into the loan amount and charges interest upon that inflated amount, thus increasing the finance charges that accrue. The lender almost invariably derives profit from those products because, even in the event of customer cancellation, the company retains that portion of the finance charge that was attributable to the cost of the insurance.

financed as long as the insurance is not required. However, state law, either found in insurance statutes or under a state consumer credit code, may make it a violation of state law to present credit life insurance as required. State law will also deal with such issues as the licensing requirements to sell credit insurance, the dollar amount against which premiums are to be calculated, and the permissible charge for credit insurance (often expressed as cents per $100 of the loan amount).[5] State law also often describes whether the insurance is "single interest" (creditor's interest only) or "dual interest" (covering the interests of the creditor and the debtor's (equity)).

The cost of credit insurance is typically far higher than an equivalent amount of insurance purchased through a traditional insurance company. For example, a credit life insurance premium to cover a $5,000 loan may be more than twice as much as the premium for $5,000 worth of term insurance purchased directly from an insurance company.

Part of the reason for the cost difference is that when credit life insurance is sold, typically none of the individual characteristics of the borrowers are considered, such as health and age (except some companies will not sell credit life insurance to an individual over 65 years old). In ordinary life insurance, the insured's age, health and habits (smoker or nonsmoker) are among the facts used to assess

    5. *See* Brian H. Redmond, Annotation, *Coverage of Insurance Transactions Under State Consumer Protection Statutes*, 77 A.L.R. 4th 991 (1990).

the risk and establish a premium. However, in the case of credit insurance, often the only requirement is that the debtor has a pulse.

Another factor that explains the level of credit insurance premiums is that typically, the loss-ratio in credit insurance is very low. The loss ratio is the percentage of each premium dollar which is paid out to insureds when claims are made. In industry studies and examinations conducted by U.S. House and U.S. Senate committees, typical loss ratios were in the range of 35% to 40%.[6] In some states, regulators watch the loss-ratios and adjust the rate charts to keep the loss-ratios more in line with benchmark ratios of 50 to 60 percent. But in other states, permissible rates are high and sticky, never moving downward.[7]

Beyond Truth in Lending and state statutes in the areas of consumer credit, banking and insurance, additional sources of state rules may also need to be explored. There are often credit insurance regulations, promulgated by individuals such as a state superintendent of banking or state insurance commissioner. There also may be informal or formal opinions from those regulators, as well as the

[6]. Credit Life Insurance Hearing Before the Subcommittee on Antitrust, *Monopoly and Business Rights of the Senate Committee on the Judiciary*, 96th Cong. 1st Sess. 48 (1979).

[7]. *See* consumer Fed'n of Am. & U.S. Pub. Interest Research Group, Most Credit Life Insurance Still a Rip–Off (1997). The source for the data is an October 1996 report from the National Association of Insurance Commissioners. *See* Nat'l Ass'n of Ins. Comm'rs (NAIC), Credit Life and Accident & Health Experience by State 1993–1995 (1996).

office of the attorney general, on matters relating to credit insurance.

3.   CREDIT LIFE INSURANCE

Credit life insurance pays off the credit obligation in the event of the debtor's death. The most common type of credit life insurance is decreasing term, where the amount of the coverage declines as the loan balance is reduced over the life of the credit transaction. The majority of the states allow the premium to be based on what is called "gross coverage." Gross coverage is written on the "total of payments" in a precomputed installment loan, where the total of payments includes both the principal and interest on the loan. If coverage can only be set to cover the principal on the loan, the term "net coverage" is used.

If gross coverage is permitted by law, there is no "legal overcharge," but there is an economic overcharge in most cases. Recall that in earlier discussions on credit math, both in Chapter Seven and in the coverage of "flipping in this chapter (Part B), when a loan is paid off early, the creditor is not entitled to keep the unearned portion of the finance charge." The creditor often calculates the "earned" portion of the finance charge through the operation of the Rule of 78's. It is also true that if a debtor dies during the term of the loan, the creditor is entitled to be paid the unpaid balance on the principal and that portion of the interest that *has been earned*, but not paid. But in almost no case, where death occurs during the loan term, would the creditor be entitled to be paid the principal and *all* of the precomputed interest. Therefore, setting the initial credit insurance premium on the total principal and precomputed interest over insures the creditor's interest.

Recognizing that gross coverage over insures the loan, some of the state allow only for net coverage. In other states, some *courts* have held that net coverage is the appropriate policy, where the state statute or regulations created an ambiguity, by allowing the coverage to be set at the "approximate amount and term of the credit." For example, in *McCullar v. Universal Underwriters Life Ins. Co.*, 687 So.2d 156 (Ala.1996), the Alabama Supreme Court held that the amount financed, rather than the total of payments, should be used in determining the credit life insurance premium in a precomputed, add-on interest loan. The court refused to make its decision prospective only, but did hold that because the defendants based their calculation on directives from the State Banking Department and State Insurance Department, the species of fraud under which the plaintiff could assert a claim is that of an "innocent/mistaken" misrepresentation. The effect of this finding was to make the defendant liable for the overcharge, but not for punitive damages. The industry had argued that because of reliance on the regulatory authorities, the court should make its decision prospective only.

A reasonable compromise on the "gross" versus "net" coverage issue is a system known as "net plus one." If a debtor died two or three weeks after the last payment was due, the creditor would have earned the interest during those two to three weeks, but the credit life insurance policy would not cover it if it was pegged only to the decreasing portion of the principal, under a pure net coverage scheme. In order to factor in this possibility, the premium could be set at the dollar amount that is the original amount financed *and* one scheduled payment. This net plus one coverage strikes a reasonable balance between under insuring and over insuring in the sale of credit life insurance.[8]

Some creditors and credit insurance companies require the debtor to fill out a few very simple health questions when the amount of the loan is very large, such as an amount over $10,000. From

8. Representative of a state statute which provides for "net plus one" coverage is Ala. Code § 5–19–20(b)(2):

(2) This subdivision (2) applies to all consumer credit transactions entered into on or after June 19, 1996. If the consumer credit transaction is schedule to be repaid in substantially equal installments which include a portion of the amount financed, the amount of credit life insurance at any time shall not exceed the greater of the approximate unpaid balance of the debt, excluding unearned finance charges, if any, or the approximate unpaid scheduled balance of the debt, excluding unearned finance charges, if any, plus the amount of one scheduled payment. The amount of credit life insurance on single payment consumer credit transactions and the amount of accident and health insurance and involuntary unemployment insurance shall not exceed the approximate amount of the total of payments. The amount of credit life insurance under an open-end credit plan shall not exceed the approximate unpaid balance of the debt from time to time. The debtor's estate or a named beneficiary shall be entitled to any excess credit life insurance benefit.

time to time there is litigation over denial of coverage when the debtor dies, but the insurance company refuses payment, claiming that the debtor was not truthful in responding to those questions. The outcome is often based on whether the creditor drew attention to the questions and the ramifications of failing to provide accurate responses. Creditors are in a weak position if their employees filled out the responses to the questions, in the rush to sell credit insurance.[9]

4. CREDIT DISABILITY INSURANCE (ACCIDENT & HEALTH)

Credit disability insurance, sometimes called accident and health insurance (A & H) picks up the monthly payments whether debtor is disabled or off work for an extended period due to an accident. Setting the premium based on "gross coverage" (principal plus interest) makes sense here, because the payments that are picked up include interest and principal.

A & H policies typically will have a "waiting period," which is the number of continuous days a person is required to be disabled before the coverage is triggered. Some policies also have a retroactivity provision, so that once the "waiting period"

9. For a discussion of the theories under which a consumer may challenge a post-claim determination of ineligibility for credit life, disability or loss-of-income insurance, *see Credit Insurance: Obtaining Relief for Postclaim Ineligibility Determinations,* Clearinghouse Review, Dec. 1994, at 891.

requirement is met, benefits are payable starting with the first day of the disability.

5. INVOLUNTARY UNEMPLOYMENT INSURANCE

Involuntary unemployment insurance covers the monthly payments under circumstances where the debtor is out of work through no fault of his or her own. Examples include a plant closing, temporary lay-off, or a strike. Specific provisions for coverage under an involuntary unemployment policy must be closely examined to know what falls within the coverage.

Some policies have limits on the duration of coverage, which may result in payments being made for only a portion of the loan's duration. For example, the coverage under involuntary unemployment insurance may be limited to 12 months, but the credit transaction may carry a 24–or 36–month maturity. This limitation on coverage, when coupled with the reality that most consumer finance contracts are for a short duration (reducing the likelihood of claims), explains why the loss-ratios are as low as they are in the credit insurance industry. Involuntary unemployment insurance is a fairly new product when compared to such insurance products as credit life and credit property. Therefore, it is hard to predict what experience consumers will have with this product.

6. CREDIT PROPERTY INSURANCE

a. Overview

Secured creditors are permitted to require that collateral be insured against losses caused by events such as theft, damage, or destruction of the property. For example, a bank that takes a security interest in a car in a secured loan may require the debtor to keep insurance on the car, and in the event the debtor allows the insurance to expire, the creditor may "force place" insurance to cover the creditor's interest. Force placed insurance usually results in the premium for the insurance being added to the loan balance.

As a *concept*, credit property insurance is probably the most valid among credit insurance products because if the debtor and creditor negotiate for a secured transaction, both parties may benefit from insurance on the collateral. The interest rate and other terms made available to the consumer may be more favorable than the terms of the transaction, were the loan to be unsecured. Similarly, the creditor has an obvious benefit in a secured transaction because the collateral has economic value, the existence of the collateral and the threat of repossession may provide needed leverage to encourage the debtor to pay, and the status of the creditor as secured generally provides an advantage should the debtor file for bankruptcy, at least when measured against a totally unsecured claim in bankruptcy. Both parties benefit from insurance on the collateral.

What a creditor has "at risk" in the insured collateral is the outstanding loan balance. The debtor may also have some equity in the car, where the fair market value of the car exceeds the amount of the outstanding debt. When the insurance covers only the creditor's interest, it is commonly referred to as Vendor's Single Interest Insurance (VSI). VSI insurance policies must be examined to understand the scope of the coverage, but the typical policy covers the lesser of the fair market value of the collateral, actual loss on the property, or the outstanding loan balance. Therefore, if the outstanding loan balance is $2,000 and the car was worth $5,000, VSI policy will pay off the debt in the event of a total loss, but the consumer's equity would not be covered. However, if the car is worth only $1,000 and the loan balance is $2,000 (which is not uncommon when older used cars are sold on subprime lots), the insurance would pay the creditor $1,000, but the consumer would still owe the remaining $1,000. When the loan balance reaches and surpasses 100 percent of the value of the car, both the debtor and creditor are at risk.

It is now common to find loan balances on used cars that exceed the fair market value of the car, and sometimes by a large margin. When the used car dealers mark up the sales price of the car to compensate for the discount that must be paid to a subprime assignee (see Chapter Six, pages 155–162, discussing buried finances in the cash price), and pack the transaction with credit insurance and add-ons, the amount financed on the transactions becomes more and more detached from the real value of the car. This risk will also be reflected in a higher interest rate. And as dealers and consumers became more comfortable with loan maturities that stretch out for as long as five or six years, loan balances diminish at a slow pace, while collateral value drops at a steeper rate.

When both the creditor's interest (loan balance) and the debtor's equity are insured, the policy is said to have dual interest coverage. Protecting both the interest of the debtor and the creditor is common in typical automobile insurance (not necessarily credit insurance), where an insurance company provides coverage for the fair market value of the car, as well as liability coverage. The interest of the creditor remains in effect because the creditor's security interest is known to the insurer, and in the event of a loss, the insurance company payment will be viewed as "proceeds" of the insured collateral. Of course, short of a total loss, the damaged car would be repaired and the creditor's security interest would remain in the collateral. Both the debtor and the creditor should be satisfied with this arrangement.

b. Excess Property Insurance Coverage

Credit property insurance is not as heavily regulated as credit life insurance. But just as the "gross coverage" concept can result in excess coverage in credit life insurance, it is not uncommon to find excess credit property insurance that far exceeds the interest of the creditor, where the excess benefit will never be realized by the debtor.

Some states prohibit the sale of credit property insurance on very small credit transactions. For example, the state law may require that the amount financed exceed $300 before credit property insurance may be required. It is also common to find state laws that limit the amount of property insurance to the loan balance, rather than the total of payments. This is the same concept at work that was discussed in the material on gross versus net coverage in credit life insurance.

A particularly egregious case of over-insurance is where the credit property insurance premium is established on the outstanding loan balance, but the insurer's liability is limited to the fair market value of the collateral on the date of the loss. If the collateral is worthless, such as in the case of many used household goods, such a credit insurance policy results in an obvious overcharge.

In cases where totally worthless collateral is identified to allegedly "collateralize" a loan, or where a security interest in household goods is an obvious violation of the FTC Credit Practices Rule restriction on non-purchase money security interests in household goods, discussed previously in this chapter, the invalidity of the credit property insurance is clear. In the one case, the creditor has no real economic risk because the collateral is worthless. In the other, the creditor's security interest is legally invalid. A non-possessory security interest in most household goods cannot be taken, under the prohibitions of the FTC rule, except in the case of a purchase money security interest.

In 1987, the Attorney General of the State of Kansas issued an opinion which sets forth appropriate limits on the sale of property insurance. (Kan. Atty. Gen. Op. No. 87–3, 1987 WL 290401 (Kan. A.G.)). The synopsis of the opinion follows:

A creditor may not contract for or receive a separate charge for insurance unless the credit insurance provides a benefit which covers a loss to property which relates to the credit transaction. Household goods cannot be related to the transaction unless a purchase money credit arrangement is involved. Nor may the creditor be named as a loss payee of a policy which covers all of a consumer's household goods, even though that creditor has a security interest in some of the property covered under the policy. The amount of insurance is limited to the lesser of either the amount of debt or the value of the property insured. If a separate charge is received for credit insurance, before the insurance may be written, the consumer must give an informed, affirmative, written request for the policy. In addition, a creditor may not sell credit insurance to a consumer if he has knowledge that an existing policy gives full coverage of the property related to the transaction, and the credit insurance would therefore be pro-rated.

Were all states to regulate credit property insurance in this way, there would be far fewer cases of abuse and excess coverage.

7.   NON-FILING INSURANCE

Probably the strangest bird in the area of credit insurance is a product called non-filing insurance, sometimes referred to as chattel mortgage non-filing insurance. In a typical secured transaction, governed by Article 9 of the Uniform Commercial Code, the creditor could perfect its security interest by filing a financing statement in the public record. A non-filing insurance product insures the creditor against monetary loss caused by the inability to repossess the collateral because the creditor *elects not to file a financing statement*. An industry publication describes the product as follows:

American Bankers Chattel Mortgage Non–Filing program indemnifies the creditor against direct loss due to:

- Inability to repossess the property, and enforcing its rights under the Chattel Mortgage or lien;

- Inability to attach secured collateral in the event that the debtor has been adjudicated bankrupt, or

- If inability to repossess is caused by the non-filing or non-recording of the lien with the proper authorities.

The advantages of non-filing insurance were described in that same industry publication, as follows:

- This policy is designed to place the creditor in the same position he would have been had he recorded or filed the lien.

- The premium charged may be passed on to the debtor. In most cases, the premium for the Chattel Mortgage Non–Filing program is less than the actual recording or filing fee, which the customer would normally pay.

- The need for a costly, time-consuming filing or recording process is eliminated.

- Charge-offs will be reduced.

- Simple premium reporting and claims procedures.

- Chattel Mortgage Non–Filing is written at the time the indebtedness is incurred, and continues in force for the full term.

Were non-filing insurance to be administered *exactly* as it was advertised and approved by state insurance commissioners, there would be little problem with it. As noted in Chapter Six, at page 155, Truth in Lending permits the cost of non-filing insurance to be excluded from the finance charge in most cases and many state laws allow for non-filing insurance. The problem has come from disclosures in litigation which show that in some cases, the claims made on the policies were not made because the creditor was unable to realize on the collateral due to its failure to file, but rather the premiums were used to build up a default pool that was paid back to the creditor to compensate for bankruptcies, skips and general defaults. In other words, the non-file programs were not being administered as advertised. In such cases, the non-filing premium is invalid as an insurance product, it does not deserve to be treated as another entry in the "amount financed," and should be more properly characterized as a finance charge.

In *Warehouse Home Furnishings v. Whitson*, 709 So.2d 1144 (Ala.1997), the Alabama Supreme Court noted that under § 9–302(d)(1) of the Uniform Commercial Code, a creditor's purchase money security interest in consumer goods is *automatically perfected*. Thus, because the retailer's security interest was automatically perfected, the non-filing insurance premium could not be "in lieu of perfecting any security interest," and should therefore be treated as part of the finance charge, in cases of purchase money transactions. An example of a purchase money transaction is where a retailer sells goods on credit and takes a security interest in the goods purchased.

The court also focused on the way the non-filing insurance program was administered. The losses on which claims would be paid under the policy in *Whitson* included losses due to bankruptcy, skips and destroyed goods. Thus, claims under the policy were not made to cover losses occurring because the retailer could not repossess the item due to the failure to file. Therefore, the non-filing premiums were for the most part building a default pool and were not being used as a means to operate "in lieu of filing a financing statement." Actions of creditors making claims based on bankruptcy, skips and destroyed goods have almost *nothing* to due with a filing concept or the risk of not filing. Therefore, the non-file premium should have been included in the finance charge because the state law tracked the concept under Truth in Lending, for excluding the non-file premium from the finance charge under appropriate circumstances.

Not all challenges to non-filing insurance have been successful. In *Mitchell v. Industrial Credit Corp.*, 898 F.Supp. 1518 (N.D.Ala.1995), the non-filing fees were held to be for proper insurance and thus could be included in the amount financed. But *Mitchell* did not involve purchase money transactions and the Alabama Supreme Court in *Whitson* distinguished *Mitchell* by noting that the court in *Mitchell* did recognize the invalidity of non-filing insurance were the creditor to be perfected by another means.

For creditors, the result in a case such as *Whitson* is particularly dangerous, where a credit insurance product is held to be invalid, and therefore, wrongfully included in the "amount financed" portion of the contract. Where there is an after-the-fact finding that a charge should have been included in the finance charge, the stakes are very high *if the creditor already charged the maximum interest rate allowed under a state usury law*. In such a case, moving the charge over from the amount financed to the finance charge will not only trigger problems under credit insurance laws, but also automatically trigger a violation of the usury laws, previously discussed in Chapter Seven.

8.   FORCE-PLACED INSURANCE

Most automobile installment sales contracts and notes secured by automobiles establish the right of the creditor to purchase property insurance on the car in the event the debtor allows his insurance to lapse. Typically, premiums are added to the loan balance and do not change the monthly payment. Force-placed insurance, even where it insures only the creditor's interest, is often very expensive because it does not take into account the individual characteristics of the driver. And in some cases, force placed insurance covers phantom risks and includes add-on coverage that go well beyond protecting the interests of the creditor.

Many states limit force-placed insurance (also called collateral protection insurance, or CPI), to a VSI arrangement, where only the amount the creditor has at risk can be covered. Many of those same states require that the creditor give written notice that the consumer's policy has lapsed and that VSI will be purchased and added to the account unless the consumer acts quickly to restore his own insurance on the car. Unfortunately, many consumers who have allowed the insurance to expire have done so because they are short of funds. Receiving a notice that insurance will be purchased and added to the loan balance to be taken care of at a later date is almost good news, no matter what the cost. But where those premiums are padded for excess coverage or an amount that exceeds the insurable interest of the creditor, force-placed insurance will come under considerable scrutiny, particularly where a large part of the deficiency after foreclosure is based on CPI policies that were stacked on the loan. Creditors who are smart will give full disclosure to the consumers *out front* that force-placed insurance will be placed on the account if the consumer allows his insurance to lapse. Full disclosure should again be made before the insurance is purchased, allowing the consumer to have sufficient time to arrange for restarting his own insurance. And the disclosures should also provide that the insurance, once placed, can be pulled off the account and unearned premiums recredited to the account in the event the consumer purchases insurance at a later date. And the insurance itself should be bare-bones, avoiding excess coverage and coverage for phantom risks.

9. VOLUNTARINESS

With the exception of credit property insurance on secured collateral, most of the other credit insurance products should be "voluntary." Truth in Lending only allows the exclusion of the credit insurance premiums from the finance charge if they are voluntary, as noted in Chapter Six. There has always been considerable controversy over whether these insurance products are indeed voluntary, even where consumers indicate that their choice to purchase the products was voluntary.

The National Consumer Law Center and the Federal Trade Commission have cited the following factors as critical in determining whether the insurance is indeed voluntary:

- The creditor's penetration rate (i.e., that portion of loans which include insurance).
- The creditor's pecuniary interest in making the sale.
- A practice of including insurance in quoting monthly repayment figures to prospective borrowers.
- The automatic pre-inclusion of premiums in loan documents.
- Placing an "x" by the authorization signature line or otherwise indicating the borrower should sign it.
- Presenting pre-typed loan agreements for signature without disclosing the purpose of the signature.
- Suggesting the loan may be delayed if the borrower does not purchase the insurance.

In some cases, the penetration rate for particular branches of finance companies exceeds 90 percent, in the sale of credit life insurance. That is, 9 out of every 10 contracts includes credit life insurance. A high percentage penetration rate, when linked with deposition testimony and other evidence can provide compelling evidence that credit life insurance is either being pushed through a hard sell, or is being illegally included in the transaction out front, with no meaningful consumer choice. There is no absolute bright line on what conclusions can be drawn from a particular penetration rate, but the higher the rate, the more likely it is that credit insurance is being sold in an improper fashion. In the deposition of an executive from a large finance company, a penetration rate of 75 percent was described as "something that would be a red flag" for further scrutiny of how credit insurance was being sold. What the employee did not know was that in discovery, branch penetration rates of over 90 percent were found to be commonplace.

The creditor's pecuniary interest in selling credit insurance is obvious and was previously discussed in the material on credit insurance packing. Not only are some of the premium dollars shared with the creditor, but the overall loan volume is increased because the credit insurance premiums are financed, with interest charged against the higher loan volume. And when the loans are flipped, the operation of the Rule of 78's in rebating credit insurance premiums works to the advantage of the creditor and the disadvantage of the borrower.

Including the credit insurance premiums in the initial monthly payment figure given to the borrower is a very common practice among consumer finance companies. In consumer finance companies, a lot of business is done over the telephone. Employees are often given what are called telephone "routes" each day that they "run," contacting existing customers, potential new customers, and making collection calls to borrowers who are behind in their payments. Training videos, training manuals and deposition testimony reveal that employees often include the whole array of credit insurance products in the original quote over the telephone, without indicating their inclusion to the borrower. As noted previously, employees in one of the largest finance companies in the country used the expression "full meal deal" when a customer bought all of the credit insurance products. If the customer does not flinch at the monthly payment and comes into the office to pick up the check, the completed loan documents are waiting, with the credit insurance premiums in tow. The check is cut reflecting a transaction with all the credit insurance products in place. If the consumer reads the documents and for the first time objects to the "voluntary" credit insurance products, he may be told that "all the paperwork needs to be redone," so he should come back later or wait an hour, so the deal can be restructured. Employees have testified that they tried to make reworking the deal as inconvenient as possible to break down the consumer's resistance to the credit insurance. And as noted previously, some employees were instructed to be told "no" at least three times (get three turn-downs on credit insurance) before they completed the paperwork without credit insurance products. Employees also use such terms as "payment protection plan" instead of credit insurance, because many people do not like pitches for the sale of insurance. And quoting the cost of credit insurance as "cents per day" is a common strategy, rather than draw attention to the total bloated premium for an overpriced product.

Finally, a common strategy is to complete the paperwork before the customer arrives (including the credit insurance premiums), and to place an "x" next to the TILA disclosure box where the consumer indicates that he wants the insurance. The paperwork is then presented with an "x" placed in various places, one of which will be the "yes" box on credit insurance. This is particularly effective if there has been no previous discussion of credit insurance products and the consumer is either rushed through the execution of the documents, or has difficulty reading.

In March of 1998 the United States Senate Special Committee on Aging held hearings on subprime lenders, flipping of consumer loans and packing of credit insurance products. A former branch manager testified as follows regarding the sale of credit insurance products:

Insurance Packing—How is it done?

Packing is taking insurance products (as many as you can), putting them on the loan and then trying to cover them up or gloss over them. Packing is shoving as much insurance onto the customer as possible without the customer's knowledge or without the customer's understanding.

We attempted to pack insurance during our
first pitch to a new customer. For example, we
were trained to tell a new retail installment customer that we had reviewed the customer's financial situation and could offer the customer a debt
consolidation loan that would save the customer
money by reducing the customer's monthly payments to creditors. The sales pitch would be substantially similar to the following: "Mr. Smith, in
reviewing your loan application, I see that you
have a lot of credit card payments. What if I could
save you $550 a month through consolidating
your debt into one loan?" I was taught that the
most effective way to sell insurance was to always
include insurance products in this quote without
telling the customer that my monthly quote included insurance. I was taught that I should
always include as many insurance products as
possible in the monthly payment quote so long as
I could quote a figure that would be less than the
customer's current outstanding debt obligation.
Using that method, if the customer did not express interest in my initial quote, I could eliminate one insurance product (without telling the
customer that I was doing this) and give a quote
for an even larger monthly savings. For example,
if the customer rejected my pitch to save him
$550 a month, I would eliminate one insurance
product and respond "Suppose I could save you
$600 per month?" Usually, the more naive the
customer, the more insurance I would pack on
the loan before I made the initial monthly pay-

ment quote. This tactic was very effective with immigrants and non-English speaking people. Don't be fooled by training manuals. The manuals are written for regulators, but finance company employees are trained to ignore the manuals if they expect to make their profit quotas and keep their jobs. For example, even though my training manuals discussed quoting a monthly payment both with, and without insurance, I was trained by my supervisors that unless my conversation was being audited, I should ignore the manuals, and *always* quote the monthly payment on a proposed loan *with* insurance unless the customer specifically asked what the cost would be *without* insurance. The tactic we used at all of the finance companies I worked for was "If they [customers] don't ask, don't tell." I heard this phrase often from many of my managers and supervisors.

The "don't ask, don't tell" policy was successful because customers were not aware, until closing (if at all), that the loan included insurance. Once the customer indicated that we could schedule a closing regarding the loan proposed in the telephone solicitation, we merely presented the loan documents with insurance included, even though insurance had not been discussed previously. Through their training and experience, finance company employees know that customers are often desperate for the money, and usually will not object to the insurance once the loan reaches closing. If customers object to the insurance at closing, we would add more pressure by telling them that if they wanted the loan without insurance, it would be necessary to re-do their loan documents and the closing would need to be rescheduled for a later date. That was a half-truth. We could re-do loan documents in a few minutes. It wasn't really necessary to reschedule the closing for a later date, but we knew that customers would be more likely to cave-in and accept the insurance if they thought that they couldn't get the money that day. In my experience, this was usually enough to persuade the customers to go through with the closing and take the insurance.

When insurance was to be included with the loan, our computer programs automatically calculated the maximum amount of insurance as provided by state law. The amount of insurance coverage on the loan was never arrived at through negotiation with a consumer.

Why did we pack insurance?

Insurance sales are very important to finance companies. My supervisors often used phrases like, "Insurance drives profits." One of my supervisors said that insurance was more important to our company's profitability than its spread on interest rates.

Because insurance sales are so important to the bottom line, finance companies require that their employees meet goals and quotas regarding insurance. Insurance sales are tracked by dollar volume, penetration rates and premium-to-volume ratios. For example, one of my employers required that its branches maintain an 80% penetration rate for credit life (that is, employees were expected to sell credit life insurance in at least 8 out of every 10 loans). My employers always made it clear that I would not keep my job unless I fulfilled my insurance sales quota.

Finance companies also provided additional rewards for employees who meet or exceed their insurance sales quotas. All of my finance company employers had a quarterly bonus system. Part of my bonus depended on whether my branch met its insurance sales quotas. All of my finance company employers also ran quarterly insurance sales contests. We would be eligible for contests awards if we exceeded quotas regarding insurance penetration and insurance sales volume.

Conclusion

I am glad that I no longer work for a finance company. If they want to keep their jobs, finance company employees must flip and pack loans. They are under enormous pressure to meet quotas regarding loan volume, repeat business and insurance sales. In fact, the pressure to produce loan volume and insurance sales is so great that on many occasions, I've seen finance company employees commit forgery on a massive scale. These employees have forged everything from insurance forms, RESPA documents, income verification forms, and even entire loan files. These practices have always disturbed me, and I hope

that something can be done to make finance
company customers more aware of these practices
so that they can keep from becoming victims of
flipping and packing scams.

D. UCC LIMITATIONS ON INTERESTS IN AFTER–ACQUIRED CONSUMER GOODS

The Federal Trade Commission Credit Practices
Rule, discussed in Part A of this chapter, limits the
ability of creditors to take a nonpurchase money
security interest in certain household goods. Consumers also receive some limited protection by certain provisions in Article 9 of the Uniform Commercial Code.

Every credit seller and every credit lender is
interested in being paid. Accordingly, every credit
seller and every credit lender is interested in any
legal device that will increase the possibility of
repayment. Security increases the possibility of repayment. Every credit seller and every credit lender
is interested in minimizing collection costs. Security
minimizes collection costs. Accordingly, creditors
are interested in obtaining security. The more the
better. For example, a seller who sells appliances
may well figure that the value of the appliance may
decline faster than the balance due, and so want
more security.

Today, in most states, the only state statute affecting security interests in household goods or other personal property is Article 9 of the Uniform

Commercial Code, and the Code generally expands rather than limits the property available to creditors' security interests.

Article 9 of the Uniform Commercial Code has often been referred to as a "floating lien" statute. The phrase "floating lien" nowhere appears in any provision of the Code. The Official Comments to section 9–204 use the terms "continuing general lien" and "floating charge" without defining either term. A floating lien (or "continuing general lien" or "floating charge") is a lien that "floats" as to the property subject to the lien (collateral) or the debt secured.

The collateral covered may include all of the personal property which the debtor from time to time owns, or all of a certain class or classes of that property, including assets not owned at the time the lien is created if the security agreement contains an after-acquired property clause.

There is an express limitation on the scope of security interest in after-acquired consumer goods. Under Section 9–204(2) of the Uniform Commercial Code, after-acquired consumer goods are covered by a security interest only if the parties so agree *and* the secured party has given value within ten days. To illustrate, (1) On January 2, D borrows $2,000 from S giving S a security interest in all of D's furniture now owned or thereafter acquired. On January 20, D buys a new china cabinet from X. S's security interest will not reach this china cabinet and (2) Same facts as No.1 except that on January

15, S loaned D an additional $100. S's security interest will now reach the china cabinet.

The debt secured may vary. A security agreement may provide that the collateral there described secures not only the present extension of credit but also all future credit transactions between the debtor and the secured party.

The classic unconscionability case, *Williams v. Walker–Thomas Furniture Co.*, 350 F.2d 445 (D.C.Cir.1965) illustrates maximum creditor use (abuse?) of unrestricted availability of consumer property as security. The consumer had purchased some 16 items totaling $1,500 from the same dealer in a five-year period. Under the contracts there involved, the seller retained a security interest in all items purchased until every item was paid in full; moreover, payments were allocated pro rata to the various items purchased so no item was paid for until all items were paid for. As a result of these contract provisions, when the consumer defaulted on the last item purchased, the seller repossessed all of the items purchased. The court remanded for a determination of whether the contract was unconscionable.

E. YIELD SPREAD PREMIUM FINANCING ARRANGEMENTS

A yield spread premium is generated when a "loan" is written by a broker (or car dealer Finance and Insurance [F and I] office) at a higher interest rate than the assignee requires. The broker (or car dealer) retains all or a portion of the differences as an "origination fee" or as compensation for handling the transaction before the paper is assigned to the mortgage lender, bank or finance company. The yield spread premium is often calculated by taking the present value of the rate spread, and is either paid directly by the assignee back to the originator, or entered in a "reserve," out which payments are periodically paid to the loan originator or car dealer. In the event there is a recourse arrangement between the loan originator (dealer) and assignee, the reserve may be tapped by the assignee in cases where the consumer loans do not pay out.

The original cases involving undisclosed yield spread premiums occurred in mortgage loans, where mortgage brokers received some of their compensation through sharing a part of the interest rate on the loans. But it was not long after the several prominent cases involving mortgage loans that lawsuits were filed against car dealers and assignees of the installment sales contracts. The essence of the claims was that the dealer and assignee owed to the consumer a duty to disclose the yield spread premium component of the deal.

As a *stand alone theory*, the "undisclosed yield spread theory" is clearly without merit. There may be individual cases where representations made by the F and I officer were fraudulent, but absent those facts there should be no liability attached to yield spread financing.

As lawyers, we often get lost in arguments involving fine points of law, immersed in statutes, cases, regulations and procedural concepts. With yield spread premium financing, it is also helpful to step back and frame the argument simply. No law requires that an automobile dealer disclose to the buyer the wholesale price of a car that is for sale at a retail price on the lot. Further, no law requires that a car dealer disclose to a buyer how the dealer's "spread" (difference between wholesale and retail) will be dispersed. Similarly, absent some requirement mandated by state or federal law, no *lender or merchant* should be required to disclose how the profit on a loan (interest) is to be shared., if the retail rate is fully disclosed to the consumer. In automobile financing, the retail rate for the cost of money is disclosed to the borrower through the TILA-mandated APR disclosure, leaving the borrower to shop for rates. In yield spread premium financing, the car dealer quotes the "retail" cost of credit, the assignee's buy rates is the equivalent of the wholesale cost in the dealer-assignee arrangement, and the borrower is free to shop for lower retail rates, which are widely quoted and circulated. There aren't many secrets in automobile financing and the competition is fierce. No one is compelled to finance through the auto dealer.

Some plaintiffs have argued that if the yield spread arrangement were disclosed, the borrower would go directly to the lender-assignee to negotiate a car loan at the "wholesale" buy rate. However, F and I offices will often match other bank rates quoted by customers and it remains to be seen whether the "buy rates" used in yield spread financing are actually available to consumers. Assignees are willing to live with a lower yield if another entity is handling the paperwork, credit approval and closing. Transaction costs are not avoided by the bank or finance company if a customer deals directly with the financial institution, and thus the buy rate quoted to dealers may not be available to a consumer who "shops direct."

Representative of yield spread litigation in automobile financing is *Ex parte Ford Motor Credit Co.*, 717 So.2d 781 Ala. (1997). The buyer purchased a vehicle from the dealer and obtained financing through Ford Motor Credit. The dealer and Ford Credit had a dealer agreement providing for the purchase of retail installment contracts and the payment of a yield spread premium in connection with the transaction. After the plaintiff selected the vehicle, the dealer advised him that the dealer would obtain the best financing available. Financing was arranged through Ford Motor Credit and the buyer was advised of the rate, but the dealer did not disclose its agreement with Ford Credit for the payment of a yield spread premium of 3% on the purchase of the retail installment contract. When the buyer asked why the cost of financing was so high, the dealer told him that the high cost had been caused by the plaintiff's poor credit history, which included a personal bankruptcy.

With respect to the fraudulent suppression claim, the buyer argued that the dealer and Ford Credit had a duty to disclose the existence of the yield spread premium. The buyer claimed he was forced to pay a higher rate of interest than he otherwise would have been required to pay if the agreement for the payment of the yield spread premium had not existed. He argued that the existence of the yield spread premium was a material fact that the dealer and Ford Credit were obligated to disclose and that if he had known about the agreement to pay the yield spread premium, he would have sought financing from another source.

The defendants argued that there is no statutory duty to disclose the existence of the yield spread premium under Alabama law or under TILA. The defendants also argued that there is no common law duty to disclose because, in the absence of a special confidential relationship, a creditor-debtor relationship does not create a duty to disclose a fact such as the existence of the yield spread premium. Ford Credit also argued that it would not be liable for actions of the dealer as there was no agency relationship between the dealer and Ford Credit.

The Alabama Supreme Court recognized that neither the Alabama Mini–Code nor TILA requires the disclosure of a yield spread premium. Moreover, the court held that no common law duty to disclose the yield spread premium arose because, in the absence of a special confidential relationship, the general creditor-debtor relationship does not impose a fiduciary duty requiring such disclosure. The court held that the plaintiff's inquiry of the dealer as to why the interest rate was so high did not impose a duty to disclose the existence of the yield spread premium. The court reasoned that the plaintiff's question was not specific enough to impose such a duty, that the dealer's answer was generally truthful and that the plaintiff's credit history did impact the available rate of interest. The court also noted that there is no common law duty of a seller to disclose the details of its pricing strategy, including the amount of profit to be earned on a sale.

With respect to the fraudulent misrepresentation claim, the buyer argued that the dealer and Ford Credit fraudulently misrepresented that the contract rate of interest was the "best" financing available and that a genuine issue of material fact existed that should have been determined by the jury. The dealer and Ford Credit argued that the plaintiff's reliance on the dealer's statement regarding the interest rate was not justifiable because the plaintiff was experienced in purchasing, selling and financing vehicles, had been offered a lower rate a month earlier and knew he could shop around for alternative financing. The Alabama Supreme Court held that the summary judgment in favor of the defendant should not have been reversed because the deposition testimony of the plaintiff did not support a claim that he requested the dealer to survey available financing and to obtain the best possible rate. The court also concluded that reliance by the plaintiff on the alleged statement by the dealer would not have been justifiable. The buyer could not close his eyes in order to rely on the dealer's representation given his experience in buying, selling and financing vehicles and the recent offer of financing on another vehicle at a lower rate of interest.

The most notable part about the decision is the holding that absent special facts, there is no duty to disclose a yield spread premium arrangement. This makes sense. The "retail" rate is what must be disclosed by TILA and what determines the monthly payments. There is no duty to disclose how the rates will be shared.

F. ADDITIONAL COMPLAINTS RE-GARDING "UP-CHARGES" AND ITEMIZATION OF THE AMOUNT FI-NANCED

Consumer complaints against credit insurance sales and yield spread premium financing arrangements share the notion that the charges are padded because the dealer is retaining a part of the charge without full disclosure to the buyer. One of the beliefs of consumer advocates is that this leads to "reverse competition" in the case of credit insurance, and padded rates in the case of yield spread premium financing. In automobile financing, there are other charges in which dealers retain a portion of the retail sales price quoted to the consumer. An example of such a charge is the premium for an extended service contract, which are often sold on used cars and appliances. Extended service contracts (ESC's) typically operate separate from any warranty on the item and provide reimbursement for certain repairs that must be made on the car. Extended service contracts are also sold on appliances, and are even offered on very inexpensive items, such as a $15 remote telephone.

The sale of ESC's is typically very profitable for retail dealers. In some cases the mark-up is 100 percent of the actual cost of the ESC, which is paid to a third party that administers the ESC program. In the case of automobiles, the consumer who buys the ESC is not required to take the car to the original seller for repairs. The car can be taken anywhere, the consumer pays the bill, then submits a claim to the ESC company for reimbursement.

Often the charge for an ESC is disclosed on an installment sales contract as an "amount paid to others" in the itemization of the "Amount Financed" under Truth in Lending (TILA), discussed previously in Chapter Six. The failure of the dealer to disclose their mark-up and the fact that not all of the premium is being "paid to others" has been the focus of recent litigation, with claims alleging fraud, violation of TILA, and violation of state UDAP laws.

In 1996 the Official Staff Commentary to Regulation Z was amended. The relevant part of Official Staff Commentary § 226.18(c)(1)(iii)–2 is as follows:

> Given the flexibility permitted in meeting the requirements of the amount financed itemization ..., the creditor in such cases *may* reflect that the creditor has retained a portion of the amount paid to others. For example, the creditor could add to the category "amount paid to others"

language such as (we may be retaining a portion of this amount.) [Emphasis added]

Some cases held that the language *may* made the disclosure optional. However, the majority of recent cases has held that creditor must disclose the fact that they are retaining a portion of the price of these add-ons, though the specific amount does not need to be disclosed.

The most prominent recent case is out of the Seventh Circuit Court of Appeals. In *Gibson v. Bob Watson Chevrolet–GEO, Inc.*, 112 F.3d 283 (7th Cir.1997), the court remanded the case to allow the consumers the opportunity to prove that the dealers charged their credit customers more of an up-charge on service agreements than they charge cash customers. But included in the opinion was the notion that the "may" in the Official Staff Commentary means "shall," and that dealers should disclose that they are retaining a portion of the fee for the ESC. This is a middle-ground position, because consumers are alerted to the fact that there is an up-charge in the ESC, but dealers are not required to disclose the amount in actual dollars and cents. In response to the litigation over yield spread premium, itemization of the amount financed and the sale of installment sales contracts at a discount, many dealer forms have blanket disclosures (although they are by no means uniform), describing the concept of up-charges, sharing of portions of the interest rate between the dealer and assignee, and the possibility that the installment sales contract may be sold to an assignee at less than par value.

G. UNCONSCIONABILITY

Section 2–302 of the Uniform Commercial Code provides;

(1) If the court as a matter of law finds the contract or any clause of the contract to have been unconscionable at the time it was made the court may refuse to enforce the contract, or it may enforce the remainder of the contract without the unconscionable clause, or it may so limit the application of any unconscionable clause as to avoid any unconscionable result.

(2) When it is claimed or appears to the court that the contract or any clause thereof may be unconscionable the parties shall be afforded a reasonable opportunity to present evidence as to its commercial setting, purpose and effect to aid the court in making the determination.

Comment 1 contains the following language:

This section is intended to make it possible for the courts to police explicitly against the contracts or clauses which they find to be unconscionable. In the past such policing has been accomplished by adverse construction of language, by manipulation of the rules of offer and acceptance or by determinations that the clause is contrary to public policy or to the dominant purpose of the contract. This section is intended to allow the court to pass directly on the unconscionability of the contract or particular clause therein and to make a conclusion of law as to its unconscionability. The basic test is whether, in the light of the general commercial background and the commercial needs of the particular trade or case, the clauses involved are so one-sided as to be unconscionable under the circumstances existing at the time of the making of the contract. Subsection (2) makes it clear that it is proper for the court to hear evidence upon these questions. The principal is one of the prevention of oppression and unfair surprise * * * and not of disturbance of allocation of risks because of superior bargaining power.

Unconscionability is not defined in the Code, nor do the views expressed in the official comment provide a precise definition. *Zapatha v. Dairy Mart, Inc.*, 408 N.E.2d 1370 (Mass.1980). Unconscionability is found when there is an absence of meaningful choice on the part of one of the parties, together with contract terms which are unreasonably favorable to the other party. "Whether a meaningful choice is present in a particular case can only be determined by consideration of all the circumstances surrounding the transaction." *Williams v. Walker–Thomas Furniture Co.*, 350 F.2d 445 (D.C.Cir.1965).

Court frequently distinguish between "procedural" unconscionability (some kind of overreaching that constitutes an abuse in the process of bargaining) and "substantive" unconscionability (some objectionable or oppressive clause).

Judge Posner discussed the issue of a lack of meaningful choice in the following passage:

There can be no objection to using the one-sidedness of a transaction as evidence of deception, lack of agreement, or compulsion, none of which is shown here. The problem with unconscionability as a legal doctrine comes in making sense out of lack of "meaningful choice" in a situation where the promisor was not deceived or compelled and really did agree to the provision that he contends was unconscionable. Suppose that for reasons unrelated to any conduct of the promisee the promisor has very restricted opportunities. Maybe he is so poor that he can be induced to sell the clothes off his back for a pittance, or is such a poor credit risk that he can be made (in the absence of usury laws) to pay an extraordinarily high interest rate to borrow money that he wants desperately. Does he have a "meaningful choice" in such circumstances? If not he may actually be made worse off by a rule of nonenforcement of hard bargains; for, knowing that a contract with him will not be enforced, merchants may be unwilling to buy his clothes or lend him money. Since the law of contracts cannot compel the making of contracts on terms favorable to one party, but can only refuse to enforce contracts with unfavorable terms, it is not an institution well designed to rectify inequalities in wealth.

Amoco Oil Company v. Ashcraft, 791 F.2d 519, 522 (7th Cir. 1986).

The focus of the unconscionability test is the situation as it existed at the time of the contract. Unlike the concept of "good faith," which is used to scrutinize the conduct of the parties at the time of contracting and throughout the course of the contractual relationship, the unconscionability test is applied only at the time of the dealmaking. The issue of unconscionability is one of law for the court. If there is a finding of unconscionability, the court may refuse to enforce the contract, enforce the remainder without the unconscionable clause, or limit the application of the unconscionable provision so as to avoid an unconscionable result. Parties generally plead unconscionability as an affirmative defense. There is no right to recover damages *solely* on an unconscionability theory, but there may be other theories such as fraud or breach of an implied covenant of good faith and fair dealing that may allow for recovery.

CHAPTER NINE

POST-TRANSACTION PROBLEMS

A. THE HOLDER IN DUE COURSE DOCTRINE

1. INTRODUCTION

As was discussed in Chapter Four, retailers often arrange for financing which furthers the sale of consumer goods. Although some retailers keep their installment sales contracts and collect the monthly payments, most retailers sell the product but assign (sell) the installment sales contract to a finance company or bank. In some cases, the consumer may have trouble with the product or have a claim against the seller, but faces an assignee—finance company that just wants to be paid and kept out of any dispute between the consumer and the retailer.

Prior to the development of the FTC Rule, discussed in the following section, consumers would often find themselves obligated to pay the holder of the note even though they might have a valid defense against the original seller. The purpose underlying the holder in due course (HDC) doctrine was first stated in the eighteenth century and was usually described as needed to promote "the growth of commerce by assuring liquidity of commercial paper."[1] That is, individuals are normally willing to finance and purchase paper only if payment is reasonably certain, or at least not subject to common disputes which occasionally arise between the buyer and seller of the goods.

The principles of the HDC doctrine were incorporated in the Uniform Commercial Code (UCC), which is now the statutory source of the doctrine. Through the application of several sections of the UCC, an assignment (usually a sale) of a note to a holder in due course[2] separates the buyer's obligation to pay from the seller's obligation to perform.

The path through the UCC starts with the requirement that before holder in due course status will be conferred, the instrument must be taken for

1. *See* Thomas J. Grendell, *Let the Holder Beware! A Problematic Analysis of the FTC Holder in Due Course Rule*, 27 Case W. Res. L. Rev. 977, 979 (1977) (containing an excellent historical analysis of the holder in due course doctrine and the development of the FTC Rule).

2. UCC § 3–302 provides:

(1) A holder in due course is a holder who takes the instrument:

(a) For value: and

(b) In good faith: and

(c) Without notice that it is overdue or has been dishonored or of any defense against or claim to it on the part of any person.

"value,"[3] "in good faith,"[4] and "[w]ithout notice that it is overdue or has been dishonored or of any defense against or claim to it."[5] Once holder in due course status is established, the holder of the instrument is shielded from an attempt by the maker to assert the so called "personal defenses," but would be subject to the few "real defenses," such as infancy, duress, illegality and minority.[6] However, consumers are only rarely in a position to assert the real defenses. Because holder in due course status

3. UCC § 3–303 provides:

A holder takes the instrument for value:

(a) To the extent that the agreed consideration has been performed or that he acquires a security interest in or a lien on the instrument otherwise than by legal process; or

(b) When he takes the instrument in payment of or as security for an antecedent claim against any person whether or not the claim is due; or

(c) When he gives a negotiable instrument for it or makes an irrevocable commitment to a third person.

4. UCC § 1–201(19) (provides: " 'Good faith' means honesty in fact in the conduct or transaction concerned)."

5. UCC § 3–302(1)(c). UCC § 1–201(25) defines notice:

A person has "notice" of a fact when:

(a) He has actual knowledge of it; or

(b) He has received a notice or notification of it; or

(c) From all the facts and circumstances known to him at the time in question he has reason to know that it exists.

A person "knows" or has "knowledge" of a fact when he has actual knowledge of it. "Discover" or "learn" or a word or phrase of similar import refers to knowledge rather than to reason to know. The time and circumstances under which a notice or notification may cease to be effective are not determined by this title. *Id.*

6. *See generally* Donald W. Garner & Darrell W. Dunham, *FTC Rule 433 and the Uniform Commercial Code: An Analysis of Current Lender Status*, 42 Mo. L. Rev. 199 (1978) (noting that in only the most extreme and statistically irrelevant cases will the consumer have a defense against the lender).

shields the holder from defenses most commonly
raised by consumers who were sold defective goods
or services, the status of a holder in due course has
sometimes been described as that of a superplaintiff.[7]

Dissatisfaction with the harsh operation of the
holder in due course doctrine in consumer transactions caused some courts to conclude that the buyer-transferee of the paper was too closely connected
to the seller-transferor to be protected by HDC
status.[8] The "closely connected" doctrine is also
sometimes described as the "party-to-the-transac-
tion rule," where holder in due course status will be
denied if the lender is viewed as so closely involved
in the underlying sale that it cannot claim the
innocence of a holder in due course.[9]

7. *See* James J. White & Robert S. Summers, Uniform Commercial Code 613 (3d ed. 1988). White and Summers describe
holder in due course status as follows:

Among such defenses are failure of consideration, the failure of
a condition, fraud and so on. In this branch of the law, the
legal effectiveness of such defenses varies depending on who
the plaintiff is, and the party able to attain the status of holder
in due course under both state and federal law qualifies as
Superplaintiff. With some exceptions, the holder in due course
is immune to defenses that prior parties to commercial paper
might assert. The holder in due course also enjoys certain
pleading and proof advantages.

Id.

8. Most commentators cite Unico v. Owen, 232 A.2d 405
(N.J.1967), as the landmark decision in what is now called the
"closely connected" doctrine.

9. *See* Jones v. Approved Bancredit Corp., 256 A.2d 739, 742
(Del.1969).

To justify denying holder in due course status to a buyer-transferee who controls or participates in the underlying contract, the courts often conclude that "the plaintiff was not in *good faith*, that the plaintiff had *notice* of underlying defenses, or that the plaintiff is the same entity as the seller-transferor and can stand in no better situation."[10] The courts have used a number of tests to assess whether the buyer-transferee of the paper will be denied holder in due course status.[11] Some of the inquiries made in deciding whether the lender is too closely connected to be granted holder in due course status include:

1. Is the buyer-transferee the alter ego of the seller-transferor? do they have the same officers, same personnel, [or] same location?

2. Who drafted the original promissory note?

3. Is the buyer-transferee mentioned in the note?

4. Does the seller-transferor sell paper to other buyers, or is the buyer-transferee the only market?

5. Did the buyer-transferee get involved in the transaction by which the note was created? did it, for instance, conduct a credit investigation of the maker?

6. Did the buyer-transferee have some knowledge of the seller-transferor's poor past per-

10. Douglas J. Whaley, Problems and Materials on Payment Law 62 (3d ed. 1992).

11. *Id.*

formance of similar contracts?[12]

Even before the development of the FTC Rule, discussed in the next section of this chapter, the courts used elements of the "closely connected" doctrine to deny holder in due course status to some lenders who were transferees of paper from home improvement contractors. For example, in *United States Finance Co. v. Jones*, 229 So.2d 495 (Ala. 1969), where the homeowner received tar paper sprayed with paint instead of aluminum siding, the Alabama Supreme Court upheld the trial court's denial of holder in due course status, citing the steep discount in the purchase price of the note and the fact that the mortgage and certificate of completion of the work were signed on the same date. The court focused on the "good faith" element of the holder in due course test, but noted that the number of transactions between the contractor and lender, along with the knowledge the lender had of the contractor's business, made it difficult to view the lender as an innocent purchaser for value without notice.

In addition to the use of the "closely connected" doctrine to limit the operation of the holder in due course rule, a number of states, both by statute and judicial decision, have limited the operation of the holder in due course doctrine where the maker of the note was a consumer. For example, in Alabama, a section of the Alabama Consumer Credit Act (the Mini–Code), which was adopted in 1971, makes an assignee subject to all claims and defenses of the

12. *Id.* at 61–62.

buyer arising out of a consumer credit sale or consumer lease.[13] However, the failure of all of the states to protect consumers, the ineffectual nature of some of the statutes, and the creative strategies used by some lenders to circumvent state regulation caused the Federal Trade Commission to respond.

2. THE LOSS OF HOLDER IN DUE COURSE STATUS IN CERTAIN CONSUMER LENDING

In 1975, the Federal Trade Commission promulgated its Trade Regulation Rule Concerning Preservation of Consumers' Claims and Defenses (FTC Rule). The FTC Rule, which became effective on May 14, 1976, requires that most consumer credit contracts contain the following provision:

NOTICE

ANY HOLDER OF THIS CONSUMER CREDIT CONTRACT IS SUBJECT TO ALL CLAIMS AND DEFENSES WHICH THE DEBTOR COULD ASSERT AGAINST THE SELLER OF

13. Ala. Code § 5–19–8 (1975) provides:

With respect to a consumer credit sale or consumer lease, an assignee of the rights of the seller or lessor is subject to all claims and defenses of the buyer or lessee against the seller or lessor arising out of the sale or lease, notwithstanding an agreement to the contrary, but the assignee's liability under this section may not exceed the amount owing to the assignee at the time the claim or defense is asserted against the assignee. Rights of the buyer or lessee under this section can only be asserted as a matter of defense to or set-off against a claim by the assignee. (Acts 1971, No. 2052, p. 3290, § 5.).

GOODS OR SERVICES OBTAINED PURSUANT HERETO OR WITH THE PROCEEDS HEREOF. RECOVERY HEREUNDER BY THE DEBTOR SHALL NOT EXCEED AMOUNTS PAID BY THE DEBTOR HEREUNDER.

The FTC spent more than five years on the development of the FTC Rule, holding three sets of hearings and accumulating approximately 10,000 pages of transcripts during that time.[14] The FTC Rule raised considerable controversy when it was promulgated.

After an extensive review of selling and lending practices in many sectors of the economy, including major appliances, home improvements, and the sale of aluminum siding, the FTC concluded that unethical merchants and lenders were victimizing consumers.[15] The operation of the holder in due course doctrine was viewed as inappropriate and outdated in consumer settings.

The statement of the Hon. John M. Murphy at the Hearings describes the operation of the holder in due course doctrine in consumer settings:

> The doctrine originally arose out of court suits involving commercial transactions between mer-

---

14. *Consumer Claims and Defenses: Hearings Before the Subcomm. On Consumer Protection and Finance of the House Comm. on Interstate and Foreign Commerce*, 94th Cong., 2nd Sess. 131 (1976) [hereinafter *Hearings*].

15. *See* Michael F. Sturley, *The Legal Impact of the Federal Trade Commission's Holder in Due Course Notice on a Negotiable Instrument: How Clever Are the Rascals at the FTC?*, 68 N.C. L. Rev. 953, 955 (1990).

chants with approximately equal bargaining power. If one merchant bought from another, paid for the article on an installment basis, and the seller of the article sold the debt obligation to a bank, the courts generally held that the buyer could not stop payment to the bank if the merchandise failed to perform as expected. The buyer could sue the seller, or could refuse to deal further with him. As between two innocent parties, the buyer and the bank—the rule did not apply if the bank had knowledge that the merchandise was faulty, the buyer was considered to be in a stronger position to deal with the seller and to solve his problem, or to cease dealing with him.

As applied to consumer transactions, however, the theory of equal bargaining power does not apply, and the consumer suffers. The consumer buys, for instance, a television set from a seller. He signs an installment contract, which the seller discounts to a finance company. The television set fails to function properly two weeks after purchase. The consumer cannot stop payment to the finance company, who is a holder in due course. The consumer is legally obligated to continue paying the creditor despite any breach of warranty, misrepresentation or even fraud by the seller. And a lawsuit against the seller is generally out of the question because of the expense and time required. Finally, because the consumer buys television sets very seldom, he cannot realistically threaten to stop doing business with the seller. He just has no leverage.

The FTC Rule was adopted specifically to prevent the seller from making the consumer's obligation to pay independent of the seller's obligation to perform the contract and comply with consumer protection laws. Private actions by the consumer against the seller of goods were often fruitless because the retailers were frequently on the move and judgment proof.[16] Further, many consumer claims were so small that attorneys would not take their cases. Consumers were thus viewed as lacking the economic muscle to enforce their rights against sellers.[17]

The FTC supported the Rule with the explanation that if the seller was out of business or sold defective merchandise, then, as between the consumer and the assignee-lender, the latter was in the best position to protect itself against dealer misconduct. Lenders had better access to information regarding the dealer and could resort to reserve or recourse agreements with the dealer in the event the consumer raised a legitimate defense. In crafting the dealer agreement, the lender could require the dealer to buy back the note if the consumer raised a defense to payment. Because the lender could transfer back to the dealer the costs of any "misconduct" that had occurred, the FTC described the Rule as one which would "internalize" the costs of the

16. Michael T. Lewis & Gregg L. Spyridon, *Preservation of Consumer Claims and Defenses: Miller's Tale Tolled By FTC (Or is it?)*, 47 Miss. L.J. 768, 781 (1976).

17. Comment, *Implied Consumer Remedy Under FTC Trade Regulation Rule—Coup De Grace Dealt Holder In Due Course?*, 125 U. Pa. L. Rev. 876, 890 (1977).

failed performance of the seller, removing that cost from the consumer.

The following passage from the Statement of Basis and Purpose helps to understand the Rule:

This rule approaches these problems by reallocating the costs of seller misconduct in the consumer market. It would, we believe, reduce these costs to the minimum level obtainable in an imperfect system and internalize those that remain. As a practical matter, the creditor is always in a better position than the buyer to return seller misconduct costs to sellers, the guilty party. This is the reallocation desired, a return of costs to the party who generates them. The creditor financing the transaction is in a better position to do this than the consumer, because (1) he engages in many transactions where consumers deal infrequently; (2) he has access to a variety of information systems which are unavailable to consumers; (3) he has recourse to contractual devices which render the routine return of seller misconduct costs to sellers relatively cheap and automatic; and (4) the creditor possesses the means to initiate a lawsuit and prosecute it to judgment where recourse to the legal system is necessary.

We believe that a rule which compels creditors to either absorb seller misconduct costs or return them to sellers, by denying sellers access to cutoff devices, will discourage many of the predatory practices and schemes discussed above in Chapter II. Creditors will simply not accept the risks generated by the truly unscrupulous merchant. The market will be policed in this fashion and all parties will benefit accordingly. Where applicable economics militate against a creditor effort to return misconduct costs to a particular seller, due to the limited or irregular nature of such costs, the rule would require the creditor to absorb such costs himself. That is, where a consumer claim or defense is valid, but limited in amount, a creditor may choose to accept less payment from the consumer to save transaction costs associated with pursuing the seller whose conduct gave rise to the claim. The creditor may also look to a "reserve" or "recourse" arrangement or account with the seller for reimbursement. In such cases, the price of financing will more accurately reflect the actual costs of sales finance.

Many in the lending community strongly opposed the FTC Rule. Members of the House and Senate received hundreds of letters from lenders, most of which were characterized as being in the Chicken–Little-the-sky-is-falling category.[18] Representative of the letters received was one from a small banker, which read in part:

> Down payments of 50 percent or higher will be required on big ticket items such as automobiles to guarantee that a buyer has a large enough equity from time of purchase that he will not default on his contract because his cigarette lighter didn't work. With today's ridiculous prices for automobiles and a required down payment of 50

18. *Hearings*, at 4.

percent, guess how this will affect the auto industry.

Lenders claimed that the rule would ruin small business, destroy many industries, and even discourage energy conservation. Years later, most of these concerns look foolish and courts have had little trouble interpreting the FTC Rule.

Although justification for the FTC Rule may be stated in terms of "internalization of costs," a more simply stated purpose is to indirectly drive dishonest dealers out of the market. It was thought that lenders who experienced losses in paper purchased from a dealer would likely cut the dealer off and not finance new contracts made between that dealer and consumers. While a lender can control bad credit risks by doing good credit and income research on the borrower, it would not be inclined to maintain a relationship with a dealer who has sold the lender notes, the makers of which, despite being good credit risks, regularly raise defenses. Because the lender is subject to consumer claims and defenses based on the underlying contract, buying paper from a bad dealer is buying trouble unless the lender is able to shift the loss back to the dealer through a provision in the dealer agreement.

The last sentence in the required notice under the FTC Rule purports to place a limit on the liability of the lender where the consumer is raising a claim or defense. The sentence reads: "[r]ecovery hereunder by the debtor shall not exceed amounts paid by the debtor hereunder." The origin of this language and its application in judicial decisions will be examined next.

The derivative and agency liability elements of the lender liability decisions discussed in Chapter Four, given the nature of the damage awards, raise interesting questions for future interpretations of the FTC Rule. Some courts have focused on the last sentence of the FTC Rule to limit the liability of the lender where the damage claim against the seller of the goods might far exceed the amount of the debt, particularly where the lender has had no primary involvement in the fraud or misbehavior of the dealer. *See, e.g., Home Savings Ass'n v. Guerra*, 733 S.W.2d 134 (Tex.1987); *Ford Motor Co. v. Morgan*, 536 N.E.2d 587 (Mass.1989).

3. SHOULD THE FTC RULE LIMIT AFFIRMATIVE RECOVERY?

It is clear from reading the transcripts of hearings on the FTC Rule that the Federal Trade Commission developed the Rule anticipating a defensive use by consumers. By sweeping away the classic holder in due course doctrine in consumer transactions, the FTC expected that consumers would commonly use the FTC Rule to assert the right to avoid future payments, and even recover payments made, based on the claim that the seller had delivered defective goods or had otherwise breached the agreement.

What the FTC might not have anticipated was a change in the way debtors viewed the lending relationship, with debtors taking on an aggressive posture in the lender liability litigation of the 1980s. Debtors in search of a deep pocket were no longer satisfied with an outcome that might simply allow them to walk away from the debt, but sought additional damages—even punitive damages—against lenders (assignees) who funded a contract where the debtor became dissatisfied.

As noted above, the FTC Rule generated considerable controversy in the five year period of its development, and even after it became the law. A congressional subcommittee held hearings on the FTC Rule just three months after its effective date, which attracted many witnesses and submissions for the record. A major concern voiced at these hearings was the failure of the Rule to expressly address tort claims in the preservation of claims and defenses language. By 1976, lenders had largely given up the fight on whether the holder in due course doctrine should be preserved in consumer lending, but were eager to have some clear statement that the FTC Rule would not authorize imposing unlimited tort liability on the lender for the acts of the dealer.

At the hearings, the Acting Director of the Bureau of Consumer Protection of the Federal Trade Commission sought to address the concerns of the lenders and suggested that the liability of the lender under the FTC Rule had clear limitations. The director noted:

The required contract provision simply preserves against the creditor any legal claims and defenses the consumer would have against the seller under applicable state law. It does not extend these claims or defenses in any other way, since the objective was to preserve existing substantive rights, not to create new ones. Thus, contrary to some unfortunate news stories, the rule does not create any new right to withhold payment. A consumer who wrongfully refuses to pay does so at the same peril he faced before—no more, no less. If a consumer has a warranty claim worth $60 based on the cost of repair, and state law gives him only a right of set-off up to this amount, he has only the right of set-off against the creditor.

Some who testified or submitted letters applauded the FTC's decision to refrain from specifically addressing the issue of tort claims in the required notice, indicating that the last sentence in the disclosure placed a clear limit on the lender's liability. At the Hearings, one consumers' rights attorney stated:

> The other issue raised by the Federal Reserve Board which seems to have been particularly troublesome to some creditors is the Rule's non-exclusion of tort claims in the preservation notice. These creditors seem to be worried that they will have to obtain costly insurance to cover the possibility of large personal injury actions against them for the seller's or manufacturer's negligence. But the Rule could simply not be more

clear that a consumer may not assert against the creditor any rights which he might have against the seller for consequential damages beyond the amounts which the consumer has already paid under the credit contract! The required Preservation Notice unequivocally announces "Recovery Hereunder Shall Not Exceed Amounts Paid By The Debtor Hereunder." Only the cost of the merchandise, plus interest, can be recovered.

Even consumer advocates expressed the view that the liability of the lender under the FTC Rule was limited, and in no instance could the consumer recover punitive damages against the lender even if the punitive damages would have been allowed against the seller of goods. A counsel for low-income consumers noted:

> In accordance with the foregoing, where a seller's conduct gives rise to damages exceeding what has been paid under the contract, the consumer may elect to sue to liquidate the unpaid balance and recover the amount already tendered or defend in a creditor collection action. In no instance can the consumer recover additional damages, of a consequential or punitive nature, for example.

However, lenders expressed considerable worry over the "all claims and defenses" language, and suggested that the word "claim" would encourage borrowers to consider theories allowing for recovery against the lender in an amount exceeding the loan contract. A leading consumer banker stated:

In connection with the point made concerning "all claims and defenses," we would assert there is no solace or comfort in the limitation on recovery without a specific limitation on type and extent of claims assertable. We would further submit that a consumer can assert his *claims* on whatever basis the *law* now permits, and that it is totally outside the scope of a project to prohibit the separation of a buyer's duty to pay from the seller's reciprocal duty to perform as promised to insert an encouragement to assert *claims* and an apparent Commission-decreed "right" to assert *claims* in a situation designed to preserve a consumer's remedies in the nature of withholding payment as a "defense" to nonadjustment of legitimate consumer complaints. In that connection, a proposed revision of the prescribed notice is suggested:

> "Any holder of this consumer credit contract is subject to all rescission and restitution rights, and all defenses, which the debtor could assert against the seller from which the subject goods or services were obtained pursuant hereto or with the proceeds hereof. Recovery hereunder by the debtor shall be limited to amounts paid by the debtor to the holder of his consumer credit contact."

Hearings, at 113 (statement of Paul L. Stansbury, President, The Consumer Bankers Association).

Shortly after the FTC promulgated the FTC Rule, the FTC staff issued Guidelines on Trade Regulation Rule Concerning Preservation of Consumers' Claims and Defenses.[19] The Guidelines do not have the force of law and do not amend the FTC Rule or the Official Statement of Basis and Purpose published with the FTC Rule. However, they do indicate how the drafters of the FTC Rule and Statement of Basis and Purpose intended the FTC Rule to operate.

In the Guidelines, the Bureau of Consumer Protection stated:

> This limits the consumer to a refund of monies paid under the contract, in the event that an affirmative money recovery is sought. In other words, the consumer may assert, by way of claim or defense, a right not to pay all or part of the outstanding balance owed the creditor under the contract; but the consumer will not be entitled to receive from the creditor an affirmative recovery which exceeds the amounts of money the consumer has paid in.

> . . .

> The limitation on affirmative recovery does not eliminate any other rights the consumer may have as a matter of local, state, or federal statute. The words "recovery hereunder" which appear in the text of the Notice refer specifically to a recovery under the Notice. If a larger affirmative recovery is available against a creditor as a matter

19. FTC Governing Prosecution of Consumers' Claims and Defenses, 41 Fed. Reg. 20,022–25 (1976) [hereinafter Guidelines].

of state law, the consumer would retain this right.

. . .

The Rule does apply to all claims or defenses connected with the transaction, whether in tort or contract. When, under state law, a consumer would have a tort claim against the seller that would defeat a seller's right to further payments or allow the consumer to recover affirmatively this claim is preserved against the holder. This is, of course, subject to the limitation of recovery under this Rule to the amounts paid in.

Guidelines, at 20,023–24.

Thus, although the testimony at congressional hearings and the many pieces of correspondence submitted into the record over the course of five years of hearings appear to place a limit on the liability of the lender if the lender is not a direct participant in the dealer's bad behavior, the Guidelines do not articulate any limitation on the claims or defenses the consumer may assert. It seems obvious in hindsight that most of the participants involved at the time of the development of the FTC Rule focused almost exclusively on the defensive use of the language required in the regulation, rather than examining the limits of liability should the borrower make a claim for affirmative recovery beyond the amount of the debt.

There are very few judicial decisions interpreting the FTC Rule in cases where consumers have made the claim for an affirmative recovery. In *Eachen v.*

Scott Housing Systems, 630 F.Supp. 162 (M.D.Ala. 1986), the court held that under the FTC Rule consumers are not limited to asserting claims against lenders only by way of defense or set-off. The court noted that if the consumer has a legitimate defense and stops payment, he may be sued for the balance due by the third party lender. The lender, however, may elect not to bring suit, especially if he knows that he would be unable to implead the seller and he knows the consumer's defenses may be meritorious. The lender may elect not to sue in hopes that the threat of an unfavorable credit report may move the consumer to pay.

In *Armstrong v. Edelson*, 718 F.Supp. 1372 (N.D.Ill.1989), the court, in denying a motion to dismiss, held that nothing in the FTC Rule itself or the commentary surrounding the rule limits the effect of the Rule to contractual claims and defenses. The court, citing the FTC Guidelines, noted that the FTC expressly included fraud in the list of claims preserved by the rule. However, in citing the FTC Rule, the court spoke in terms of the consumer raising the claim or defense to defeat or diminish the right of a creditor to be paid. There was no discussion of recovery that might exceed the amount of the loan.

In *Tinker v. DeMaria Porsche Audi, Inc.*, 459 So.2d 487 (Fla.Dist.Ct.App.1984), the court held that under the FTC Rule, the fraud found to have been perpetrated by the seller constituted a complete defense to the bank's counterclaim for the balance owed on the installment sales contract. The court agreed with the verdict in favor of the bank on the direct fraud claim, stating that the facts justified the finding "that the Bank was not so closely related with the seller as to be responsible for its fraudulent acts. However, the borrower could assert the fraud perpetrated by the seller to defeat the right of the bank to receive payment."

The Texas Supreme Court has held that a creditor's derivative liability for seller misconduct is limited to the amount paid by the consumer under the contract. The court stated the issue in *Home Savings Ass'n v. Guerra*, 733 S.W.2d 134 (Tex. 1987), as whether an assignee of a retail installment contract can be held derivatively liable for the seller's misconduct in excess of the amount paid by the buyer. In finding a limit on the creditor's liability, the court traced the development of the FTC Rule and reasoned that a rule of unlimited liability would place the creditor in the position of an absolute insurer or guarantor of the seller's performance.

However, for purposes of the attempted application of the FTC Rule to the home improvement cases discussed in Chapter Four, it is important to note that the Texas Supreme Court specifically commented that its finding does not limit or foreclose a consumer's right of recovery against the creditor based on independent state law grounds. The court noted that all the jury findings pertained to wrongful acts committed solely by the contractor and that the plaintiff had premised the lender's liability strictly on its admission that it was the holder of the note.

In examining the plaintiff's derivative liability theories and the result in the agency cases, one might first conclude that if the finding of liability was based solely on a derivative (agency) theory, then the application of the FTC Rule would shield the lender from a punitive damage claim in excess of the amount of the loan. The possibility of tort claims flowing through to the assignee was definitely on the minds of lenders as they looked at the proposed FTC Rule. A number of participants in the proceedings surrounding the development of the FTC Rule gave assurance that lenders would not face derivative tort liability.

Nevertheless, the decisions to date dealing with the FTC Rule where debtors are using it affirmatively, as well as the guidance coming from the FTC staff in the mid–1970s, suggest no such limited liability was intended if the plaintiff's theory was based on independent state law grounds and not on the FTC Rule. Thus, the characterization of the house improvement and dealer cases as the simple application of fraud and agency concepts does not appear to conflict with the analysis in cases employing the FTC Rule where some limit on derivative liability was found.

If the two principal reasons for the FTC Rule are to reduce seller misconduct and to internalize the costs of any seller misconduct that remains, the punitive damages awards in the dealer cases involving agency concepts reach the same end, but through different theoretical means. The results in the agency cases will cause dishonest contractors to be driven from business and lenders who deal with them to police their dealer agreements more closely or withdraw from home improvement dealer agreements more closely or withdraw from home improvement dealer financing altogether. Others would argue that the punitive damage awards and further regulation will merely cause lenders to withdraw from the market, leaving a void in the credit market for borrowers who are often starved for credit.

It does not appear the FTC staff and others gave sufficient consideration of the possibility of "offensive" debtor actions against assignees of consumer notes. However, if the application of simple fraud and agency analysis under state law leads to results like those discussed in Chapter Four, it would be ironic if a federal rule intended to benefit consumers could be invoked to their detriment.

B. DEFENSES IN CREDIT CARD TRANSACTIONS

1.   DEFENSES ARISING FROM THE UNDERLYING TRANSACTION

Bob purchases a lawnmower from Sears on his Sears credit card. He takes the lawnmower home but is unable to get the mower to start. So, Bob returns the mower to Sears and demands a refund. The fact that Bob used the Sears card does not affect his rights as to Sears. But, what if Bob purchased the lawnmower with a VISA card? Now, there are three parties and there contracts involved.

The first contract is between Bob and the VISA card issuer which arose when Bob applied and accepted the VISA card. The credit card agreement between Bob and VISA authorizes VISA to pay money to Sears (or another merchant) when it presents VISA with a "sales slip." In exchange for this payment, the agreement also contains the terms upon which Bob is to repay VISA for the credit so extended, such as the finance charged involved, grace period and minimum payment, as discussed in Chapter Six. Second, is the contract between VISA and Sears. That agreement, among other things, sets forth the terms and conditions whereby VISA will accept sales slips presented by Sears. And, the third contract is between Sears and Bob. That contract is contained in the sales slips which Bob signed for the purchase of the mower. Since there are three parties now, can Bob assert the same product defense against VISA, rather than against Sears? Consumers groups say yes. Credit card issuers vary and the Truth-in-Lending Act say yes in certain situations.

Consumers generally agree that credit card issuers are better able to police sellers and bear the costs of merchandise risks than they are as the credit card holders. Therefore, consumers argue that they should be able to make a direct attack against the seller simply by not making their credit card payment. Although, many credit card issuers have agreements with merchants to obtain charge-backs from merchants if merchandise claims arise, credit card issuers have two principal arguments as to why they should not be liable. First, the issuer has nothing to do with and, therefore, should be completely insulated from any claims or defenses the cardholder may have against the seller. Second, a credit card is a payment, rather than a credit device so that defenses should be assertable only where there is a credit transaction. Congress attempted to establish a compromise between these two positions by enacting 15 U.S.C. § 1666(i) of the Truth in Lending Act.

Under 15 U.S.C. § 1666(i) consumers can assert product defenses against a credit card issuer if the merchant is located in the same home state as the cardholder or within 100 miles of his address. This geographic limitation, however, may be considered as waived by the issuer if it agrees to assist a cardholder in a dispute with a foreign merchant. *See Hyland v. First USA Bank*, 1995 WL 595861 (E.D.Pa.) In mail-order cases the question of where a particular transaction took place is determined according to the applicable state law. *See Izraelewitz v. Manufacturers Hanover Trust Co.*, 465 N.Y.S.2d 486 (NY Civ. Court. 1983). Although the geographic limitation may seem harsh, especially, when card holders use credit cards for purchases made while traveling out of state or even out of the country, courts have declined to make any such exception to the statute. *See Singer v. Chase Manhattan Bank*, 890 P.2d 1305 (Nev.1995).

Additionally, before the cardholder can assert any defense against the issuer he must make "a good-faith attempt to obtain satisfactory resolution of a disagreement or problem relative to the transaction from the person honoring the credit card."[20] And, the purchase price must be greater than $50 because a transaction for $50 or less is treated as if it had been a cash transaction.[21] If a consumer, however, has already paid the disputed balance, he loses any further rights to assert claims and defenses other than billing errors. *See* Official Staff Comment § 226.12(c). The claims and defenses that are available against the issuer because they are available against the seller is determined by the applicable state law.

The other limitation placed on consumers by the Truth in Lending Act is that the cardholder may only withhold payments up to the amount of credit outstanding from the property or services that gave rise to the dispute and any finance or other charges imposed on such amount. That amount is determined at the time the cardholder first notifies the

20. The provisions of this section do not apply to the use of a check guarantee card or a debit card in connection with an overdraft credit plan or to a check guarantee card used in connection with cash advance checks. Rev. Reg. Z § 226.129(c), FN 24.

21. The dollar and geographic limitations do not apply when the person honoring the card: (1) is the same person as the card issuer; (2) is controlled by the card issuer directly or indirectly; (3) is under the direct or indirect control of a third person who also directly or indirectly controls the card issuer; (4) controls the card issuer directly or indirectly; (5) is a franchised dealer in the card issuer's products or services; or (5) has obtained the order for the disputed transaction through a mail solicitation made by or participated in by the card issuer. *See* Rev. Reg. Z § 226.12(c)(3)(ii), FN 26.

card issuer or the person honoring the card of the existence of a claim or defense.

Rather than going after the cardholder for non-payment of a disputed purchase, the issuer has a much quicker remedy against the merchant. Generally, issuers, particularly issuers of general bank credit cards, have agreements with merchants whereby the issuers may charge-back the merchant's account for charges made where the purchaser disputes the sale of merchandise or services performed or for the non-delivery or the return of merchandise. The charge-back simply involves the issuer bank pulling the merchant's account and reversing the credit originally given by the bank on receipt of the "sales slip" signed by the consumer. However, this does not mean that problems don't arise between the issuer and cardholder. The cardholder may still be liable for a disputed purchase to the issuer where the merchant has a fair no refund policy and where the holder has other remedies available. *See Izraelewitz v. Manufacturers Hanover Trust Co.*, 465 N.Y.S.2d 486 (NY Civ. Court. 1983).

2. UNAUTHORIZED USE

An unauthorized use of a credit card is the use of the card by someone "other than the credit card holder who does not have actual, implied, or apparent authority for such use and from which the cardholder receives no benefit." 15 U.S.C. § 1602(*o*). The burden falls upon the card issuer to show that the use was authorized. 15 U.S.C.

§ 1643(b). To meet its burden the card issuer must set forth facts that permit a reasonable person to conclude that the cardholder authorized the use of the card or that the conditions for liability for unauthorized use have been met. *See Elder–Beerman v. Nagucki,* 55 Ohio App.3d 10, 561 N.E.2d 553 (1988).

15 U.S.C. § 1643(a)(1) of the Truth in Lending Act limits the liability of the cardholder for unauthorized use. That section provides that a cardholder is liable for the unauthorized use of a credit card *only if*:

(1) the card is an accepted card;

(2) the liability is not greater than $50;

(3) the card issuer gave adequate notice to the cardholder of the potential liability;

(4) the card issuer provided the cardholder with a description of a means by which the card issuer may be notified of loss or theft of the card;

(5) the unauthorized use occurred before the card issuer was notified of the unauthorized use and

(6) the card issuer provided a method whereby the user of such card can be identified as the person authorized to use it.

A consumer may be found to have authorized the use of his credit card even without actual intent to give such authorization. For example, in *Stieger v. Chevy Chase Sav. Bank*, 666 A.2d 479 (D.C.Ct.App.

1995), the court had to answer the question of whether a credit cardholder who permits a third person to use his credit card for a specific purpose is liable for other uses not specifically authorized. The court held that the holder was liable for the extra charges where the signature on the sales slips matched the signature on the back of the card and where the holder voluntarily relinquished the card to the third party. Therefore, the court based its decision on a finding of "apparent authority." *See also, Towers World Airways, Inc. v. PHH Aviation Systems, Inc.,* 933 F.2d 174 (2nd Cir. 1991). The issue of authority is very fact specific and must be determined on a case by case basis. *See, e.g., Universal Bank v. McCafferty,* 624 N.E.2d 358 (Ohio Ct. App. 1993) (apparent authority is not proven by the conduct of the agent, but by the acts of the principal that cloak the agent with apparent power to bind the principal); *Fifth Third Bank/ Visa v. Gilbert,* 478 N.E.2d 1324 (Ohio Mun. Ct. 1984); *Transamerica Insurance Co. v. Standard Oil Co.,* 325 N.W.2d 210 (N.D.1982); *Blaisdell Lumber Co. v. Horton,* 575 A.2d 1386 (N.J. Super.App.Div. 1990).

In enacting section 133, Congress contemplated and most courts have agreed they will defer to basic principals of agency law to determine the liability of cardholders where there is an alleged unauthorized use. Under general principals of agency law, the authority of an agent "is the power of the agent to do an act or to conduct a transaction on account of the principal which, with respect to the principal, he is privileged to do because of the principal's manifestations to him." *See* Rest. (Second) Agency § 7. As the statute indicates this authority may be either implied or express or be apparent. Implied or express authority can be ascertained by looking at the written or spoken words or the conduct of the principal. Apparent authority, however, is much harder to grasp because it is normally created through the words or conduct of the principal as they are interpreted by a third party.

In *Minskoff v. American Express Travel Related Services Co.*, 98 F.3d 703 (2d Cir. 1996), the court found that apparent authority existed even where an assistant had fraudulently obtained credit cards in the name of her boss without either implied or express authority because the cardholder negligently failed to examine the bank statements sent by the issuer itemizing the charges made by the secretary. The court held that by his negligent acts or omissions the cardholder created an appearance of authority in the third party to use the card. Therefore, the holder was not limited to the $50 amount as provided for in § 1643, but was held liable for all the charges made by the secretary after the credit card statements were issued. *See also, Draiman v. American Express Travel Related Service Co.*, 892 F.Supp. 1096 (N.D.Ill.1995).

If a card issuer intends to impose liability on the cardholder for unauthorized use, it must investigate the claim in a reasonable manner. This duty is reciprocal on the cardholder, however, because the cardholder must cooperate with the card issuer in conducting its investigation or the issuer may terminate its investigation. Steps which may be taken in conducting a reasonable investigation include:

(1) reviewing the types or amounts of purchases made in relation to the cardholder's previous purchasing pattern;

(2) reviewing where the purchases were delivered in relation to the cardholder's residence or place of business and

(3) reviewing where the purchases were made in relation to where the cardholder resides or normally has shopped. *See* Rev. Reg. Z § 226.12(b), Official Staff Commentary.

C. ELECTRONIC FUND TRANSFER ACT

The Electronic Fund Transfer Act was Congress's response to provide rights for consumers in the new electronic age of banking. Most banking transactions can now be conducted exclusively through the use of machines. Customers deposit and make withdrawals during all hours of the day and night via the automated teller machines. Employees have their pay checks directly deposited into their accounts and insurance companies automatically draw on a consumer's account for payment of monthly premiums. Consumers can transfer money from one account to another, pay for utilities and other bills through their home computer or telephone. These transactions are conducted through electronic debits and credits without the consumer ever writing a check. Rather the debits and credits are processed by an automated clearinghouse or (ACH).

Electronic Fund Transfer is a payments system in which the processing and communications necessary to effect economic exchange, and the processing and communications necessary for the production of services incidental or related to economic exchange, are dependent wholly or in large part on the use of electronics. The EFTA, 15 U.S.C. § 1693 provides a "basic framework establishing the rights, liabilities and responsibilities" of EFT participants in a number of areas. These areas include: disclosure of the terms and conditions with respect to EFT consumer accounts; documentation of EFT transactions; error resolution; consumer liability for unauthorized withdrawals and liability for failing to make transfers ordered by consumers and to comply with orders to stop payment of preauthorized transfers; and the suspension of a consumer's obligation when an EFT system malfunctions.

The scope of the EFTA is determined by looking at the definition of an electronic fund transfer. The Act only applies to electronic fund transfers. The statute defines an electronic fund transfer as "any transfer of funds, other than a transaction originated by check, draft, or similar paper instrument, which is initiated through an electronic terminal, telephonic instrument, or computer or magnetic tape so as to order, instruct or authorize a financial institution to debit or credit an account." 15 U.S.C. § 1693(a)(6). It includes point-of-sale transfers, automated teller machine transactions, direct deposits or withdrawals of funds, and transfers initiated by telephones. All of the examples discussed above are included. The definition also includes a list of transactions which are not considered as an electronic fund transfer. One clear exception is a check authorization or guarantee service which does not directly result in a debit or credit to a consumer's account. For example when a consumer writes a check at the grocery store, the clerk generally feeds the check through a check scanner or Accucheck machine. The scanner informs the clerk whether to accept or deny the check, but no corresponding debit is made to the consumer's checking account. This transaction is specifically excluded from the definition of EFT, as is a transaction whereby funds are transferred from a savings account to a demand account to cover an overdraft or maintain an agreed upon minimum balance. The list of exclusions also includes the exceptional or emergency transfer which is generally initiated by telephone between a customer and an officer or employee of the bank which is not pursuant to a prearranged plan and under which periodic or recurring transfers are not contemplated.

Assume that an employer transfers electronically the consumer's wages of $400 into the consumer's account. What must the bank do to insure the accuracy of electronic funds transfers *e.g.*, to insure that $400 is credited to the consumer's account rather than $4,000? Section 1693(d) deals with the documentation of transfers. It requires that at least monthly the financial institution send a statement to each consumer having an account that may be accessed by means of an electronic fund transfer. 15 U.S.C. § 1693(d)(c). The statement must include information regarding transactions other than electronic fund transfers and shall set forth, with regard to each EFT during the period, the amount of any fee assessed during the period, the balances in the consumer's account at the beginning and close of the period and the address and telephone number to be used by the consumer to contact the financial institution about errors. *Id.* Additionally, for each transfer initiated by the consumer the financial institution must make available to the consumer, at the time of the transfer, written documentation of the transfer. 15 U.S.C. § 1693(d)(a). This document, as all other documentation required by this section regarding an electronic fund transfer, is evidence of the transfer and is prima facie proof that the transfer was made. 15 U.S.C. § 1693(d)(f). For example, when the employer transfers the consumer's pay, this section requires the financial institution to notify the consumer either each time the preauthorized transfer is made or, at the institution's election, only when the transfer is not made. 15 U.S.C. § 1693(d)(b).

If the consumer believes that an error has been made in the documentation required to be provided to him by this section, the consumer should follow the error resolution procedure provided for in Section 1693(f). First, the consumer is to notify the financial institution of such error. If the notice is received by the financial institution within 60 days of sending the documentation to the consumer, the financial institution must conduct an investigation concerning the error. If, however, the consumer fails to notify the creditor within the 60 day period, the creditor is under no obligation to conduct any investigation. The results of the investigation must be mailed to the consumer within 10 business days. The statute provides that the consumer may orally give notice of an error to the financial institution. However, the financial institution may instruct the consumer to also provide written confirmation of the oral notice within 10 days. If the consumer does not comply with the written confirmation within 10 days then the financial institution does not have to provisionally re-credit the consumer's account and will not be held liable for treble damages.

The financial institution may extend its investigation period beyond the 10 day period if the institution provisionally re-credits the consumer's account for the amount alleged to be in error. That extension, however, cannot exceed 45 days. The provisional credit must be at the disposal of the consumer until the investigation is concluded. If the institution discovers that an error did in fact occur then the institution must "promptly" re-credit the consumer's account. The institution can take no longer than one business day to make such a correction. Should, however, the institution learn that no error has been made, the institution must supply the consumer with an explanation of its findings within 3 business days after the conclusion of its investigation. The explanation must include a notice that the consumer can request copies of any documents the financial institution relied upon to reach its determination.

The EFTA provides substantial incentive for a financial institution to comply with the documentation requirements and error resolution procedures and all other provisions of the Act. A financial institution which fails to comply with an EFTA provisions with respect to a consumer is liable under section 1693(m) (the general civil liability provision) for actual damages suffered by the consumer, a minimum penalty (from $100 to $1,000 in an individual action), and the costs of the action plus a reasonable fee for the consumer's attorney. In addition, the section prescribing the error resolution procedure, section 1693(f), provides that in certain cases the consumer can recover treble his actual damages. Treble damages are recoverable if the financial institution did not provisionally credit the amount of the alleged error to the consumer's account and either failed to make a good faith investigation of the alleged error or did not have a reasonable basis for believing that the consumer's account was not in error. Treble damages are also authorized under Section 1693(f) in any case where a financial institution concluded that an error was made when that conclusion could not reasonably have been inferred from the evidence available to the institution at the time of its investigation.

The EFTA also imposes criminal liability for a number of offenses, including knowing and willful failure to comply with any of its provisions. Another criminal offense under Section 1693(n) of the Act is knowingly and willfully giving false information or failing to provide information which the EFTA requires to be disclosed. The maximum penalties for these offenses are a $5,000 fine or imprisonment for one year, or both.

Discussed on pages 364–368, *supra*, was the consumer's liability in the event of unauthorized use of the consumer's credit card. Similarly, the EFTA has a provision governing the consumer's liability when a thief steals the consumer's access card and, at an automated teller machine, withdraws cash from the consumer's account. The general rule is that the consumer incurs no liability for such unauthorized use except as provided for in Section 1693(g). That section imposes three requirements for a consumer to be liable. First, the access card must have been "accepted" by the consumer. That means that the consumer must have requested the card, received the card, signed the card and used the card or authorized someone else to use it. Secondly, the card issuer must have provided a means to identify the user of the card as the person authorized to use it *e.g.*, provided the consumer with a personal identification number (PIN). Finally, the card issuer must have given the consumer the disclosures required by Section 1693(c) at the time the consumer contracted for the EFT service. Those disclosures are "(1) the consumer's liability for unauthorized electronic fund transfers and, at the financial institution's option, notice of the advisability of prompt reporting of any loss, theft or unauthorized use of a card, code or other means of access; (2) the telephone number and address of the person or office to be notified in the event the consumer believes an unauthorized transfer has been or may be effect."

The burden is on the financial institution to establish the above preconditions for unauthorized transfers. This burden may at times be difficult, and yet, the rewards are only minimal. The EFTA provides that *in no event* shall the consumer's liability exceed $50. That phrase is, however, not as rigid as it may sound. In fact, the consumer can and may be liable for considerably more than $50 in certain cases. For example, the consumer is liable for the losses that could have been avoided had the consumer notified the financial institution of the loss or theft of a means of access within 2 business days after the consumer learned of it. The consumer is responsible for losses which occur between the close of the 2nd business day after he learns about the theft or loss and the day he finally notifies the financial institution. The limit of liability in this circumstances is not $50 but $500 (or the amount of the unauthorized transfers, whichever is less). Additionally, the consumer is liable for all losses resulting from his failure to notify the financial institution, within 60 days after he receives his account statement, of unauthorized transfers or error which appear in that statement. In this case the consumer bears unlimited liability for losses occurring after the 60–day period (but before the bank is finally notified) which the financial institution can prove would have been avoided had the consumer given timely notice. Also, similar to the "apparent authority" provisions of the TILA, the EFTA does not include within its definition of unauthorized transfers, a situation in which the consumer entrusted his access card to a person who uses it to effect transfers beyond those actually authorized by the consumer. Where such is the case, the consumer is liable for all the transfers made by that third party.

Section 205.6 of Regulation E (the regulations accompanying the EFTA) provides that all three tiers of liability ($50, $500 and unlimited) can apply to a series of unauthorized transfers. For example, a consumer could be liable for $50 for transfers that occurred before the close of two business days after the consumer learned of the loss or theft of his card; for another $450 for transfers occurring after the close of the 2 business days and before the lapse of the 60 day period following the transmittal of a periodic statement; and for an unlimited amount of liability for transfers occurring after the close of the 60 day period, if the financial institution can prove when the consumer learned of the loss or theft, and that the losses occurring after the close of 2 business days and after the close of the 60 days would not have occurred but for the failure of the consumer to notify the financial institution.

Assume that a consumer has authorized his bank to transfer monthly payments from his account to the account of GMAC to pay for an automobile he purchased pursuant to a retail installment sales contract. (This is considered as a preauthorized transfer and is permitted by the EFTA pursuant to

Section 1693(c).) What is the bank's liability if the bank's EFT system malfunction and it failed to make the transfer for one month? Under the terms of the retail installment contract, the non-payment would be considered as a default and GMAC could repossess the car.

Section 1693(h) makes the bank "liable to a consumer for all damages proximately caused by . . . the financial institution's failure to make an electronic fund transfer, in accordance with the terms and conditions of an account, in the correct amount or in a timely manner when properly instructed to do so by a consumer." There are some exceptions, however. A financial institution's liability will be limited to "actual damages proved" when the failure to make the transfer was unintentional and resulted from a bona fide error despite the existence of procedures designed to avert such errors. A financial institution will have a complete defense to liability if it can show that the failure make the transfer resulted from either "(1) an act of God or other circumstance beyond its control, that it exercised reasonable car to prevent such an occurrence, and that it exercised such diligence as the circumstances required; or (2) a technical malfunction which was known to the consumer at the time he attempted to initiated an electronic fund transfer or, in the case of a preauthorized transfer, at the time such transfer would have occurred."

In the example, the most significant damage to the consumer would be the repossession of his car. However, the creditor may not have the right to repossess the car, regardless of the terms of the retail installment contract, where the failure to make the transfer is caused by an EFT system malfunction. Section 1693(j) provides that "if a system malfunction prevents the effectuation of an electronic fund transfer initiated by the consumer to another person, and such person has agreed to accept payment by such means, the consumer's obligation to the other person shall be suspended until the malfunction is corrected and the electronic fund transfer may be completed." In this situation, the creditor cannot repossess because there has been no default in payment since the consumer's obligation is suspended. Rather, the creditor must wait until the EFT system is fixed, unless he subsequently makes in writing a demand for payment by some other means.

Assume now that a consumer, through his personal computer, instructed his financial institution to transfer $1,000 from his savings account to his checking account, using software supplied by the institution. The transfer, however, is not made and subsequently, checks drawn on the consumer's account are dishonored by the bank because of insufficient funds. Is the bank liable and for what amount? To answer that question, the first issue to resolve is which law governs. Does the EFTA Section 1693(h) govern or is the bank's liability determined by the Uniform Commercial Code Section 4–402? Although both sections provide that the banks is liable for actual damages for the wrongful dishonor of a "properly payable" instrument, the issue of which law applies is an important one for three reasons.

First, the bank has certain defenses under the EFTA which are unavailable under the UCC. Second, the EFTA may allow the consumer to recover certain sums e.g, attorney's fees and costs, of a successful wrongful dishonor action, which are not recoverable under the UCC. Section 1693(m), the general civil liability provision of the EFTA, is not limited exclusively to disclosure violations and failure to comply with the error resolution procedures. The section does not expressly preclude its applicability from cases where the consumer is injured by a financial institution's failure to effect a fund transfer despite proper instructions. The only limitation in the section provides that "[e]xcept as otherwise provided in this section and Section 1693(h)." And, Section 1693(h) does not otherwise provide that attorney's fees and costs are not recoverable. Another important distinction involves jurisdiction. Cases brought under the UCC will be brought in state court, absent diversity of citizenship and satisfaction of the federal jurisdiction amount. While, cases brought under the EFTA may be brought in federal district court without regard to the amount in controversy.

Since the UCC is state law and the EFTA is federal law, the next issue that arises is the issue of preemption. The federal EFTA preempts applicable state law only "to the extent that those laws are inconsistent with the provisions of this [EFTA], and then only to the extent of the inconsistency." Section 1693(q) also provides that "State law is not inconsistent ...if the protection such law affords is greater than the protection afforded by [the EFTA]." The determination of whether a state law is inconsistent with the act is relegated to the Board of Governors of the Federal Reserve System. "If the Board determines that a State requirement is inconsistent, the financial institution shall not incur liability under the law of that State for a good faith failure to comply with that law, notwithstanding that such determination is subsequently amended, rescinded or determined by judicial or other authority to be invalid for any reason."

Similar to the UCC provision for stopping payment, a stop payment may be issued by a consumer under the EFTA. The stop payment provision, however, is very limited. A stop payment may be made on preauthorized transfers such as a payment to an insurance company if the consumer notifies the bank at least three business days before the scheduled transfer. The notification can be given orally and is non-waiveable even if the agreement with the bank provides that written notification must be given.

Since commerce on the Internet is now as common as commerce through mail-order catalogues, the FTC may apply consumer protection statutes to the on-line community. One of the statutes which must be adhered to by on-line users is the EFTA and its implementing Regulation E. Companies that provide on-line banking services or any other method of on-line payment involving direct deposits and automatic draws affecting a consumer's account must comply with the EFTA. One of the most recent issues concerning the internet and the EFTA is the failure of internet companies who receive recurring payments from consumers via electronic fund transfer to obtain the consumer's written authorization in advance and failure to notify the consumers in advance if the amount of a particular transfer will vary from the pre-authorized amount or range of amounts.[22] For example, AOL which was one of the target companies of the FTC's investigation, may debit a consumer's account $9.95 one month and $38.95 another month for miscellaneous fees. The EFTA was enacted before the World Wide Web and Cyberspace became a household name. Therefore, as on-line transactions, including debits and credits, become more common than going to the bank down the street, the EFTA will have to adapt accordingly.

D. BILLING PROBLEMS

1. FAIR CREDIT BILLING ACT

The Fair Credit Billing Act (FCBA) became effective in 1975 and is codified as 15 U.S.C. §§ 1666 to 1666(j). The Act sets forth an orderly procedure for identifying and resolving disputes between a cardholder and a card issuer as to the amount due at

22. *See* Roscoe B. Starek, III and Lynda M. Rozell, *A Cyberspace Perspective: The Federal Trade Commission's Commitment to On-line Consumer Protection,* 15 J. Marshall J. Computer & Info. L. 679 (1997).

any time. *See Gray v. American Express Co.*, 743 F.2d 10 (D.C. 1984). Therefore, the Act applies only to open-end credit accounts e.g., credit card accounts, revolving charge accounts and overdraft checking accounts. But, the FCBA does not encompass loans or credit sales which are paid according to a fixed schedule until the entire amount is paid back. Although the Act governs a variety of do's and don't's as to issuers and holders of open-end credit plans, two of the more significant parts of the Act are discussed below:

a. Billing Errors

Basically, the FCBA billing error provisions (1) establish procedures for consumers to use in complaining about certain billing errors and (2) require creditors to provide explanations or corrections for the alleged errors. The FCBA allows consumers to dispute a creditor's statement of accounts in the consumer's name and seek correction and resolution of the dispute in a timely and orderly manner. The Act begins by defining billing errors as any of the following:

(1) an extension of credit which was not made or was not in the amount reflected on the statement;

(2) an extension of credit for which the card holder requests additional clarification;

(3) bills for goods or services not accepted by the cardholder;

(4) failure of the card issuer to reflect on a statement a payment made by the holder;

(5) computation error;

(6) failure to transmit the statement to the last address provided for by the holder unless the address was provided less than 20 days before the end of the billing cycle and

(7) any other errors described in regulations by the Board. 15 U.S.C. § 1666(b).

In the event that an error is discovered, the Act requires the credit issuer to furnish the consumer with procedures for complaining about billing errors. Therefore, Section 1637(b)(10) requires the issuer to disclose on its periodic billing statements the address to which the cardholder may send billing inquiries. Additionally, Section 1637(b)(7) requires that at the time that the consumer opens the account and at semi-annual intervals, thereafter, the credit issuer must furnish to the consumer a statement in the form prescribed in Reg. Z § 226.7(a)(9) explaining the consumers rights and obligations under the FCBA.

The latter information is particularly important as the billing error provisions of the Act are triggered only by a communication from the consumer that meets the following six requirements of Section 1666:

(1) the notice must be in writing;

(2) the notice must be received at the address indicated by the issuer;

(3) the notice must enable the creditor to identify the name and account number of the obligor;

(4) the notice must indicate the obligor's belief that the statement contains a billing error;

(5) the notice must set forth the amount of the billing error and

(6) the notice must set forth the reasons for the obligor's belief that the statement contains a billing error.

The obligor may use the back of a payment stub or other payment medium supplied by the creditor to state his complaint if the creditor stipulates such method of notice in its disclosure.

After the creditor receives a proper claim of error, the creditor has thirty days to either provide a written acknowledgment of receipt or a written response. If the creditor issues a written acknowledge of receipt, then it must provide a written response no later than ninety days after the receipt of the notice of a claim of error. 15 U.S.C. § 1666(a)(3)(A) & (B).

The written "response" can be in two forms. If the creditor concludes that an error was made then the creditor must make the appropriate corrections to the obligor's account, including crediting the account for any finance charges on the amounts erroneously billed and transmit to the obligor "a notification of such corrections." If the amount corrected is different from the amount claimed of as in error by the obligor, then the creditor must provide an explanation of such change (the obligor can request documentation evidencing the obligor's indebtedness in such changed amount.) 15 U.S.C. § 1666(a)(3)(B)(i). However, should the creditor conclude that in fact no error was made, then the written response will be in the form of a written explanation or clarification "setting forth to the extent applicable the reasons why the creditor believes the account of the obligor was correctly shown in the statement and, upon request of the obligor, provide copies of documentary evidence of the obligor's indebtedness." 15 U.S.C. § 1666(a)(3)(B)(ii). Should the amount in dispute be about undelivered goods, the creditor cannot conclude that the amount is correct unless the creditor determines that such goods were actually delivered, mailed or otherwise sent and provides the obligor with a statement setting forth such determination.

Until the creditor provides the obligor with a "response," there are a number of restrictions placed on the creditor. For example, under § 1666(a), the creditor may not take any action to collect the disputed amount. The section does not prohibit the creditor from sending a statement to the obligor reflecting finance charges on the disputed amount as along as the creditor also notes on the statement that the obligor is not responsible for the payment of such amount until the creditor provides a response concerning the error. Secondly, the creditor may not restrict or close the obligor's account solely because the obligor refuses to pay the amount in dispute. The creditor, may however, apply the disputed amount against the credit limit on the obligor's account. Finally, the creditor cannot use the non-payment of the disputed amount to tarnish the obligor's credit report. The section prohibits the creditor from reporting or threatening to report to a third party that the disputed amount is delinquent. Rather, the section requires the creditor to provide not only a response to the claim of error but allow the obligor not less than 10 days to make payment of the disputed amount.

If the consumer disagrees with the creditor's response and sends the creditor further written notice that the amount is still in dispute, rather than sending a payment, the creditor may not report the amount as delinquent unless the creditor also reports that the amount is in dispute. At the same time, the creditor must also provide the obligor with a list of the names of addresses of each party to whom the creditor is reporting the information about the delinquency. And if subsequently, the matter is resolved, such resolution must be communicated to the all parties who were initially informed about the delinquency.

If a creditor fails to comply with the requirements set forth in §§ 1666 or 1666(a), above, the creditor forfeits its right to collect the amount in dispute, whether or not such amount was in fact in error. The creditor also loses the right to collect any corresponding finance charges, provided that the amount so forfeited does not exceed $50 for each item or transaction on a periodic statement indicated by a customer as being in error. 15 U.S.C.

§ 1666(e). Because of the very low limit placed on the creditor's liability, a question remains as to the effectiveness of the FCBA. Creditors may see more of an incentive to violate the Act if compliance would cost more than non-compliance. But if the consumer does file suit, noncompliance can be costly. Such an action could result in the creditor being liable for twice the finance charge (minimum of $100, maximum of $1,000) plus court costs and reasonable attorney's fees. 15 U.S.C. § 1640(a).

b. Billing Period

Many credit card agreements provide for a "grace period" during which the consumer may avoid paying finance charges if he pays the full amount of the bill within that period of time. Although credit card companies do not have to provide consumers with a "grace period," the TILA requires that any such period be disclosed. *See* Reg. Z § 226.7(a)(1).

The problem is that very few consumers are actually able to take advantage of this "grace period." Assume the following information: (1) the buyer could avoid all finance charge by paying the entire balance within 20 days after the date ending the billing cycle, (2) the billing cycle ends on the last day of the month and (3) the creditor does not mail out statements until the 10th of the month. That means, that the grace period is largely illusory because few consumers will able to act quickly enough to take advantage of it. In essence, rather than a 20 day grace period the consumer only has about a five day grace period. Consumer advocate groups label this concept as the "shrinking billing period" problem.

Section 1666(b) deals with this problem. It requires that bills be mailed early enough to permit consumers to take advantage of any "grace periods" offered by the creditor. Specifically, if the creditor wants to offer a "grace period," the creditor must transmit billing statements at least "fourteen days prior to the date specified in the statement by which payment must be made in order to avoid imposition of that finance charge." If the bills are not timely mailed, the creditor cannot collect the finance charge even though the consumer does not pay the full amount of the bill until long after the grace period is over.

The following is a hypothetical which illustrates the application of Section 1666(b). A credit plan provides for a finance charge based on an APR of 18%. It further provides that no finance charge will be imposed if the debtor pays the full amount of the balance within 20 days after the end of the billing cycle, which is the last day of the month. The debtor makes the following purchases and payments:

February 10—$100 purchase of clothes

March 10—creditor sends statement

March 25—debtor pays $10 minimum payment

Even though the debtor did not pay the debt in full within the grace period, section 1666b will prevent the creditor from collecting any finance charge since the creditor mailed the bill too late. The creditor should have mailed the bill by March 6th—fourteen days prior to the date specified in the statement by which the payment must be made in order to avoid imposition of that finance charge if it wanted to collect a finance charge.

2.　BILLING SYSTEMS

The type of billing system used by a credit company determines the amount of a consumer's credit card bill. There are up to seven methods, but only four will be discussed in this chapter: (1) the average daily balance, (2) the two-cycle average daily balance, (3) the adjusted balance method and (4) the previous balance method. The Federal Reserve Board recognized these four methods as the most commonly used methods when it enacted 12 C.F.R. § 226.5a(b)(6). That provision of Regulation Z requires credit card companies to disclose the balance computation method it uses on credit card applications. The creditors may refer to the one of the four methods listed above by name-only but must explain any other method.

Probably, the most controversial is the previous balance system. Under this method, the finance charge is computed without first deducting partial payments because the periodic finance charge rate is applied to the balance at the beginning of the billing cycle. From the earlier hypothetical, assuming that the only outstanding balance was $100, under the previous balance method, the April bill would reflect $91.50 as the new balance. [($100–10) + (.015 x $100)].

The previous balance method, although allowed by the TILA, has been attacked because it does not consider payments or credits made during the current billing period. On the other hand, the method also does not consider new purchases made during the current billing period. For example, even if the debtor paid $99 of the $100 balance, the finance charge would still be computed as against the $100. But, if the debtor made $99 worth of new purchases, then the finance charge would still be computed as against the $100 balance.

Zachary v. R.H. Macy & Co., 31 N.Y.2d 443, 293 N.E.2d 80 (1972) is the leading case addressing the legality of the previous balance method. In upholding the method, the court stated that "the outstanding indebtedness [from month to month against which finance charges are computed] merely requires that finance charges be computed at consistent monthly intervals on the customer's outstanding indebtedness at that time." And, that time can be at the beginning of the billing cycle as easily as at the end. There have not been any more recent cases addressing the previous balance method since *Zachary*. This may be due in part to the fact that some state legislatures have chosen to prohibit the use of the previous balance method as an available method through state statutes. For example, Kansas only allows for computation by the average daily balance or the adjusted balance. *See* K.S.A. § 16a–2–202. The same is true for Michigan, Massachu-

setts, Arizona and New York which have also prohibited the use of the previous balance method. *See*
M.C.L.A. § 445.862; M.G.L.A. 255D § 27; AZ Stat.
§ 44–1205; NY Pers. Prop. § 413.

Today, the most common method of computation
is the average daily balance method. There are two
variations of this method because the creditor can
either include or exclude new purchases. If the
creditor includes new purchases then the balance is
figured by adding the outstanding balance (including new purchases and deducting payments or credits) for each day in the billing cycle, and then
dividing by the number of days in the billing cycle.
In other words, to compute a debtor's balance, the
creditor totals the beginning balance for each day in
the billing period and subtracts any credits made to
the debtor's account that day. The resulting daily
balances are added for the billing cycle and the total
is divided by the number of days in the billing
period to attain the "average daily balance." (The
average daily balance excluding new purchases
works in the same fashion except that new purchases and credits will be excluded.) Using the
average daily balance method on the example above,
the balance for April would be $98.33. [(25 days x
$100) + (5 days x $90)/ 30 days] Every state statute
allows for computation using the average daily balance.

The other methods of computation most commonly used are the two-cycle average daily balance
method and the adjusted balance. Similar to the
average daily balance, the two-cycle average daily

balance can either include or exclude new purchases. The only difference with the two cycle method is exactly what the name comports, the average balance is the sum of the average daily balances for two billing periods. Unlike the average daily balance methods, the adjusted balance method is a modification of the previous balance method. The balance is computed by deducting payments and credits made during the billing cycle from the outstanding balance at the beginning of the billing cycle. This method is attractive because it allows consumers to avoid a part of the finance charge by making a partial payment even though he cannot take advantage of the grace period by paying the balance off in full. And, although credits for payments are considered, new purchases are still excluded. From the above example, the April balance would be $91.35 under the adjusted balance method. [($100–10) + (.015 x $90)]

Another method, which until the 1980's, was quite common and has been displaced to some extent by the two-cycle average daily balance method is the ending balance method. That method picks up both payments and purchases during the billing period.

The following table illustrates the difference that using one computation method versus another can make with respect to the amount of finance charges actually paid on an account:

	Average Daily Balance (including new purchases)	Average Daily Balance (excluding new purchases)	Adjusted Balance	Previous Balance
Monthly rate	1 1/2 %	1 1/2 %	1 1/2 %	1 1/2 %
APR	18%	18%	18%	18%
Previous Balance	$400	$400	$400	$400
New purchases	$50 on 18th day	$50 on 18th day		
Payments	$300 on 15th day (New balance = $100)	$300 on 15th day (new balance = $100)	$300	$300
Average Daily Balance	$270*	$250**		
Finance charge	$4.05 (1 1/2 % × $270)	$3.75 (1 1/2 % × $250)	$1.50 (1 1/2 % × $100)	$6.00 (1 1/2% × $400)

* To figure average daily balance (including new purchases):
($400 x 15 days) + ($100 x 3 days) + ($150 x 12 days)/ 30 days = $270
** To figure average daily balance (excluding new purchases)
($400 x 15 days) + ($100 x 15 days) / 30 days = $250

As the table illustrates, the amount of finance charge can vary from $1.50 to $6.00 depending on the type of billing system that a credit card company uses, even though the interest rate is the same. The most expensive is the previous balance and the least expensive is the adjusted balance. But remember, the most common is the average daily balance.

E. DEFAULT

Chapter Four provided some insights into the explosive growth in the use of open-end and closed-end credit in our economy. Many of the consumer laws included in this Nutshell describe the disclosures that must be made at the start of the consumer credit transaction. However, as the use of consumer credit expanded among households and creditors took on riskier borrowers through the development of the subprime credit market, there was also the need to more thoroughly police accounts, and in some cases, use judicial and extra-judicial methods to enforce credit obligations. That is, some of the focus shifted away from disclosures made at the inception of the debtor-creditor relationship, to the post-transaction relationship as outstanding balances were being collected and foreclosures were being pursued.

1. COMMON LAW LIMITATION ON COLLECTION EFFORTS

Because of the delay and expense involved in litigation, the creditor is likely initially to employ extra-judicial tactics to obtain payment. The extra-judicial collection method most generally used is the collection letter. This letter, containing a request for payment, can be either cordial or hostile depending on the policy of the creditor and the length of time that the debt is outstanding. Debtors often do not respond to a polite request for payment. Consequently, creditors seek other methods to recover the money due and owing, including telephone calls, personal visits, threats of litigation, and communications with the debtor's employer. Occasionally the creditor or his agent becomes overzealous, particularly when the debtor is weak and vulnerable.

The following excerpt from the court's statement of facts in *Duty v. General Finance Co.*, 273 S.W.2d 64 (Tex.1954), illustrates how a collector can "hassle" a debtor:

"The harassments alleged may be summarized as follows: Daily telephone calls to both Mr. and Mrs. Duty which extended to great length; threatening to blacklist them with the Merchants' Retail Credit Association; accusing them of being deadbeats; talking to them in a harsh, insinuating, loud voice; stating to their neighbors and employers that they were deadbeats; asking Mrs. Duty what she was doing with her money; accusing her of spending money in other ways than in payments on the loan transaction; threatening to cause both plaintiffs to lose their jobs unless they made the payments demanded; calling each of the plaintiffs at the respective places of their employment several times daily; threatening to garnishee their wages; berating plaintiffs to their fellow employees; requesting their employers to require them to pay; calling on them at their work; flooding them with a barrage of demand letters, dun cards, special delivery letters, and telegrams both at their homes and their places of work; sending them cards bearing this opening statement: 'Dear Customer: We made you a loan because we thought that you were honest.'; sending telegrams and special delivery letters to them at approximately midnight causing them to be awakened from their sleep; calling a neighbor in the disguise of a sick brother of one of the plaintiffs, and on another occasion as a stepson; calling Mr. Duty's mother at her place of employment in Wichita Falls long distance, collect; leaving red cards in their door, with insulting notes on the back and thinly-veiled threats; calling Mr. Duty's brother long distance, collect, in Albuquerque, New Mexico, at his residence at a cost to him in excess of $11, and haranguing him about the alleged balance owed by plaintiffs.''

Overzealous extra-judicial collection efforts have resulted in law suits based on defamation, invasion of the right to privacy, and intentional infliction of mental anguish. Recoveries on these theories, however, are relatively rare. It is difficult to match the facts of a debt collection effort with the elements of these torts.

Defamation is aimed at publication of *false* material that results in injury to reputation. Truth is thus a defense—in most jurisdictions, an absolute defense. A statement truthfully disclosing that a debt is due, owing and unpaid is not actionable. A statement that falsely imputes a *general* unwillingness to pay debts or unworthiness to obtain credit may be the basis of a defamation action.

Another defense to defamation is privilege. A communication will be privileged if it pertains to a matter in which the recipient of the communication has a legitimate interest. Informing an employer that his employee has not paid his debts is a common collection tactic to induce payment through indirect pressure on the employee. Employers want to avoid the bother and costs of wage garnishment. Courts are divided as to whether employers have a sufficient interest to cause the communication to be privileged.

Debtors have also sued on invasion of privacy for injuries resulting from creditors' communications with employers—generally with little success. Public disclosure of private facts is one form of invasion of the right to privacy. However, as a general rule, reasonable oral or written communications to an employer have not been viewed as a sufficient disclosure of private facts; as with defamation, the communication is privileged based on the employer's interest in his employee's debts.

Some courts have granted recovery where the creditor has done more than inform the employer that a debt is overdue—for example, contacting the employer on numerous occasions. Additionally, there are cases finding an invasion of privacy by communications such as calls to the debtor's neighbors, publication of the debtor's name and amount of debt in a newspaper, and posting a notice of the indebtedness at the creditor's place of business.

A second form of violation of the right to privacy is a wrongful intrusion on the solitude of the debtor. Obviously, every creditor contact, every intrusion, is not actionable. The creditor has the right to contact the debtor—has the right to try and collect the debt. The problem is one of balancing the respective interests. Only unreasonable intrusions are actionable. In determining reasonableness, courts generally consider factors such as the content, nature, number and time of communications.

Where these communications are "extreme and outrageous" and result in emotional distress, the debtor may be able to recover on a theory of *intentional infliction* of mental distress. Several difficulties inhere in such an action. As the "name" of the tort indicates the debtor faces the problem of proving intent. The debtor must show that the collector intended the mental distress. The collector's actions must be beyond all bounds of decency. Another difficulty attending this cause of action is the requirement that the emotional stress be severe. The normal strain caused by contact with a collection agency is not sufficient. The debtor has to establish serious mental stress. Finally, a number of courts are still hesitant to impose liability for mental distress alone, and insist on some form of physical injury. Even if the debtor is able to establish all of the elements of one of the above discussed common law causes of action, he or she still faces the problem of proving damages.

In addition to common law claims, many states have statutes which regulate debt collection activities. Some of the statutes are comprehensive, while others are weak tea.[23] Commonly found in the state laws are provisions for licensing of collection agencies, lists of prohibited practices, and the range of penalties provided for violation of the state law. In some states, statutory damages and attorney fees for successful consumers are available. However, it was the lack of meaningful legislation on the state level that led to the enactment of the Fair Debt Collection Practices Act of 1978 (FDCPA).

23. For a summary of many of the state debt collection statutes, *see* Fair Debt Collection, National Consumer Law Center, Appendix L (3d ed. 1996).

2. THE FAIR DEBT COLLECTION PRACTICES ACT

a. Introduction

The Fair Debt Collection Practices Act (FDCPA) became effective on March 20, 1978, and is codified at 15 U.S.C. §§ 1692–1692o. Many of the cases and the Federal Trade Commission informal staff letters cite to particular provision in Public Law 95–109, rather than the United States Code. Therefore, individuals using the law are well advised to have a cross-reference table available to research the issues before them, moving from the Public Law section to the U.S.C. section. The most recent amendments to the FDCPA occurred in 1996, when Congress amended 15 U.S.C. § 1692e(11), dealing with required disclosures in communications with the debtor.

The purposes of the FDCPA are to eliminate abusive debt collection tactics and to insure that ethical debt collectors are not competitively disadvantaged. The FDCPA prohibits debt collectors from using harassing or abusive conduct, false or misleading representations, or any unfair means to collect a consumer debt.

b. Persons and Transactions Covered

Only consumer debts are covered by the FDCPA. A consumer debt is one where a natural person is obligated to pay a debt arising out of a transaction that is primarily for personal, family or household purposes, whether or not such obligation has been reduced to judgment. 15 U.S.C. § 1692a(5). A consumer debt can include an obligation that is not the typical consumer loan or credit transaction. For example, in *Ladick v. Van Gemert*, 146 F.3d 1205 (10th Cir. 1998), an attempt to collect a condominium association assessment was held to trigger the provisions of the FDCPA. And in *Snow v. Jesse L. Riddle, P.C.*, 143 F.3d 1350 (10th Cir.1998), an attempt to collect on a dishonored check was held to be within the protections of the FDCPA.

Only debt collectors are covered by the Act. A debt collector is defined in 15 U.S.C. § 1692a(6) as:

> any person who uses any instrumentality of interstate commerce or the mails in any business the principal purpose of which is the collection of any debts, or who regularly collects or attempts to collect, directly or indirectly, debts owed or due or asserted to be owed or due another. (T)he term includes any creditor who, in the process of collecting his own debts, uses any name other than his own which would indicate that a third person is collecting or attempting to collect such debts.

The most significant exception to the definition of debt collector is a creditor collecting its own debt in the name of that creditor. 15 U.S.C. § 1692a(6)(A). Also, an assignee who purchases a debt after the debt is in default is considered a debt collector and subject to the provisions of the FDCPA. The definition of "debt collector" also includes an attorney who regularly collects or attempts to collect, directly or indirectly, consumer debts. *Heintz v. Jenkins*,

514 U.S. 291, 115 S.Ct. 1489, 131 L.Ed.2d 395 (1995).

c. Validation of Debts

Section 1692g requires a debt collector, either in the initial communication, or within five days after the initial communication, to send the debtor a written notice disclosing:

(1) the amount of the debt;

(2) the name of the creditor to whom the debt is owed;

(3) a statement that unless the consumer, within thirty days after receipt of the notice, disputes the validity of the debt, or any portion thereof, the debt will be assumed to be valid by the debt collector;

(4) a statement that if the consumer notifies the debt collector in writing within the thirty-day period that the debt, or any portion thereof, is disputed, the debt collector will obtain verification of the debt or a copy of a judgment against the consumer and a copy of such verification or judgment will be mailed to the consumer by the debt collector; and

(5) a statement that, upon the consumer's written request within the thirty-day period, the debt collector will provide the consumer with the name and address of the original creditor, if different from the current creditor.

If within 30 days the consumer notifies the debt collector in writing that the debt is disputed, all collection activity must cease until written verification of the debt is sent to the consumer. 15 U.S.C. § 1692g(b). Failure of the consumer to dispute the debt is not an admission of liability. 15 U.S.C. § 1692g(c).

d. Prohibitions Against False or Misleading Information

Section 1692e includes a general prohibition against the use of false, deceptive or misleading information. The section also includes a list of sixteen specific representation or actions that are considered a violation of the FDCPA. The prohibitions that are most frequently at issue in the cases include the following:

(1) the false representation or implication that the debt collector is affiliated with the United States or any state;

(2) the false representation of the amount, character or legal status of a debt;

(3) the false implication that the collector is an attorney or that the communication is by an attorney;

(4) the representation that nonpayment of the debt will result in the arrest of the person or the seizure, garnishment, or sale of any property unless the action is lawful and the debt collector intends to take the action;

(5) a threat to take any action that is illegal or unintended;

(6) the false representation that the consumer committed a crime or other conduct to disgrace a consumer;

(7) threatening to communicate or communicating to another person credit information which is known or should be known as false; and

(8) the use of any company or business name other than the true name of the debt collector's company or business.

The 1996 amendment deals with § 1692(e)(11). Formerly, section 1692e(11) stated that, except when acquiring location information from a third party, the debt collector had to disclose in all communications that the communication was for the purpose of collecting a debt and any information received would be used for that purpose. Significant case law examined exactly what was required by this section.

15 U.S.C. § 1692e(11) was amended to read:

1692e ... the following conduct is a violation of this section:

(11) The failure to disclose in the initial written communication with the consumer and, in addition, if the initial communication with the consumer is oral, in that initial oral communication, that the debt collector is attempting to collect a debt and that any information ob-

tained will be used for that purpose, and the
failure to disclose in subsequent communications that the communication is from a debt
collector, except that this paragraph shall apply
to a formal pleading made in connection with a
legal action.

The amendment became effective December 29,
1996. Consequently, for all communications beginning December 29, 1996, section 1692e(11) provides
that the debt collector must disclose the previously
required information only in its initial written communication with the consumer and, if the initial
communication with the consumer is oral, in the
initial oral communication as well. Under the new
provision, the collector has to disclose in subsequent
communications only that the communication is
from a debt collector. The provision previously had
required the full disclosure and warning in all communications with the consumer.

e. Harassment or Abuse

Section 1692d includes a prohibition on tactics
that harass or abuse consumers. Without limiting
the general application of the section, the following
conduct is a violation of the section:

(1) The use or threat of violence or other criminal means to harm the person, reputation or
property of the person.

(2) The use of obscene or profane language.

(3) The publication of lists of consumers who
allegedly refuse to pay debts.

(4) Causing a telephone to ring or engaging any person in telephone conversation repeatedly or continuously with the intent to annoy, abuse or harass.

f. Additional Restrictions on Communications With the Debtor

Without prior consent of the debtor or express permission by the court, a debt collector cannot communicate with a debtor "at any unusual time or place or a time or place known or which should be known to be inconvenient to the consumer." The FDCPA states the convenient time for communication is after 8:00 a.m. and before 9:00 p.m. In addition, the FDCPA restricts communication with a debtor represented by an attorney, 15 U.S.C. § 1692(a)(2) and at the debtor's place of employment "if the debt collector knows or has reason to know" the employer prohibits the communication. 15 U.S.C. § 1692(a)(3).

g. Civil Liability and Bona Fide Error Defense

Violations of the FDCPA may result in liability for actual damages, additional statutory damages up to $1,000, attorney fees and costs. 15 U.S.C. § 1692K(a)(2)(A). Even without evidence of actual damages, attorney fees and costs may be awarded for a violation.

The Act also provides that a debt collector will not be liable upon proving by a preponderance of the evidence that the violation is unintentional and results from a bona fide error, despite maintaining procedures to avoid the error. 15 U.S.C. § 1692K(c). This bona fide error defense is an affirmative defense that the debt collector has the burden to prove at trial.

3. OTHER STATUTES

There are a number of statutes affecting extra-judicial collection; the problem is that few if any of the statutes affect extra-judicial collection very much.

There are federal regulations governing the use of the mail and the telephone. For example, collection abuses involving use of the mails have been prosecuted under 18 U.S.C.A. § 1341 and 18 U.S.C.A. § 1718. And, there are some general state laws such as those dealing with assault, libel and blackmail that are some help in extreme cases. The only other relevant legislation in most states are the provisions licensing and regulating collection agencies. Generally, the licensing serves as a source of revenue for the state, and little more.

4. JUDICIAL COLLECTION EFFORTS

There is little in the law of judicial collection that is peculiar to consumer credit transactions. All creditor have essentially the same collection remedies; the same statutes apply to commercial and consumer debts. In most jurisdictions, judicial collection remedies are conditioned on the filing of a law suit.

Until the suit is filed, the creditor is limited to the extra-judicial collection methods mentioned above.

There are several post-filing/*pre-judgment* creditor remedies that can be used *in certain statutorily prescribed situations*. Garnishment is perhaps the best known collection remedy available prior to judgment.

Garnishment is a collection remedy directed not at the defendant/debtor but rather at some third person, the garnishee, who owes a debt to the principal debtor, has property of the principal debtor, or has property in which the principal debtor has an interest. Garnishment is a warning or notice to the garnishee that the plaintiff/creditor claims the right to have such debt or property applied in satisfaction of his claim, and that the garnishee should hold such property until the creditor's suit has been tried and any judgment satisfied. For example, if C brought an action against D to collect a debt that was due and owing and C learned that G held property of D, C might garnish this property. Then, if C was successful in her action against D, C's judgment could be satisfied by the property of D held by G, and, if G no longer had such property, C could recover from G personally. The most common examples of garnishees are the employer of the principal debtor and the bank in which the principal debtor has a savings or checking account.

It is also possible to reach property held by the debtor himself or herself prior to judgment through use of attachment and replevin or sequestration. In attachment, the sheriff levies, *i.e.,* seizes, non-exempt property of the debtor sufficient to satisfy the creditor's claim and holds such property pending the outcome of the collection suit. Replevin or sequestration (also known as claim and delivery in a few states) differs from attachment in that the property so seized is specific property that the creditor claims a right to or an interest in. To illustrate, S sells D an appliance on time and reserves a security interest in the appliances. D defaults; S files suit. S can attach any of D's non-exempt property; S can replevy or sequester only the appliances subject to S's security interest. In some jurisdictions, replevin or sequestration also differs from attachment in that the creditor holds the seized items pending final judgment.

These prejudgment remedies are of limited availability. A creditor can make use of attachment or garnishment or replevin only if it satisfies the statutory condition precedents. If the creditor prevails in the lawsuit, then the creditor has a *right* to obtain a writ of execution directing the sheriff to seize and sell sufficient non-exempt property of the debtor to satisfy the judgment.

5.   EXEMPT PROPERTY

a.   State Law

Today all states constitutionally or statutorily restrict creditor recourse to certain property. A three-pronged purpose is commonly attributed to these exemption statutes: protection of the debtor, protection of the family of the debtor, and protection of society. By allowing the debtor to retain certain property free from appropriation by creditors, exemption statutes extend to a debtor an opportunity for self-support so that he will not become a burden upon the public.

There are two notable characteristics of state exemption statutes: (1) obsolescence and (2) extreme variety. Nevertheless, certain generalizations are possible. All states exempt certain personal property from creditor process. In some jurisdictions, the exempt property is identified by type (*e.g.*, the family bible, the family rifle); in others, by value (*e.g.*, personal property of a value of $500). In most states, some specific provision is made for the exemption of life insurance (both the proceeds of the policy and the cash surrender value thereof) and wages.

The procedure for asserting rights under an exemption statute also varies from state to state. The burden usually is on the debtor to claim his exemption, and usually the statute sets a limit on the space of time after the levy in which he may claim his exemption. Where the statute is of a "value" type—*e.g.*, personal property of a value of $500— the statute generally provides for the appointment of appraisers who value property selected as exempt by the debtor. Where the statute specifies items of property that are exempt, courts are often confronted with the problem of applying a 19th century statute to 20th century property—*e.g.*, whether a television set comes within a statutory exemption for a "musical instrument" or whether an automobile is a salesman's "tool of trade."

Almost all states also have legislative provisions, commonly referred to as homestead laws, designed to protect the family home from the reach of certain classes of creditors. Homestead laws only protect real property interests of the debtor and so are of no aid to the urban apartment dweller. Moreover, not all real property interests of the debtor may be the subject of a homestead claim. Common statutory limitations include the requirements that the debtor have a family, that the property be occupied and used as a residence (an almost universal limitation), that the owner have a specified interest (usually present, possessory) in the property, and (in a few states) that there be a formal declaration that the property is a homestead.

The protection afforded by an exemption statute is not absolute. A federal tax claim may be satisfied from "exempt property." A number of states make similar exceptions for state taxes, claims for alimony and child support, materialman and mechanics liens. By statute in most states, case law in others, purchase money mortgages and security interests are generally not affected by an exemption statute. Thus, the bank that finances the purchase of a home or car will be able to seize and sell the property notwithstanding the fact that the property is covered by an exemption statute. And, most states treat nonpurchase money mortgages and security interests similarly: a debtor may in the absence of statutory provisions to the contrary mortgage or pledge exempt property, thereby destroying the exemption. So, if D gives C a second mortgage on his home to secure a loan, C can, on D's default, foreclose on D's home. On the other hand, an executory agreement to waive the benefit of an exemption has generally been held to be invalid as against the public policy, notwithstanding some obvious similarities between such a waiver and a nonpurchase money mortgage.

There are also federal statutes that exempt property from the reach of creditors in either federal court or state court. Most of the federal provisions relate to the benefits of federal social legislation such as money paid under social security and veteran's benefits. The most significant federal exemption provision is Title III of the Consumer Credit Protection Act which provides a statutory minimum exemption of wages from garnishments.

b. Title III of the Consumer Credit Protection Act

Title III of the Consumer Credit Protection Act provides a statutory minimum exemption of wages from garnishments. Under Title III, "ordinary" creditors may garnish in the aggregate only 25% of a person's weekly "disposable earnings" or the amount by which his disposal earnings exceed thirty times the minimum hourly wage, whichever is less.

"Disposable earnings" is statutorily defined as salary less deductions "required by law." The following hypothetical illustrates the operation of Title III. X's salary is $10,800 a year. X does not, however, receive $900 a month. Rather, X's "take-home pay" is only $700 a month because of the following deductions: $130 for taxes, $50 for social security, $20 for Blue Cross. Only the $130 for taxes and the $50 for social security are deductions "required by law." X's "disposable earning" is thus $720 a month or $180 a week. Title III limits the amount that X's creditors can garnish to $45.

Note that the 25% limitation affects not only the amount that can be garnished by one of the debtor's creditors but also the amount that can be garnished by all of the debtor's "ordinary" creditors. If, for example, X owes Swil–Mart, the Brick Shirthouse, and April Showers Massage Parlor, only $45 of his wages can be garnished by these creditors.

If X also owes federal taxes, none of his wages are protected by Title III. The restrictions of section 303 do not apply in the case of "any debt due for any State or Federal Tax." And, if X also owes child support or alimony, less of his wages are protected. Title III permits garnishment of up to 60% of disposable earnings to satisfy a support order. If the debtor is supporting either or both a spouse and a dependent child and the garnishment for support concerns someone else, *i.e.*, a former spouse or another dependent child, then only 50% of the disposable earnings is subject to garnishment.

Where there is a garnishment for support as well as a garnishment for "ordinary" debts subject to the 25% limit, the priority of the garnishments is a matter of state law. State law almost invariably gives claims for alimony and child support priority over commercial claims. A support order is almost always going to have priority over an "ordinary" creditor even though the "ordinary" creditor obtained its wage garnishment order first. If the garnishment for support has priority and results in the withholding of 25% or more of the debtor's disposable earnings, then the garnishment for ordinary debts take nothing.

Title III does not pre-empt state statutes "prohibiting garnishments or providing for more limited garnishment than are allowed under [Title III]." Where state restrictions are stronger, it will be state law which regulates. Title III also makes provision for state law to apply in lieu of the wage garnishment provisions of Title III where the Secretary of Labor determines that the laws of that state provide restrictions on garnishment which are "substantially similar" to those provided in the Act.

Title III of the Consumer Credit Protection Act also affords protection to a debtor from discharge because of garnishment. The Act prohibits the discharge of any employee "by reason of the fact that his earnings have been subjected to garnishment for any *one* indebtedness." Thus if D is indebted to C, and C garnishes D's wages several times in an attempt to satisfy his claim, D's employer cannot discharge him because of these garnishments. On the other hand if D is indebted to both C and E and both garnish D's wages, D's employer can discharge him because of the garnishments.

There is not private remedy provision in Title III. Rather the "exemption" and discharge provisions are to be enforced by the Secretary of Labor. There have been several reported cases that have considered implied private action contentions. The cases are split on the question. *E.g., Stewart v. Travelers Corp..*, 503 F.2d 108 (9th Cir.1974) (private right of action for wrongful dismissal); *Smith v. Cotton Brothers Baking Co., Inc.*, 609 F.2d 738 (5th Cir. 1980) (no private claim for wrongful dismissal).

6.   OBTAINING JUDGMENTS

A creditor often wants to obtain the judgment quickly and as inexpensively as possible. A default judgment is thus preferable to a judgment resulting from prolonged litigation. Most consumer collection actions result in a default judgment for the creditor. Some creditors increase the chances for judgment by default by never delivering the summons and complaint and executing a false and fraudulent affidavit of personal service. [This is commonly called "sewer service" to indicate the probable resting place of the process papers.]

A number of states permit service of process by private individuals. In such states, private process servers are generally paid only for completed service and this has resulted in widespread sewer service. Criminal prosecution for perjury and violation of civil rights under color of law has had a limited deterrent effect. More promising is the prospect of civil actions instituted by the federal government for the benefit of debtors deprived of due process by reason of sewer service.

Filing a collection action in a distant forum also significantly increases the chances of a default judgment. For example, an Arkansas debtor is more likely to default if the collection action is filed in King of Prussia, Pennsylvania, instead of Little Rock, Arkansas.

Spiegel, Inc. v. FTC, 540 F.2d 287 (7th Cir.1976), held that the Federal Trade Commission has the power to prevent creditors from suing consumers in inconvenient forums. Spiegel, a catalog retailer with its principal place of business in Chicago, regularly sued in Illinois courts to collect delinquent accounts of out-of-state consumer customers. The Illinois long-arm statute granted jurisdiction for such suits. Nevertheless, the FTC issued a "cease and desist order." The Seventh Circuit held that the "unfair practice" language of section 5 of the Federal Trade Commission Act empowers the FTC to enjoin distant forum abuse of consumer debtors.

Section 1692i of the Fair Debt Collection Practices Act protects consumers from suits by *"debt collectors"* in inconvenient forums. Actions by debt collectors to enforce a lien on real property may be filed only in the county in which the real property is located. Other "debt collector" collection actions may be brought only where the debtor resides or where the contract is signed.

7. SPECIAL RIGHTS OF LIEN CREDITORS

a. Repossession in General

The preceding pages focused on rights available to *all* creditors by extra-judicial collection and the judicial process. Some creditors have rights in addition to those already discussed. There are two major sources of such additional rights: contracts and statutes. The debtor and the creditor may agree that the creditor is to have a *lien* on certain personal property (security interest) or real property (mortgage) of the debtor. Statutes are the other common source of liens: tax liens, artisans' liens, innkeepers' liens are but a few of the statutory liens that directly affect consumers.

A creditor with a consensual or statutory lien has special rights in the property subject to its liens, *i.e.*, collateral. These rights include a right of foreclosure—the right to proceed directly against the collateral without resorting to the judicial process. For example, almost every state has a statutory innkeepers' lien. When a hotel or boarding house has the benefit of an innkeepers' lien, it may summarily seize the baggage of a guest who has not paid his or her bill and hold it or possibly sell it. Landlords' liens give landlords similar rights as to the property of a tenant behind on his or her rent.

Holders of consensual liens also enjoy this right to repossession of the collateral without recourse to the judicial process. Section 9–503 of the Uniform

Commercial Code provides: "Unless otherwise agreed a secured party has on default the right to take possession of the collateral. In taking possession, a secured party may proceed without judicial process if this can be done without breach of the peace * * *."

b. Actions Under Article 9

(1) "Breach of the Peace" Under Section 9–503

Section 9–503 of the Uniform Commercial Code authorizes the secured party or its agent to repossess without judicial process only where such repossession can be accomplished without a "breach of the peace." This phrase, "breach of the peace," is nowhere defined in the Code or the Official Comments thereto.

"Breach of the peace" is, of course, not a phrase peculiar to Article 9 of the Uniform Commercial Code. The classic criminal definition is "an act of violence or an act likely to produce violence." This standard has been generally applied to UCC self-help repossessions: An act of actual violence has not been required, merely an act likely to produce violence.

Most reported cases that have found a breach of the peach for purposes of Section 9–503 have involved either an unauthorized entry by the secured party or the secured party's agent into the debtor's residence *or* objections by the debtor.

The majority of cases takes the position that unauthorized entry into the debtor's home poses a danger of exciting a violent response—sanctity of the home, likelihood of forcing the debtor into a confrontation in his/her role as family protector. The courts apparently feel that trespassing on the driveway is not likely to product the same response; courts have been virtually unanimous in upholding repossessions of cars from the driveways, absent objection by the debtor.

Where the car is taken from the driveway over the debtor's protests, there is a breach of the peace. If the debtor is there and is objecting to the taking, this is a situation likely to produce violence. Remember the effect of so treating a debtor's protest is not to preclude repossession of the collateral; it merely precludes self-help repossession.

(2) Retention or Resale Under Article 9

What happens after repossession depends on the type of lien. Since an Article 9 security interest is the type of lien most often involved in consumer transactions, this book will focus on the post-repossession provisions of Article 9—more particularly sections 9–504 through 9–507.

Under section 9–506, the debtor has a right to redeem property that has been repossessed. This right is subject to two very important limitations: time and price. The right of redemption is terminated by the occurrence of any one of the following events: (1) disposition or entry into a contract for disposition of the collateral by the secured party, (2) acceptance by the secured party of the collateral in satisfaction of the debt under section 9–505 (dis-

cussed below) or (3) signing a written waiver of the
right of redemption after default.

In order to redeem, the debtor must "tender
fulfillment of all obligations secured by the collateral as well as the expenses reasonably incurred by
the secured party. * * *" The comment to 9–504
emphasizes that "all obligations means all obligations". If, as is common, the security agreement
contains a clause accelerating the entire balance
due on default in one installment, the debtor will
have to tender the entire balance plus expenses in
order to redeem. In this focus, the right of redemption is of limited practical significance.

In the event that repossession is not followed by
redemption, the secured party may either retain the
collateral or sell it. There are both practical and
legal limitations on retention of the collateral, *i.e,*
strict foreclosure. The primary practical limitation
is that if the secured party chooses to keep the
collateral, it keeps the collateral in satisfaction of
the debt. Accordingly, strict foreclosure will be used
when the collateral is worth more than the amount
due on the debt and the repossession costs. If the
collateral has depreciated rapidly in proportion to
the payments made on it [or if the secured party
does not want to keep the collateral], the secured
party will sell after repossession.

The legal limitations are set out in section 9–505.
Section 9–505(1) provides that where a consumer
debtor has paid 60% of the cash price in the case of
a purchase money security interest in consumer

goods or 60% of the loan in the case of another security interest in consumer goods, a secured party may not use strict foreclosure unless the debtor after default consents to such retention. Absent this "post-default" consent, the secured party must sell the collateral within 90 days of repossession. Where the collateral is consumer goods but debtor hasn't paid 60%, the secured party must send a notice of his intention to retain the collateral to the debtor unless the debtor has after default consented to such retention. By sending the secured party a written objection to the proposed retention the debtor can prevent the secured party from retaining the collateral, and can cause the secured party to have to sell the collateral.

Because of these limitations on retention, repossession is generally followed by resale of the collateral. If the proceeds of the sale are not sufficient to satisfy the indebtedness the debtor is liable for any deficiency, absent an agreement to the contrary. In seeking recovery of such deficiency, the creditor has all of the rights of a general creditor. In the unlikely event that the sale yields a sum greater than the amount owed by the debtor, the secured party must account to the debtor for any surplus.

c. Limitations on Deficiency Judgment

The theory underlying the secured party's right to recover deficiencies is simple. The debtor has undertaken an obligation to pay X dollars. The debtor should pay X dollars. If the sale of the repossessed collateral yields less than X dollars, the

debtor should be required to make up this difference.

The problems commonly raised when deficiency
judgments are pursued are that (1) the resale value
of most consumer goods is considerably less than
the original purchase price and (2) repossession
sales do not always yield the fair value of the
repossessed collateral.

The Uniform Commercial Code tries to require
secured parties to conduct a sale that will yield the
fair market value of the collateral. Section 9–504
requires that "reasonable notice" of the sale must
be given to the debtor unless the collateral is per-
ishable or threatens to decline in value or is of a
"type customarily sold on a recognized market."
More important, section 9–504 requires that every
aspect of the sale be "commercially reasonable."

The Code does not have a definition of "commercially reasonable." "Obviously, each case will turn
on its facts. Generally, evidence as to every aspect
of the case, including the amount of advertising
done, normal commercial practices in disposing of
particular collateral, the length of time elapsing
between repossession and resale, whether deteriora-
tion of the collateral has occurred, the number of
persons contacted concerning the sale, *and even* the
price obtained," *Clark Leasing Corp. v. White
Sands Forest Products, Inc.*, 87 N.M. 451, 535 P.2d
1077 (1975).

The Code nowhere expressly states that a sale is
not "commercially reasonable" because the price is

too low. To the contrary, section 9–507 (2) states that the fact that a better price could have been obtained is not "of itself sufficient to establish that the sale was not made in a commercially reasonable manner." Notwithstanding the above quoted language from *Clark Leasing* and section 9–507(2) that low resale price alone is not enough, the primary issue in most cases seems to be the sufficiency of the price. This is not to say that courts expressly reject section 9–507(2); rather, little more than an unusually low resale price is needed to establish that the sale was not commercially reasonable.

Section 9–507 imposes liability on a secured party who fails to give "reasonable notice" or hold a "commercially reasonable sale." The measure of damages is losses caused by the secured party's failure to comply with the requirements. Because of the difficulty of establishing such losses, a minimum recovery is guaranteed to consumers: an amount measured by the finance charge plus ten percent of the principal.

The Uniform Commercial Code nowhere mentions denial of the right to a deficiency judgment as a remedy available to a debtor where the secured party has not completely complied with the requirements of Part 5 of Article 9. Nevertheless, a number of reported cases hold that noncompliance with Part 5 of Article 9 deprives the secured party of his right to a deficiency judgment. There are, of course, many cases to the contrary, cases holding that the secured

party is entitled to the deficiency minus the amount
of loss caused by the violation. A third line of cases
has taken a middle position: violation of Part 5 of
Article 9 creates a rebuttable presumption that the
loss is equal to the deficiency.

A number of states have statutorily restricted the
right of a creditor with a security interest in consumer goods to repossess, resell *and* collect a deficiency judgment. Most of the statutes are modeled
on the 1968 version of the Uniform Consumer Credit Code. Under section 5.103, of the UCCC, the
creditor must elect between repossessing the collateral and enforcing a personal judgment against the
consumer in a consumer credit *sale* where the cash
price was $1,000 [raised to $1,750 by the 1974
Official Text]. If the seller repossesses or voluntarily accepts surrender of the collateral, the buyer is
not liable for the unpaid balance. If instead of
repossessing, the seller sues on the debt and obtains
a judgment he may not repossess the collateral, and
the collateral is not subject to levy or sale on
execution. Be sure you understand what the UCCC
anti-deficiency judgment provision does and does
not do. It does require *some* sellers to *choose* between pursuing the collateral and pursuing the
debtor. It does not limit these sellers to the collateral. It does not in any way affect the sellers of new
cars or other items costing more than $1,000
($1,750, as amended). It does not in any way affect
creditors who make secured *loans*.

F. WARRANTIES

1. UNIFORM COMMERCIAL CODE

Warranties accompanying the sale of consumer products are governed by the Uniform Commercial Code.[24] Three warranties under the Code have the broadest impact on consumer transactions: express warranty, implied warranty of merchantability and implied warranty of fitness.

Section 2–313 describes a number of actions of the seller which may result in an express warranty. Of course, an express warranty may be created as a result of a statement made by the seller to the buyer. The statement need not include the words "warrant" or "guarantee." For example, a statement by a boat dealer that a boat is new constitutes an express warranty. The statement need not be in writing, although oral statements present obvious parol evidence problems. The statement must be an "affirmation of fact" or "promise" as contrasted with an "affirmation of value," "opinion" or "commendation." Phrases such as "perfect condition," "last a lifetime," and "as good as anyone's" have been regarded as "puffing" rather than warranties.

An express warranty can also be created by description or sample. In order for a statement, description or sample to give rise to an express warranty, it must be part of the "basis of the bargain."

24. For a detailed treatment of warranties, lemon laws and the Magnuson–Moss Act, *see* Consumer Warranty Law, National Consumer Law Center (1997).

The phrase "basis of the bargain" is not defined in the Code. Comment 3 to Section 2–313 does, however, indicate that proving "basis of the bargain" does not require establishing reliance. For a statement, description or sample to be a part of the "basis of the bargain" it is only necessary for it to come at such time that they buyer *could* have relied on it. While the buyer does not have to prove reliance, the seller may negative the warranty by proving that the buyer did not *in fact* rely.

Under section 2–314, a warranty of merchantability is implied in every sale of goods by a merchant seller. Section 2–314(2) sets out a nonexclusive listing of the attributes of merchantability. The key concept is that the goods must be "fit for the ordinary purposes for which such goods are used." For example, there is an implied warranty of merchantability that hair tonic will not cause "chemical haircut." Failure to satisfy this standard is the usual claim in merchantability litigation.

Section 2–315 contains the implied warranty of fitness for a particular purpose. This warranty arises whenever any seller, merchant or not, has reason to know (1) the *particular* purpose for which the goods are to be used and (2) that the buyer is relying on the seller's skill and judgment to select suitable goods. For example, if customer describes his needs to seller, failure of the hot water heater recommended by seller to produce sufficient hot water is a breach of warranty.

To recover on an implied warranty theory a consumer must show not only (1) the existence of a warranty but also (2) breach, (3) causation, (4) privity and (5) notice.[25] A consumer who satisfies these five requirements can cancel the contract and recover any down payment. Alternatively, such a consumer can bring an action for damages; the measure of damages is the difference between the fair market value of the goods as delivered and their value had they been as warranted, section 2–714. (Note the contract price is not a part of the breach of warranty damages formula). Additionally, should

25. The action for breach of warranty was originally tortuous in nature. With the development of the action of assumpsit, however, warranty came to be recognized as a part of the law of sales. The most notable bar to recovery imposed by the law of sales is the requirement of privity, *i.e.,* a direct contractual relationship between the injured plaintiff and the defendant. Where a consumer sues the manufacturer, *e.g.,* an action against General Motors because the car doors don't open, there is no privity.

Today in most states there is no privity requirement in warranty actions for *personal injuries*. The courts following the lead of the New Jersey Supreme Court in Henningsen v. Bloomfield Motors, Inc., 32 N.J. 358, 161 A.2d 69 (1960), judicially abolished the requirement.

The drafters of the Uniform Commercial Code were not as bold. The Code's privity provision, section 2–718, contains three alternatives. The most widely adopted alternative is silent as to possible defendants, *i.e.,* whether the injured plaintiff can sue the manufacturer as well as the seller, *i.e.,* vertical privity. The alternative does deal with horizontal privity, *i.e.,* possible plaintiffs, *i.e.,* whether anyone other than the purchaser can be a plaintiff. Warranty protection is extended to family, household or house guests of the consumer buyer "if it is reasonable to expect that such person may use, consumer or be affected by the goods and is injured *in person* by breach of warranty."

a consumer choose the damages route, he or she can recover consequential damages such as specific economic loss and injury to person and property caused by the breach based on section 2–715.

It is very difficult to disclaim *express* warranties. The disclaimer must be express and must *not* be inconsistent with the express warranty. Section 2–316 allows for easy elimination of *implied* warranties. An implied warranty can be excluded or modified by course of dealing, course of performance or usage of trade. Examination or refusal to examine the goods can also destroy implied warranties. When the buyer has, before entering into the contract, examined the goods or a sample or model as fully as he or she desired or has refused to examine the goods, there is no implied warranty with regards to defects which an examination ought in the circumstances to have revealed. And, of course, implied warranties can be disclaimed by language of the contract.

There are two types of language that can be used to modify or exclude implied warranties: (1) specific language that satisfies the requirements of section 2–316(2) or (2) general language that satisfies the requirements of section 2–316(3). Under section 2–316(2) a disclaimer of an implied warranty of merchantability must mention merchantability and, *if in writing*, must be conspicuous. A term or clause is conspicuous when it is so written that a reasonable person against whom it is to operate ought to have noticed it, § 1–201(10). For example, "SELLER MAKES NO WARRANTY OF MERCHANTABILI-

TY WITH RESPECT TO GOODS SOLD UNDER THIS AGREEMENT."

Section 2–316(2)'s requirements for disclaimer of warranties of fitness are quite different. The disclaimer *must be in writing* and conspicuous but need not specifically mention fitness. For example, "THERE ARE NO WARRANTIES WHICH EXTEND BEYOND THE DESCRIPTION ON THE FACE HEREOF."

Despite the specific and different requirements in section 2–316(2), section 2–316(3) provides for disclaimer of *all* implied warranties by words of general disclaimer. The words of general disclaimer must be "as is," "with the faults" or similar language which "calls the buyer's attention to the exclusion of warranties and makes it clear that there is no implied warranty." Unlike section 2–316(2), section 2–316(3) does not expressly require that the language of disclaimer be "conspicuous"; a number of consumer cases, however, have relied on the above quoted phrase to require that section 2–316(3) general disclaimers be conspicuous.

Where a warranty has been successfully disclaimed the buyer has no cause of action for a supposed breach of that warranty—no remedy. Also, a seller can, without disclaiming implied warranties, substantially reduce a buyer's warranty protection. Section 2–719 allows contractual limitations of remedies. For example, "it is expressly understood and agreed that the buyer's sole and exclusive remedy shall be repair or replacement of defective parts, and that the seller shall not be liable for damages, for injuries to person or property."

In order for such a limitation to be effective it must not cause the contract to "fail of its essential purpose." Comment 1 to section 2–719 explains that this requirement applies "because of circumstances fails in its purpose or operates to deprive either party of the substantial value of the bargain." For example, in *Riley v. Ford Motor Co.*, 442 F.2d 670 (5th Cir.1971), a new car purchaser was permitted to recover a sum far in excess of the cost of repair and replacement of defective parts which was the exclusive contract remedy. This exclusive remedy failed of its essential purpose because even after numerous attempts to repair, the car did not operate as a new car should, free of defects. Also, in *Lewis Refrigeration Co. v. Sawyer Fruit, Vegetable and Cold Storage, Co.*, 709 F.2d 427 (1983), the sales contract contained a clause excluding consequential damages, clauses limiting the available remedies to rescission or repair by the plaintiff, and performance warranties. The seller was unable to promptly repair the freezer to meet performance warranties, and rescission would have caused the buyer to suffer extreme financial loss. Thus, the remedy provided failed of its essential purpose.

Section 2–719(3) expressly provides for the limitation of consequential damages "unless the limitation or exclusion is unconscionable." It also provides that any limitation of consequential damages is prima facie unconscionable when the goods are consumer goods. For example, Brad Majors purchases new tires; the printed form sales contract excluded recovery for consequential damages. One of the tires is defective. Majors' right rear tire fails, causing the car to go out of control and roll over, seriously injuring Majors. He sues on a breach of implied warranty of merchantability theory. Unless the seller comes forward with evidence rebutting the presumption of unconscionability, Majors can recover for personal injuries. Majors, however, must establish unconscionability in order to recover for the damage to his car.

Notwithstanding the preceding hypothetical, section 2–719(3) is, at best, a mixed blessing for consumers. Some commentators and courts have relied in part on section 2–719(3) to support the position that an unconscionability attack *cannot* be made on a warranty disclaimer that satisfies section 2–316. Section 2–719(3) expressly mentions unconscionability. Not only does section 2–316 not mention section 2–302, the unconscionability provision, the cross references to section 2–316 make no reference to 2–302.

2.   THE MAGNUSON–MOSS WARRANTY ACT

The Magnuson–Moss Act was designed to promote consumer understanding of warranties. The disclosure provisions under Magnuson–Moss were intended to increase the warranty coverage available to consumers, and to make it possible for consumers to compare the warranty coverage available by standardizing and clarifying the language of warranties.

In proposing federal warranty legislation, Senator Moss stated:

> * * * [W]arranties have for many years confused, misled, and frequently angered American consumers * * * Consumer anger is expected when purchasers of consumer products discover that their warranty may cover a 25–cent part but not the $100 labor charge or that there is full coverage on a piano so long as it is shipped at the purchaser's expense to the factory. * * *

> * * * [T]he bill is designed to promote understanding. Far too frequently, there is a paucity of information supplied to the consumer about what in fact is offered him in that piece of paper proudly labeled 'warranty.' Many of the most important questions concerning the warranty are usually unanswered when there is some sort of product failure. Who should the consumer notify if his product stops working during the warranty period? What are his responsibilities after notification? How soon can he expect a fair replacement? Will repair or replacement cost him anything? There is a growing need to generate consumer understanding by clearly and conspicuously disclosing the terms and conditions of the warranty and by telling the consumer what to do if his guaranteed product becomes defective or malfunctions.

Congress passed the Magnuson–Moss Warranty Act and it was signed into law on January 4, 1975; the law became effective on July 4, 1975. It applies to manufacturers and sellers of consumer products who make express "written warranties."[26]

Magnuson–Moss is basically a disclosure statute. Sellers and manufacturers are not required to make any express warranties at all. If, however, a "consumer product firm" issues a "written warranty" it must comply with the disclosure requirements of the Act as supplemented by rules promulgated by the Federal Trade Commission.

Under 15 U.S.C. § 2302 of the Act, any "supplier", *i.e.*, manufacturer or seller, using a written warranty in connection with sale of a product costing more than $5 must, to the extent required by FTC rules, "fully and conspicuously disclose in simple and readily understandable language the terms

26. The Magnuson–Moss phrase "consumer products" is different from the UCC phrase "consumer goods." UCC section 9–109 focuses on the particular use of the particular item by the particular debtor. For example, if Warren Pease buys a pick-up truck for week-end fishing trips, it is "consumer goods" under UCC section 9–109. If, on the other hand, Burt Rentals Co. buys a pick-up to use in its rental business, the truck is not "consumer goods" under UCC section 9–109. Under Magnuson–Moss, it does not matter how a particular buyer uses the particular goods. If goods of this type are normally used for personal, family, or household purposes, the goods are "consumer products" under Magnuson–Moss. 15 U.S.C. § 2301(1)

The Magnuson–Moss phrase "written warranty" is also different from the UCC phrase "express warranty." For example, a promise to repair would be a "written warranty" under 15 U.S.C. § 2301, but not an "express warranty" under section 2–313.

and conditions of such warranty." The contents of the warranty disclosure are to be regulated by the FTC; 15 U.S.C. § 2302 empowers the FTC to promulgate disclosure requirements. These rules are set out in section 701.3 of the FTC Regulations.

Magnuson–Moss requires that all written warranties of consumer products costing more than $10 be designated as either "FULL" or "LIMITED", clearly and conspicuously. Remember, Magnuson–Moss does not require a manufacturer or a seller to make a written warranty. If no written warranties are issued, Magnuson–Moss does not apply. A warranty can be designated "FULL" only if it completely complies with the requirements of 15 U.S.C. § 2304; a supplier can avoid complying with these requirements by designating the warranty as "LIMITED".

The Magnuson–Moss Warranty Act is not purely a disclosure statute. By reason of 15 U.S.C. § 2304(a)(i) a "warrantor" (under most standard forms, both the manufacturer and the dealer) who gives a FULL warranty must fix a product that is defective or otherwise fails to conform to the written warranty. The warrantor must fix the product within a reasonable time and without charge.

In essence, 15 U.S.C. § 2304 is an anti-lemon provision. Under a FULL warranty, if repeated repair efforts fail to remedy the product, the consumer must be given a choice of a refund or replacement without charge.

The "anti privity" provision of Magnuson–Moss is 15 U.S.C. § 2304. The section provides that the protection of a FULL warranty extends to "each person who is a *consumer* with respect to the consumer product." "Consumer" is a statutorily defined term. Under 15 U.S.C. § 2301(c), "consumer" includes at least second buyers and bailees and also includes bystanders, if warranty protection under state law extends to bystanders.

Section 2304(a)(3) is a troublesome provision; it states that a FULL warranty may not "exclude or limit consequential damages * * * unless such exclusion or limitation conspicuously appears on the face of the warranty." "Consequential damages" includes personal injuries, section 2–715(2)(b). Section 2–719(3) provides that a limitation of consequential damages for personal injuries is prima facie unconscionable. Does the Magnuson–Moss provision replace section 2–719(3)? Will a conspicuous exclusion of personal injury liability be effective? 15 U.S.C. § 2311 of Magnuson–Moss—"nothing in this title shall invalidate or restrict any right or remedy of any consumer under State law"—would seem to call for a negative answer. Moreover, an affirmative answer would be inconsistent with sections 2304(b) and 2308.

Under § 2308, suppliers who make express warranties, FULL or LIMITED, *cannot disclaim* implied warranties. A manufacturer or seller who does not make any express warranties can still disclaim implied warranties by complying with the requirements of section 2–316. Section 2308 applies to both

FULL warranties and to LIMITED warranties. A supplier who gives only a LIMITED warranty can restrict the duration of implied warranties to the duration of the express warranty if it satisfies the following three requirements: (1) such limitation is conscionable, (2) in clear and unmistakable language and prominently displayed on the face of the warranty, and (3) the duration is reasonable.

Section 2310 is the remedies provision. A violation of any of the Act's warranty requirements is a violation of section 5 of the Federal Trade Commission Act, 15 U.S.C. § 2310. Section 2310 gives consumers the right to bring private actions for breach of written warranty, implied warranty, or service contract covered by the Act.

What does 15 U.S.C. § 2310 add to the rights that an aggrieved consumer already had under state warranty law? Section 2310 creates a very limited right of access to federal courts. It also provides for class actions. And, it confers a right to sue for violations of Magnuson–Moss.

When will a consumer exercise this right? What relief can a consumer obtain because a warrantor failed to designate a warranty as a FULL or LIMITED warranty? Rescission? The rights under a FULL warranty?

Perhaps the most significant right provided by section 2310 is the right to recover litigation costs including attorney's fees, 15 U.S.C. § 2310(d)(2). This right to costs extends to what are essential state actions under state warranty law. For example, Linda Tripp buys a piano from Justin Tune, Inc. for her daughter Lisa to practice on. Linda believes that the piano is defective and sues Tune in state court for breach of implied warranty of merchantability. By claiming not only her rights under UCC section 2–314 but also her rights under Magnuson–Moss § 2310(d)(2), Ms. Tripp can recover both damages and litigation costs.

Ms. Tripp can recover her litigation costs only if she "prevails" in her warranty claim and if she brings her action under 15 U.S.C. § 2301(d). There are two restrictions on bringing private actions under Magnuson–Moss § 2310 (and thus two restrictions on recovery of litigation costs by successful warranty claimants.) First, the warrantor must be "afforded a reasonable opportunity to cure" the breach of warranty, 15 U.S.C. § 2310(e). Thus, Tune would have the opportunity to repair or replace the piano. Second, if Tune has established informal dispute settlement procedures that comply with 15 U.S.C. § 2310(b) and FTC regulations promulgated pursuant thereto, Ms. Tripp must first exhaust the informal settlement procedures before seeking judicial redress under section 2310(d).

This is not to say that Ms. Tripp can not sue Justin Tune for damages under UCC 2–314 without first affording it the opportunity to cure or without first exhausting informal settlement procedures. Such litigation would not, however, be "under" § 2310 and so Ms. Tripp could not recover litigation costs under 15 U.S.C. § 2310(d)(2).

INDEX

References are to Pages

-A-

Add-on interest, 252, 287–289
Annual percentage rate (APR), 162, 252
Arbitration, 35
    American Arbitration Association, 38
    Consumer Due Process Protocol for Mediation and Arbitration of Consumer Disputes, 38
Assignment of wages, 277
Attorney general, 13
Attorney's fees, 22, 26
    Truth in Lending Act, 196
Auto leases, 61
    Consumer Leasing Act, 220–223
Auto sales repair regulations, 59
Automated clearinghouse, 369
Automobile title pawn, 67

-B-

Bait and switch advertising, 45
Billing systems, 389–393
    Average daily balance method, 391
    Previous balance method, 389
    Two-cycle average daily balance method, 391
Breach of the peace, 417

Buried finance charges, 155–162

-C-

Celebrity endorsements, 47
Class actions, 29
    Abuse in class actions, 33
    Deceptive advertising, 52
    National Association of Consumer Advocates' Standards and
        Guidelines for Litigating and Settling Class Actions, 34
    Requirements for certification, 30
Closed-end credit, 144
Common law remedies, 3, 40
Confession of judgment, 277
Consumer Credit Protection Act, 6
Consumer Leasing Act, 220–224
Consumer lending industry, 65
Cosigner, 275
Cost of Credit, 235
Credit bureaus, 99
Credit cards, 360
    Defenses based on merchant dealings, 360
    Unauthorized use, 364
Credit insurance, 153–155, 294–322
    Accident and health, 301
    Credit life insurance, 298–301
    Credit property insurance, 303
    Force-placed insurance, 312
    Involuntary unemployment, 302
    Non-filing insurance, 308
    Packing, 317
    Penetration rates, 314
    Regulation, 295
    Truth in Lending, 153
    Voluntariness, 313
Credit Repair Organizations Act, 124
Credit reports, 98
Credit sales, 244
    Time-price doctrine, 245

-D-

Dealer-arranged financing, 75

Dealer-arranged financing—Cont'd
    Control liability, 77
    Dealer paper, 76
    Home improvement dealers, 79
    Lender liability, 76
    Unfair lending practices, 86
Debt collection, 394
    Breach of the peace, 417
    Defamation, 396
    Deficiency judgment, 420
    Exempt property, 408
    Fair Debt Collection Practices Act, 399
    Garnishment, 407
    Intentional infliction of emotional distress, 397
    Invasion of privacy, 396
    Judicial collection efforts, 406
    Redeeming collateral, 418
    Repossession, 416
Defamation, 101
    Debt collection, 396
Default, 393
Depositary Institutions Deregulation and Monetary Control Act,
        136, 250
Discrimination in access to credit, 127
Door-to-door sales, 53

-E-

Electronic Funds Transfer Act, 368–381
Equal Credit Opportunity Act, 8, 127–134
    Discrimination in evaluating credit applications, 129
    Discrimination in obtaining information, 128
    Effect on state law, 132
    Notification, 131
    Remedies, 133
    Scope, 127
Equity theft, 88
Exemptions (property), 277, 408–414

-F-

Fair Credit and Charge Card Disclosure Act, 136, 174
Fair Credit Billing Act, 8, 381–389

Fair Credit Reporting Act, 7
  Administrative remedies, 118
  Civil liability, 120
  Criminal remedies, 119
  Requirements for consumers credit reporting agencies, 107
  Requirements for furnishers of information, 105
  Requirements for users of consumer reports, 110
  Rights of consumers, 114
  Scope, 102
Fair Debt Collection Practices Act, 8, 399–406
  Civil liability, 405
  False or misleading information, 402
  Harassment or abuse, 404
  Persons and transactions covered, 399
  Restrictions on communications, 405
  Validation of debts, 401
False advertising, 42
Federal Reserve Board, 137
Federal Telephone Consumer Protection Act, 11, 55
Federal Trade Commission, 15
  Credit Practices Rule, 273–280
  History, 15
  Industry guides, 16
  Regulation of advertising, 42
  Statement of Basis and Purpose, 80
  Trade Regulation Rule Concerning Preservation of Consumers' Claims and Defenses, 343–360
  Trade regulation rules, 17
Federal Trade Commission Act, 9, 43
  Section 5(9), 18
  Section 12, 42
Federal Trade Commission Improvement Act, 9
Finance charge, 149
Finance companies, 66
Financing dealer contracts, 83
Flipping, 280–293
Fraud, 3
Fringe banks, 66

-G-

Garnishment, 407
  Restrictions on garnishment, 411–414

-H-

Holder in due course doctrine, 337–343
    FTC Rule, 343–350
Limitations on affirmative recovery, 350
Home improvement dealers, 79
    Deceptive practices, 80
Home Ownership and Equity Protection Act, 8, 229–234
HUD, 227

-I-

Identity Theft Protection Act, 9, 122
Infomercials, 46
Installment debt, 63
Internet, 380
Interest Rates, 251
    Add-on, 252, 287–289
    Charges included, 263
    Computation problems, 255
    Discounted, 253
    Rule of 78's, 287
Interstate Land Sales Full Disclosure Act, 224
Invasion of privacy, 101, 396

-J-
-K-
-L-

Late charges, 276
Leasing, 220
    Consumer Leasing Act, 220–224
Loan origination fees, 264

_-M-

Magnuson–Moss Act, 10, 20, 430–436
Mail or Telephone Order Merchandise Rule, 57

-N-

Nader's raiders, 19

National Association of Consumer Advocates (NACA), 34
National Bank Act, 249
Non-purchase money security interest in household goods, 278

-O-

Official Staff Commentary, 137
Open-end credit, 144, 174–187
    Billing systems, 389–393
    Defenses based on merchant dealings, 360
    Fair Credit Billing Act, 381–387
    Litigation in marketing of consumer goods, 180
    Marketing flaws, 181
    Spurious open-end credit, 186
    Unauthorized transactions, 364

-P-

Pawnshops, 67
Payday loans, 67
Personal identification number (PIN), 374
Prepayment penalties, 266
Primary lender, 93
Private actions, 21
Puffing, 4
Pyramid sales, 59
Pyramiding late charges, 276

-Q-
-R-

Racketeer Influenced and Corrupt Organizations Act (RICO), 27
    Advertising provisions, 51
Rate ceilings, 239
Real Estate Settlements Procedures Act, 10, 226–228
Real estate transactions and TILA, 187
Referral sales, 58
Regulation E, 376
Regulation Z, 137
Reliance, 4
Rent-to-own, 68
Repossession, 416

Residential mortgage transactions, 168

-S-

Satellite–TV reception financing and open-end credit, 180
Secondary lender, 93
Securitization, 73
Security interests, 172
    Household goods, 278
Spurious open-end credit, 186
State agency enforcement, 12
Subprime credit market, 72
    Abusive lending practices, 74
    Discount financing, 157
    Securitization, 73
    Senate testimony, 317

-T-

Telemarketing, 54
Telemarketing and Consumer Fraud and Abuse Prevention Act,
    11, 55
Telephone Disclosure and Dispute Resolution Act, 11, 56
Time-price doctrine, 245
Title pawn, 67
Truth in Lending Act, 6
    Advertising provisions, 50
    Annual Percentage Rate (APR), 162
    Buried finance charges, 155
    Closed-end credit, 144, 147
    Consumer Leasing Act, 220–224
    Consumer remedies, 194–215
    Credit insurance, 153–155
    Criminal actions, 193
    Damages, 195–216
    Defenses, 216
    Discount financing, 157
    Federal enforcement of TILA, 191
    Finance charge, 149
    General disclosure requirements, 145
    Location of disclosures, 171
    Official Staff Commentary, 137
    Open-end credit, 144, 174–187, 360–368

Truth in Lending Act—Cont'd
    Real estate transactions, 187
    Regulation Z, 137, 143
    Residential mortgage transactions, 168
    Security interests, 172
    Scope of application, 138
Truth in Lending Simplification and Reform Act of 1980, 136
Truth in Savings Act, 9, 218–220

-U-

UDAP statutes, 21
    Attorney's fees, 26
    Deceptive advertising, 48
    Remedies, 25
Unconscionability, 330–336
Unfair or deceptive acts and practices, 10
Uniform Commercial Code, 11
    Breach of the peace, 417
    Holder in due course doctrine, 337
    Limitations on after-acquired consumer goods, 322
    Unconscionability, 333–336
    Warranties, 424–430
Uniform Small Loan Law, 238
United Nations Guidelines for Consumer Protection, 2
United States Senate Special Committee on Aging, 72
    Hearings on Subprime Lending, 281, 317–322
Unsolicited goods, 58
Up-charges, 330
Used Car Rule (FTC), 60
    Buyer's Guide, 60
Usury Laws, 236, 242–272
    Federal preemption, 249
    Prepayment penalties, 266
    Remedies, 271

-V-

Vendor's single interest insurance, 304

-W-

Warranties, 424–426

Warranties—Cont'd
    Disclaimer, 427
    Express warranty, 424
    Fitness for a particular purpose, 425
    Magnuson–Moss Act, 430
    Merchantability, 425

-X-
-Y-

Yield spread premium financing, 324–330

-Z-